The Low-Fat

Indian

Vegetarian Cookbook

Other titles by the same author

Vegetarian Balti Cooking
30 Minute Vegetarian Indian Cookbook
Quick Vegetarian Curries

The Low-Fat

Indian

Vegetarian Cookbook

MRIDULA BALJEKAR

Thorsons

in association with

COBRA नाम
PREMIUM BEER

In loving memory of my late parents, Dwarka Nath and
Kusum Hazarika, who always believed that a healthy diet
was the key to a healthy body and mind.

Thorsons
An Imprint of HarperCollins*Publishers*
77–85 Fulham Palace Road,
Hammersmith, London W6 8JB

™

and *Thorsons*
are trademarks of
HarperCollins*Publishers* Ltd

The Thorsons website address is: www.thorsons.com

Some of the recipes in this volume have been
published previously in *Vegetarian Balti Cooking*

10 9 8 7 6 5 4 3 2 1

© Mridula Baljekar 2002

Mridula Baljekar asserts the moral right to be
identified as the author of this work

A catalogue record of this book is
available from the British Library

ISBN 0–00–714049–5

Printed and bound in Great Britain by
Scotprint, Haddington, East Lothian

Contents

About the Author

Mridula Baljekar is a highly regarded Indian chef and cookery writer. Born and raised in North Eastern India, Mridula began cooking in the family kitchen with her mother and grandmother, later learning about more complex traditional Indian cookery with her family's resident professional chef.

After many years of training and building her experience, Mridula is now one of the UK's best known Indian cooks. She is the star of Carlton Food Network's Indian cookery series, which was filmed partly in the UK and partly 'on the road' in hotels and cafés throughout India – an experience which Mridula enjoyed immensely and hopes to repeat soon!

Mridula is also in demand as a cookery consultant for major food companies including Tesco where she helped shape their range of curries and Indian dishes. Her creative work with Tesco led to her being described as *'the cook who spiced up a superstore'!* Her innovative approach to recipe writing has ensured the success of her several Indian cookery titles, including the best-selling *Complete Indian Cookbook*. Her unique style shows most clearly though, in the menus of her award-winning Indian restaurant, The Spice Route, in Windsor, UK, where traditional Indian flavours are presented with brilliant new twists in dishes that include Venison Tikka and Turkey and Guinea Fowl Kebabs.

Introduction

I believe that food is one of the greatest gifts of love. Food brings people together, and this book is all about getting the most enjoyment out of this togetherness.

Indian food is based on ancient Ayurvedic principles. Food is seen as a gift from nature. Eating rituals are important to create and maintain harmony of body, mind and soul. The food eaten must be healthy and nutritious and has to be enjoyed in the company of friends and relations. Mealtimes must be joyous and almost ceremonial occasions.

A Matter of Fat

In this book, great care has been taken to make low-fat vegetarian food just as tasty as fatty food. Fat is a wonderful flavour enhancer, and we all need small amounts of it for the repair and growth of cells. It is also a great source of energy, but excessive amounts have negative effects on our body. Excess fat is stored by the body and results in weight gain. Fatty food is a major cause of heart disease, the biggest killer of modern times. A low-fat diet is sensible for adults who wish to minimize the risk of heart disease as well as stay in shape.

The two main types of fat are saturated and unsaturated. Saturated fat is derived from animal sources. High consumption of saturated fat raises the level of blood cholesterol, which in turn leads to an increased risk of heart disease. Foods naturally rich in cholesterol include eggs, shrimps, lamb, beef and pork. Foods high in saturated fats, such as butter, lard, cream, whole milk and hard cheese, are also high in cholesterol. Avoiding high-cholesterol foods, or consuming them only in small quantities, will help to maintain a normal level of blood cholesterol.

Unsaturated fats are divided into two groups: polyunsaturates (found in oily fish and walnuts) and monounsaturates (found in cooking oils such as sunflower, vegetable and olive). These are also known as essential fatty acids and are important in maintaining good health. The majority of the recipes in this book contain unsaturated fats in small amounts. Half-fat versions of fatty foods are also used, except in Chapter 10, 'High Days and Holidays'.

With the magical power of Indian spices to elevate humble ingredients to gourmet status, it is easy to create exciting low-fat vegetarian dishes. The secret lies in using the right combination of these spices in the correct proportion. Numerous combinations are possible and this makes it easier to create the right flavour for your chosen dish. A greater variation can be achieved by using different cooking techniques.

Vegetarian Cooking

Vegetarian food is naturally low in fat. Indian vegetarian food can be a very enjoyable and exciting experience. In India, vegetarianism has been a way of life for thousands of years. Although this was mainly due to religious beliefs, the findings of modern scientific research have confirmed the benefits of following a vegetarian diet. 'You are what you eat', and a vegetarian diet promotes a healthy body as well as a healthy mind.

I have never been a strict vegetarian myself, but having grown up in India with its abundance of fresh vegetables, fruits, beans and pulses, eating meat has never been very important. We enjoyed eating meat and poultry dishes, but only in small quantities, along with generous helpings of deliciously spiced vegetables, lentils, beans and salads.

The stressful pace of modern life limits the time we spend in the kitchen. Vegetarian food is not only quick to prepare and cook, but is also very economical. It saves time and effort and allows you to rustle up delicious meals even if you have not visited the shops for a few days. As long as your store cupboard is well stocked with the basic spices and ingredients, like lentils and beans, a quick and easy meal is always at your fingertips.

Before you make a start on any dish, have a quick glance at the slow-cooking or simmering times in the recipe. You will save time by using these gaps to make preparations for the next dish. A simple job like boiling water in a kettle rather than waiting for it to boil in a saucepan will save time. Using hot or warm water also helps to enhance the flavours of the spices. Adding cold water to carefully blended spices impairs their taste.

I have created the recipes in this book with great care, keeping three main points in mind:

1 speedy cooking time
2 easy preparation and
3 taste and essential nutrients.

The Store Cupboard

Indian cooking will be as effortless as any other if you equip your store cupboard first. It is worth making one trip to an Indian shop to save time and money. As Indian cuisine is so vast and varied, you will never be short of ideas for quick and delicious family meals or when entertaining friends at short notice. Listed below are the ingredients I always keep in my store cupboard.

Standard Whole Spices

These should be stored in air-tight jars, away from direct light.

Bay leaves

Black cumin seeds (*shahi jeera*)

Black mustard seeds

Cinnamon sticks

Coriander (cilantro) seeds

Cumin seeds

Curry leaves (Available dried and fresh. Dried variety will keep well in a moisture-free jar for several months. Fresh ones can be frozen and used straight from the freezer.)

Dried red chilli peppers (small ones and long slim ones)

Fennel seeds

Fenugreek seeds

Green cardamom pods

Nutmeg

Onion Seeds

Poppy seeds, white

Sesame seeds

Sunflower seeds

Whole black peppercorns

Whole cloves

Standard Ground Spices

These should be stored as for whole spices.

Chilli powder

Coriander (cilantro)

Cumin

Garam masala

Paprika

Turmeric

Standard Fresh Ingredients

Coriander (cilantro) leaves (Keep the roots immersed in a jug of water to preserve the leaves for 6–7 days. If you wrap the roots in a damp cloth and put the coriander in a large plastic food bag, it can be stored in the salad drawer of your fridge. Put the bunch root side down and tie the bag loosely, making sure no air is trapped. Alternatively, remove the roots, wash and chop the leaves, freeze and use from frozen.)

Fresh green chilli peppers (Will keep for 3–4 weeks if the stalks are removed and the chillies are stored in a jam jar in the fridge. They can also be frozen and used from the freezer.)

Garlic (Store in a cool, dry place, ideally with the potatoes.)

Onions

Root ginger (Store like garlic.)

Non-standard Fresh Ingredients

Half-fat single (half and half) and
   double (heavy) cream (long-life
   variety)

Dry Ingredients

Atta or chapatti flour

Basmati rice

Chickpea flour (besan)

Cornmeal or polenta

Green lentils

Ground rice

Plain (all-purpose) flour

Red split lentils (*masoor dhal*)

Semolina (cream of wheat)

Skinned and split mung beans (*moong
   dhal*)

Yellow split lentils (*toor* or *tuvar dhal*)

Yellow split peas (*channa dhal*)

Canned Goods

Chopped tomatoes

Canned chickpeas (garbanzos)

Canned butterbeans

Canned red kidney beans

Miscellaneous Items

Coconut milk (canned, reduced-fat)

Coconut milk powder

Creamed coconut

Desiccated coconut

Passata (Italian sieved tomatoes)

Tamarind concentrate

Tamarind juice

Tomato purée (paste)

Rooh Afza or rose-flavoured syrup

Sunflower or light olive oil

Kitchen Tools

Make the most of modern kitchen gadgets. Onion, ginger and garlic purée (paste) can be made in a blender or food processor. To make garlic purée, for example, simply blend peeled cloves of garlic; no other ingredients are necessary. I keep these in a set of airtight containers in the fridge for frequent use. I also store a good quantity in small containers in the freezer. Use 1½ teaspoons of puréed garlic when a recipe calls for 3–4 cloves of garlic. Similarly, use 1½ teaspoons of puréed root ginger for a 2.5cm/1 inch cube. A little more or less garlic or ginger will not have a dramatic effect on your dishes.

Of course, you can buy ginger and garlic purée (paste) ready to use, but they will not have the wonderful flavour you get by making your own.

You can chop fresh coriander (cilantro) in the food processor and freeze it in a suitable container. Break off small portions and use as required. Fresh green chilli peppers can be frozen and used straight from the freezer too. They will keep better if you freeze them with the stalks intact.

A coffee mill is essential for grinding dry spices.

If you have a pressure cooker, use it to cook lentils, dried beans and peas quickly and efficiently. These can be frozen and used for your chosen dishes as and when required.

Freezing Cooked Food

The majority of dishes in this book will freeze successfully, as long as you are careful about what and how you freeze.

Vegetables such as potatoes (except when mashed), and to a certain extent aubergine (eggplant), do not freeze very well. Most other vegetables will freeze better if they are absolutely fresh when used.

All peas, beans and lentil dishes are excellent for freezing. Cooked rice dishes and all breads also freeze very well.

When cooking for the freezer, it is wise to undercook the vegetables slightly. Cool the dish quickly and chill before freezing. Spicy dishes taste even better when defrosted and reheated.

Always thaw the dish thoroughly before reheating. Do not panic if you find that your thawed dish has a lot of water content. This is because a certain amount of separation takes place when a dish is thawed. Do not attempt to drain it off as the vegetables will reabsorb all the water during reheating.

When the dish is thawed and reheated, you may find that you need to adjust the salt and garam masala. Here is a simple tip you can follow to give your defrosted dish an absolutely fresh appearance and flavour.

Heat about 2 teaspoons of cooking oil or ghee in a karahi or wok. Add ¼–½ teaspoon garam masala, depending on the amount of food you have, and a pinch of salt. Add the thawed dish and stir-fry until heated thoroughly, adding a little warm water if it becomes too dry. Stir in about 1 tablespoon of chopped fresh coriander (cilantro) leaves.

The dish will taste as fresh as if you have just cooked it!

Storing Indian Dishes in the Fridge

Indian dishes can be stored safely in the refrigerator for 3–4 days, sometimes longer. Indian spices have natural preserving qualities. So, when planning for a dinner party, you can cook ahead of time, reheat and present your food with absolute confidence.

Make sure the food is cold and put in an airtight container before storing in the fridge. Dishes containing acid ingredients like tomatoes, tomato purée (paste) and lemon juice will preserve the food for 48 hours, or longer, in perfect condition. Other dishes will keep well, though some vegetables may turn softer and the dish may look paler.

Follow the tips I have given for 'freshening up' frozen dishes.

How to Serve an Indian Meal

Traditionally, Indian meals do not consist of several courses. Everything that is cooked for a particular meal is generally put on the table for diners to help themselves as they wish. However, Western influence has changed this practice to a certain extent. Starters are served in all Indian restaurants. It is entirely up to you as to what style you want to adopt.

Rice and bread are both served at dinner parties and large family gatherings. Generally, one starts off with bread with all the other dishes on offer and finishes with a little rice with the same curries.

Knives and forks are not normally used; you simply break off a small piece of bread and scoop up the curries with them, but many people prefer to use a fork or both spoon and fork to eat rice.

How to Store Spices

Whole spices have a much longer shelf life than ground. All spices, whole or ground, should be stored in airtight containers in a cool, dark place. Ground spices lose their flavour very quickly, even when stored properly.

The best way to preserve the flavour of spices is to heat them gently before storing. Simply preheat a heavy-based pan, add your chosen spice and stir until it releases its aroma. As soon as this happens (usually about 1 minute), remove the pan from the heat and spread the spice on a large plate or tray.

Allow to cool thoroughly before storing in an airtight container. Ground spices treated this way will keep fresh for up to 12 months – whole spices even longer.

If you wish to buy whole spices and grind them yourself (this will always give you the best results), heat them gently as above, then cool and grind them. This heating not only enhances their flavour, but will also make them easier to grind.

Cooking with Spices

The secret of success lies in cooking and blending the spices correctly. The famous 'wet trinity' (onion, garlic and ginger) need specific cooking times with regulated heat to achieve the right flavours and textures. They also take much longer to cook than dry spices. Do not rush this stage and follow instructions carefully.

For cooking dry spices, always start on a medium or low-medium heat. Do not allow the oil to overheat as the spices will burn quickly, imparting an unpleasant, slightly bitter flavour to the dish. Spices need gentle heat to enhance their flavours. Overheating can cause them to lose their natural oils, which impairs the flavours.

Using Salt

In Indian cooking, salt is used more as a spice than a seasoning agent. The quantity of salt used may appear excessive to the Western cook, but a certain minimum amount of salt is required to balance the flavour of the spices. Without this, the dishes do not have the same authentic flavour. However, reducing salt in all food is essential to healthy living. Salt on its own is not the culprit; it is the sodium that causes concern. If you prefer, use low-sodium salt, which is now readily available. You'll need to use a little more than you would with normal salt.

Special Ingredients

The following is a list of the most commonly used ingredients in Indian and Pakistani cooking. You will also find hints about storing spices that require special care and attention.

Atta or chapatti flour: this is a very fine whole-wheat flour used to make all Indian unleavened bread. It is rich in dietary fibre because, unlike other wholemeal flour, atta is produced by grinding the whole wheat kernel to a very fine powder.

Ajowan or carum: ajowan is native to India and looks rather like a celery seed. It is related to caraway and cumin, though in flavour it is more akin to thyme. All Indian grocers stock ajowan. The seeds will keep for a number of years if stored in an airtight container. Only tiny amounts are used in pulse dishes and fried snacks. Ajowan helps to prevent wind.

Bay leaf (*tej patta*): bay leaves used in Indian cooking are obtained from the cassia tree. They are quite different to Western bay leaves, which come from the sweet bay laurel. Indian bay leaves are rarely available in the West; standard bay leaves have become a popular substitute.

Black peppercorns (*kali mirchi*): fresh green berries are dried in the sun to obtain black pepper, which is widely available in supermarkets. The green berries come from the pepper vine native to the monsoon forests of southwest India. Whole peppercorns will keep well in an airtight jar whereas ground black pepper loses the wonderful aromatic flavour very quickly. It is best to store whole pepper in a pepper mill and grind it only when required. Pepper is believed to be a good remedy for flatulence.

Cardamom (*elaichi*): cardamom has been used in Indian cooking since ancient times. Southern India produces an abundance of cardamom, which found its way to Europe through the Spice Route. There are two types of cardamom: the small green ones (*choti elaichi*) and the big dark-brown variety (*badi elaichi*). In the West, we also see a third variety with a milder flavour, which is obtained by blanching the small green cardamom. Whole cardamom pods are used to flavour rice and different types of sauce. Ground cardamom, used in many desserts and drinks, can be bought from most Asian stores. It is best to grind small quantities at home using a coffee mill. Prolonged storage dries out the essential natural oils and destroys the flavour.

Cinnamon: cassia, used as cinnamon in Indian cooking, is one of the oldest spices. It is the dried bark of a tropical plant of the same name. Cinnamon is obtained from the dried bark of a tropical plant related to the laurel family. Cinnamon stick is indigenous to Sri Lanka, which has complete monopoly. Cassia, on the other hand, grows all over the tropical countries. They produce similar flavours, but cinnamon is sweeter and more mellow.

Chilli peppers (*mirchi*): it is difficult to judge the strength of chilli peppers as different shapes and sizes will produce varying degrees of pungency. Generally, the small thin ones are hot and the large fleshy ones tend to be milder. As most of the heat comes from the seeds, it is best to remove them if you want a gentle kick without too much heat. One way to do this is to slit the chilli pepper in half lengthwise and scrape the seeds away under running water. Use a small knife for this. Another way is to hold the chilli pepper between your palms and roll it for a few seconds. This will loosen the seeds. You can then slit the chilli without cutting it through and simply shake out the seeds. The following types are normally used in Indian cooking:

- **Fresh green chilli peppers** (*hari mirchi*): the long, slim, fresh green Indian chilli peppers are sold in Indian stores. Similar looking ones are sometimes sold in local greengrocers but these are usually from the Canary Islands and tend to be much milder than the Indian chilli peppers.
- **Jalapeño and serrano chilli peppers:** from Mexico, these chilli peppers are more easily available from supermarkets. Although these are not ideal for Indian cooking, they can be used when a recipe calls for fresh green chilli peppers to be chopped or ground with other ingredients. When intended to be left whole, the long Indian variety looks more attractive.

◇ **Dried red chilli peppers (*lal mirchi*):** when green chilli peppers are ripe, their colour changes to a rich red. These are then dried to obtain dried red chilli peppers. One cannot be substituted for the other as the flavour, when the chilli pepper is dried, changes completely. The dried red 'Bird's eye' chilli peppers, which are small and pointed, are extremely hot, and these are normally used whole to flavour cooking oil. Long slim ones are much weaker and are used ground with other spices. Dried red chilli peppers are ground to a fine powder to make chilli powder. Crushed dried chilli peppers are obtained by grinding dried red chilli peppers to a medium-coarse texture.

Cloves (*lavang*): cloves are unopened dried buds of a southern Asian evergreen tree. They have a strong, distinctive flavour and are used both whole and ground. In India, cloves are used as a breath freshener, and clove oil is used to remedy toothache.

Coconut (*nariyal*): coconut palms grow in abundance in southern India. Fresh coconut is used in both sweet and savoury dishes. In the West, convenient alternatives are desiccated coconut, creamed coconut and coconut milk powder.

Coriander (cilantro), fresh (*hara dhaniya*): a much-used herb in Indian cooking, the fresh leaves of the coriander plant are used for flavouring as well as garnishing. They also form the basis of many chutneys and pastes. The fruit produced by the mature coriander plant is the seed used as a spice, and from which fresh coriander is grown.

Coriander (cilantro), seeds (*dhaniya*): this is one of the most important ingredients in Indian cooking. The sweet mellow flavour blends very well with vegetables.

Cumin seeds (*jeera*): like many spices, cumin can be used either whole or ground. It is powerfully pungent and the whole seeds are used to flavour the oil before the vegetables are cooked in it. A more rounded flavour is obtained if the seeds are roasted and then ground. Because of their strength, they need to be used in measured quantities. There are two varieties: black (*kala jeera*) and white (*safed jeera*). Each has its own distinct flavour and one cannot be substituted for the other. Black cumin is sometimes confused with caraway.

Curry leaf (*kari patta*): grown extensively in the foothills of the Himalayas, these have quite an assertive flavour. Sold fresh and dried by Indian grocers, they are used to flavour vegetables and pulses. Dried curry leaves should be stored in an airtight jar; the fresh ones, which have a better flavour, can be frozen and used as required.

Dhanna-jeera powder: this is simply a mixture of coriander (cilantro) and cumin seeds, which are ground together. The mix produces a different flavour from using ground coriander and cumin individually. This is because, when the seeds in dhanna-jeera powder are mixed and ground together, their natural oils combine at the same time. If you cannot get the mix, you can make your own by using 60 per cent coriander seeds and 40 per cent cumin seeds.

Dried fenugreek (*Kasoori methi*): a strong and aromatic herb characteristic of northern Indian and Pakistani cuisines. It is native to the Mediterranean region and is cultivated in India and Pakistan. Both the seeds and leaves (fresh and dried) are used in cooking.

Fennel seeds (*saunf*): these greenish-yellow seeds, slightly bigger than cumin, have a taste similar to anise. They have been used in Indian cooking since ancient times. In India, fennel is used as a breath freshener. The seeds are also chewed to settle an upset stomach.

Garam masala: the main ingredients of garam masala are cinnamon, cardamom, cloves and black pepper. Other spices are added to these, according to preference. Garam masala is available in the shops.

Garlic (*lasoon*): fresh garlic is indispensable to Indian cooking. Dried flakes, powder and garlic salt cannot create the same authentic flavour. Garlic is always crushed or puréed as these two methods produce more flavour. Garlic is beneficial in reducing the level of cholesterol in the blood, and its antiseptic properties aid the digestive system.

Ghee (clarified butter): ghee has a rich, distinctive flavour and is used liberally in Mogul food. There are two types of ghee: pure butterfat ghee and vegetable ghee. Butterfat ghee is made from unsalted butter; vegetable ghee is made from vegetable shortening. Ghee can be heated to a high temperature without burning. Both types of ghee are available from Indian stores, and vegetable ghee is sold by some supermarkets. It is simple to make your own ghee (*see recipe on page xviii*).

Ginger (*adrak*): fresh root ginger, which has a warm, woody aroma, is vital to Indian cooking. Dried, powdered ginger cannot produce an authentic flavour. Ginger is believed to improve circulation of the blood and reduce acidity in the stomach.

Mint (*pudina*): mint is native to Mediterranean and western Asian countries. It is easy to grow and also available in most supermarkets. Dried mint, however, is a good substitute. Bottled mint sauce, which has a lovely fresh aroma, works very well in many recipes.

Mustard seeds (*sarsoon* or *rai*): these are an essential ingredient in vegetarian cooking. Out of the three types, black and brown mustard seeds are commonly used in Indian cooking, and lend a nutty flavour to a dish. White mustard seeds are reserved for making pickles, and the green leaves are used as a vegetable.

Nutmeg (*jaiphal*): the nutmeg plant is unique as it produces two fruits in one: nutmeg and mace (*javitri*). Nutmeg has a hard, dark-brown shell with a lacy covering. This covering is mace, which is highly aromatic. It is removed from the nutmeg before being sold. The best way to buy nutmeg is whole. Pre-ground nutmeg loses the lovely aromatic flavour quickly. Special nutmeg graters are available with a compartment to store the whole nutmegs.

Onion (*pyaz*): this is one of the oldest flavouring ingredients and rarely is any Indian cooking done without it. Brown, red and snow-white onions are grown and used extensively; the use of shallots and spring onions (scallions) is also quite common.

Onion seeds (*kalonji*): these tiny black seeds are not produced by the onion plant. They are referred to thus because they have a striking resemblance to onion seeds. Kalonji, available from Indian stores, are used whole for flavouring vegetables and pickles and to flavour Indian breads.

Paneer: paneer is often referred to as 'cottage cheese' in India, but it is quite different from Western cottage cheese. The only Western cheese that resembles paneer in taste is ricotta, but paneer can withstand much higher cooking temperatures. Paneer is made by separating the whey from the milk solids and is an excellent source of protein. It is available from Asian stores.

Paprika: Hungary and Spain produce a mild, sweet strain of pepper. Dried and powdered, this is known as paprika. 'Deghi Mirchi', grown extensively in Kashmir, is the main plant used for making Indian paprika. A mild chilli pepper, it tints the dishes brilliant red without making them excessively hot.

Poppy seeds (*khus khus*): the opium poppy, grown mainly in the tropics, produces the best poppy seeds. There are two varieties, white and black, but only the white seeds are used in Indian recipes. They are either ground, or roasted and ground, and help to give a nutty flavour to most sauces while also acting as a thickening agent.

Rose water: a special edible rose is grown in many parts of the country. The petals are used for garnishing Mogul dishes. They can also be crushed to extract their essence. This is diluted to make rose water, which is utilized in savoury and sweet dishes.

Saffron (*kesar*): the saffron crocus grows extensively in Kashmir. Close to 250,000 stamens of this crocus are needed to produce just 450g (1lb) of saffron. It is a highly concentrated ingredient and only minute quantities are required to flavour any dish.

***Shahi jeera* (royal cumin):** this is different from normal cumin, and is sometimes known as black cumin seeds. It is a rare variety and, in India, grows mainly in Kashmir. It is also more expensive but its delicate and distinctive flavour is well worth the extra money. The seeds will keep well almost indefinitely if stored in airtight jars.

Sesame seeds (*til*): these pale creamy seeds, with a rich and nutty flavour, are indigenous to India. They are the most important of all the oil seeds grown in the world, and India is the largest exporter of sesame oil to the West. The seeds are sprinkled over naan before baking, and are also used in some sweets and vegetables. They are an effective thickening agent for sauces.

Tamarind (*imli*): resembling pea pods when tender, tamarind turns dark brown with a thin, hard outer shell when ripe. Chocolate-brown flesh is encased in the shell, which needs to be seeded before use. The required quantity of the flesh is soaked in hot water, made into a pulp and used in several dishes. These days, life is made easier by the availability of ready-to-use concentrated tamarind pulp. Lentils, peas, vegetables and chutneys benefit from its distinctive, tangy flavour.

Turmeric (*haldi*): fresh turmeric rhizomes are dried and ground to give a rich yellow powder. India produces the largest amounts of turmeric. The quantity used in dishes has to be just right to prevent a bitter taste.

Vanilla: second only to saffron in terms of plant-to-shop costs, vanilla pods retain their flavour for years. They are usually stored embedded in sugar. The sugar, with a strong vanilla flavour, can be used in desserts. Vanilla essence is an effective alternative.

Yogurt (*dahi*): made with fresh whole milk, yogurt in India is almost always home-made. With a mild flavour combined with a creamy texture, it is a very useful ingredient in many dishes.

Ghee (clarified butter)

Melt 450g/1lb/2 cups unsalted butter over a low heat and allow it to bubble gently. After a while, the spluttering will stop, indicating that most of the moisture has evaporated. Continue to heat the butter until the liquid is a clear, golden colour and you can see the sediment (milk solids) at the bottom of the pan. This process can take up to 45 minutes, depending on the quality of butter you are using. Once the liquid and milk solids have separated, cool the butter slightly and strain it into a storage jar through fine muslin. Ghee can be stored at room temperature. Vegetable ghee can be made in the same way using margarine made with vegetable oils.

Chapter 1

Starters and Appetizers

Though not a traditional Indian practice, having starters and appetizers makes a meal much more interesting. Your dinner guests will wait with curious anticipation for the main course to follow.

The vast range of snack dishes that exists within the diversity of Indian cuisine makes it very easy to divide a meal into two or three courses. With a little salad garnish and one or two chutneys, any Indian snack can be enjoyed as an appetizer. The same snacks can also be served as part of a buffet meal.

In the following pages you will find a small selection of low-fat starters and appetizers that are bursting with flavours. They have been carefully chosen to give you a range of different tastes, textures and flavours.

Spiced Potato Canapés

Preparation time: 20 minutes
Cooking time: 15–20 minutes to boil the potatoes   Serves 4–6

Spicy potatoes with three sauces on deep-fried crispy bread, known as *Papri Chaat,* is one of north India's most popular snacks. The word *chaat* means finger-licking good – and don't be surprised if you find yourselves smacking your lips too! In keeping with low-fat cooking, I have chosen water biscuits to serve with these potatoes.

225g/8oz potatoes
½ teaspoon chilli powder
½ teaspoon ground cumin
1 small green chilli pepper, seeded
    and finely chopped
1 tablespoon coriander (cilantro)
    leaves, finely chopped
1–2 tablespoons red onion, finely
    chopped
1 teaspoon salt or to taste
125g/4oz/½ cup low-fat set yogurt
1 teaspoon sugar
1 quantity Mint and Onion
    Chutney *(page 37)*
1 quantity Instant Tamarind
    Chutney *(page 37)*
Water biscuits to serve

1   Boil the potatoes until tender, then peel and chop them very finely. While the potatoes are still hot (to ensure they absorb all the flavours), add the chilli, cumin, green chilli, coriander (cilantro) leaves, onion and half the salt. Mix thoroughly.

2   Beat the yogurt with the sugar and remaining salt. Pile approximately two teaspoons of the potato mixture on each biscuit and top with the yogurt. Drizzle over the Mint and Onion Chutney followed by the Tamarind Chutney and serve. Alternatively, arrange the potato and chutneys in individual serving dishes and serve the biscuits separately.

Savoury Potatoes with Chilli and Tamarind

Preparation time: 20 minutes
Cooking time: 20–25 minutes to boil potatoes

Serves 4–6

This street-style snack from north India is popular all over the country. Known as *Aloo Chaat,* it has a wonderful savoury, tangy-hot flavour and is served cold in small bowls. A combination of black salt and coarse sea salt is used here. Black salt is known to aid digestion, but if you cannot get it, use just the sea salt.

680g/1½lb potatoes

2 tablespoons chopped coriander (cilantro) leaves

2 tablespoons fresh mint leaves or 1 teaspoon bottled mint sauce

1 fresh green chilli pepper, seeded and chopped

½ teaspoon chilli powder (optional)

¼ teaspoon black salt

Sea salt to taste

1½ tablespoons tamarind juice or 2 tablespoons lime juice

1 small red onion, finely chopped

1 Boil the potatoes in their jackets, cool thoroughly then peel and dice into 1cm/½-inch pieces.

2 Put the remaining ingredients, except the onion, into a blender and blend until smooth. Pour this mixture over the potatoes and add the onion. Mix thoroughly.

3 Spoon into individual serving dishes and serve.

Carrot and Spinach Pancakes

Preparation time: 15 minutes
Cooking time: 15 minutes

Makes 6

Carrots and spinach contain a considerable amount of useful nutrients including betacarotene (the plant form of vitamin A), which is believed to help fight cancer. These pancakes are easy to make and truly gorgeous. Unlike traditional pancakes, the batter here is quite thick. As you finish each pancake, keep it warm on a baking sheet in an oven set at 110°C/225°F/Gas Mark ¼. Do not pile them up or they will turn soggy. Place each pancake on an individual baking tray or wire cooling rack.

125g/4oz/2 cups chopped spinach
125g/4oz/¾ cup grated carrot
125g/4oz/1 cup finely chopped
   onion
2 green chilli peppers, seeded and
   chopped
1 teaspoon aniseed or fennel seeds
1 tablespoon ground coriander
   (cilantro)
½ teaspoon chilli powder
1 teaspoon ground turmeric
¾ teaspoon salt or to taste
125g/4oz/1 cup chickpea flour
   (besan), sieved
50g/2oz/⅓ cup semolina (cream of
   wheat) or fine polenta
1 teaspoon baking powder
Oil for shallow frying

1 In a large mixing bowl, mix all the ingredients, up to and including the salt.

2 Mix together the chickpea flour (besan), semolina (cream of wheat) or polenta and baking powder and add to the above mixture. Gradually add 300ml/10fl oz/1⅓ cups cold water while you stir and mix with a wooden spoon. Mix until you have a thick batter of spreading consistency.

3 Heat a tablespoon of oil over a medium heat in an iron griddle or heavy-based non-stick frying pan. Add 2 tablespoons of the pancake mixture. Spread it so that the pancake is approximately 18cm/7 inches in diameter, cover with a lid and cook for a minute or two or until the pancake is set and the underside is lightly browned. Brush the uncooked side with a little oil and turn it over. Reduce the heat to low and cook for 3–4 minutes or until browned.

4 Fold the pancake into a triangular shape and serve garnished with a little salad and a chutney.

Spiced Mixed Fruit

Preparation time: 25–30 minutes   **Serves 4**

This is a delicately spiced combination of exotic fruits. Known as *chaat,* it can be served as an appetizer or at the end of your meal instead of a dessert. Try other combinations of fruits, such as ripe mango and fresh lychees.

⊱⊰⊱⊰⊱⊰⊱⊰⊱⊰⊱⊰⊱⊰⊱⊰⊱⊰⊱⊰

2 ripe pomegranates
1 large ripe papaya (pawpaw)
1 small or ½ medium pineapple
175g/6oz/1 cup seedless green
   grapes
175/6oz/1 cup seedless black
   grapes
½ teaspoon ground dry ginger
¼ teaspoon freshly milled black
   pepper
½ teaspoon ground cumin
Pinch of chilli powder
½ teaspoon dried mint or 6–8 fresh
   mint leaves, finely chopped
½ teaspoon salt
Fresh mint sprigs, to garnish

1   Halve the pomegranates and remove the seeds by peeling off the outer skin like you would peel an orange. If you find this difficult, gently ease away the seeds with a fork and discard the outer skin. Remove white pith and skin next to the seeds and reserve the seeds.

2   Halve the papaya (pawpaw) lengthways and remove the black seeds, scraping off the white bits you will find under the seeds. Cut the papaya into 2.5cm/1-inch cubes.

3   Peel the pineapple and remove the eyes with a small, sharp knife. Cut off the hard core and chop the fruit into bite-sized pieces.

4   Halve the grapes and combine all the prepared fruits in a large mixing bowl. Add the rest of the ingredients, except the salt, and mix thoroughly. Chill for 1–2 hours. Stir in the salt and serve garnished with the sprigs of mint.

Mung Bean Rolls

Preparation time: 30 minutes plus soaking
Cooking time: 45 minutes

Makes 8

Mung beans are low in fat and a great source of protein and fibre. You can buy them in supermarkets and health-food stores. These rolls are similar to Chinese spring rolls in shape and size. I have used filo pastry and baked them in the oven to keep the fat content low.

125g/4oz/⅔ cup mung beans, washed and soaked for 3–4 hours

2 tablespoons sunflower or olive oil plus a little extra for brushing over the pastry sheets

½ teaspoon black mustard seeds

125g/4oz/⅔ cup leeks, finely sliced

2.5cm/1-inch cube of root ginger, finely grated

2 fresh green or red chilli peppers, seeded and finely chopped

½ teaspoon salt or to taste

50g/2oz/¼ cup sweet red pepper, finely chopped

50g/2oz/¼ cup sweet yellow pepper, finely chopped

175g/6oz/1½ cups cauliflower florets, cut into small dice

½ teaspoon ground turmeric

16 sheets filo pastry

1 Drain the mung beans, put into a small saucepan with 200ml/7fl oz/¾ cup hot water and bring to the boil over a high heat. Reduce the heat to low and simmer, covered, for 10 minutes. Dry off any liquid by cooking without a lid, then remove from the heat and set aside. You can cook the beans in advance and store them in the fridge for up to two days.

2 Heat the oil in a wok over a medium heat and throw in the mustard seeds. As soon as they start popping, add the leeks, ginger and chilli peppers. Add the salt to encourage the leeks to release their juices, then stir-fry for 2–3 minutes.

3 Add the peppers and cauliflower and continue to stir-fry for 2–3 minutes.

4 Add the cooked mung beans and turmeric. Stir-fry for about 2 minutes then remove from the heat and allow to cool completely.

5 Preheat the oven to 190°C/375°F/Gas Mark 5. Place a sheet of filo pastry on a board and brush lightly with oil. Place a second sheet of pastry on this, then spoon two tablespoons of the mung bean mixture on the upper part of the pastry. Leave a border of about 5cm/2 inches at the top and 2.5cm/1 inch on each side.

6 Fold the sides and the top of the pastry and gently roll down to the bottom to make a neat roll. Seal the edges by brushing with some cold water. Place the roll, joined side down, on a baking sheet lined with greased greaseproof (waxed) paper or baking parchment. Brush the rolls with some more oil. Bake in the centre of the oven for 25–30 minutes or until browned evenly. Serve with a chutney or a salad.

Savoury Triangles filled with Spiced Vegetables

Preparation time: 30–40 minutes
Cooking time: 25–30 minutes

Makes 16

These are the ever-popular samosas, here made with low-fat filo pastry. Freeze any extra ones before frying and they can be fried straight from the freezer.

꧁꧂꧁꧂꧁꧂꧁꧂꧁꧂꧁꧂꧁꧂꧁꧂꧁꧂

2 tablespoons sunflower or light olive oil plus a little extra for brushing

½ teaspoon black mustard seeds

½ teaspoon cumin seeds

½ teaspoon onion seeds (kalonji)

1 red onion, finely chopped

1–2 fresh red chilli peppers, finely chopped (seeded if wished)

1cm/½-inch cube root ginger, finely grated

1½ teaspoons ground cumin

1 teaspoon ground coriander (cilantro)

½ teaspoon ground turmeric

275g/10oz/1⅓ cups boiled and diced potatoes

50g/2oz/¼ cup grated carrots

50g/2oz/¼ cup frozen garden peas

1 teaspoon salt or to taste

2 tablespoons finely chopped coriander (cilantro) leaves

16 sheets filo pastry

1 In a wok or other non-stick pan, heat the oil over a medium heat. When the oil is hot, but not smoking, throw in the mustard seeds. As soon as they pop, add the cumin and onion seeds and let them sizzle for 15–20 seconds.

2 Add the onion, chillies and ginger. Fry for 4–5 minutes until the onion is soft. Add the spices and cook for about a minute.

3 Add the vegetables and salt. Stir and cook for 2–3 minutes and reduce the heat to low. Sprinkle 2–3 tablespoons of water on the vegetables, cover the pan and cook for 4–5 minutes. Stir in the coriander (cilantro) leaves and remove from the heat. Allow to cool completely. You can refrigerate the mixture overnight at this stage.

4 Preheat the oven to 180°C/350°F/Gas Mark 4 and line a baking sheet with non-stick baking parchment.

5 Place a sheet of filo pastry on a flat surface and brush lightly with oil. Fold both long edges of the pastry sheet inwards so they just meet in the centre.

6 Place a tablespoon of filling on the bottom right-hand corner of the strip and fold to form a triangle. Continue to fold up to the top end, maintaining the triangular shape. Seal the edges with cold water. Place on the prepared baking sheet and brush over with some oil. If you find it difficult to form a triangle, just fold them into rolls. Bake for 20–25 minutes until crisp and golden brown. Serve immediately with a chutney such as Mint and Onion *(page 37)*. The samosas lose their crisp texture if left to cool, but will revive quickly in a hot oven.

Savoury Vegetable Loaf

Preparation time: 15–20 minutes
Cooking time: 50 minutes

Serves 4

This delicious and wholesome bake contains essential vitamins and minerals. Serve it with a chutney. Accompanied by Minted Yogurt and Coriander Sauce *(page 40),* this also makes an ideal main course.

~~~~~~~~~~~~~

175g/6oz/1 cup chickpea flour
   (besan), sieved
1 teaspoon salt or to taste
½ teaspoon baking powder
1 red onion, finely chopped
2 fresh red or green chilli peppers,
   seeded and finely chopped
2–3 tablespoons coriander
   (cilantro) leaves, finely chopped
2 small garlic cloves, crushed to a
   fine pulp
1 teaspoon ground cumin
2 teaspoons ground coriander
   (cilantro)
½ teaspoon fennel seeds
125g/4oz/⅔ cup finely grated
   carrot
175g/6oz/1 cup white cabbage,
   finely chopped
½ teaspoon chilli powder
200ml/7fl oz/¾ cup tomato juice
2 tablespoons olive oil

1 Preheat the oven to 190°C/375°F/Gas Mark 5. Line a 900g/2lb loaf tin with greased greaseproof (wax) paper or baking parchment.

2 In a large mixing bowl, mix the chickpea flour (besan), salt and baking powder. Add the remaining ingredients except the tomato juice and oil. Mix the ingredients together and gradually add the tomato juice until the mixture resembles that of a fruit cake.

3 Spoon the mixture into the prepared loaf tin and bake in the centre of the oven for 50 minutes or until firm to the touch. Allow to cool in the tin then turn out and cut into 1cm/½-inch slices.

4 In a non-stick frying pan (skillet), heat a little of the oil over a medium heat and brown a few slices of the vegetable loaf at a time until you have finished browning them all. Keep the fried slices hot in a low oven until ready to serve with Minted Yogurt and Coriander Sauce and any bread.

Spiced Corn on the Cob

Preparation time: 10–15 minutes
Cooking time: 15 minutes

Serves 4

In India, we use fresh corn, but you can use frozen too. Thaw slightly in the microwave to make them easier to slice. If using olive oil, choose plain rather than virgin or extra virgin.

⌇⌇⌇⌇⌇⌇⌇⌇⌇⌇⌇⌇

4 corn on the cob (corncob), fresh or frozen

140ml/¼ pint/⅔ cup reduced-fat coconut milk

2–4 dried red chilli peppers, chopped

1 teaspoon salt or to taste

1 tablespoon sunflower or plain olive oil

½ teaspoon black mustard seeds

½ teaspoon cumin seeds

2–3 green chilli peppers, seeded and chopped

1 tablespoon chopped coriander (cilantro) leaves

1½ tablespoons lemon juice

1 Slice the corn into 1cm/½-inch rounds.

2 Put the coconut milk and chillies into a roomy pan with the corn and add the salt. Add 90ml/3fl oz/⅓ cup water and bring to a slow simmer, cover and cook for 10 minutes, stirring halfway through.

3 Meanwhile, heat the oil in a small saucepan over a medium heat. When hot, but not smoking, add the mustard seeds, followed by the cumin. Let them pop for 5–10 seconds and pour the contents over the corn.

4 Add the green chilli peppers, fresh coriander (cilantro) and lemon juice. Stir until all the liquid dries up and the coconut sauce coats the corn. Remove from the heat and serve as a starter, snack or side dish.

Oven-roasted Spiced Walnuts

Preparation time: 5 minutes
Cooking time: 12–15 minutes

Serves 4–6

Recent research has shown that walnuts are beneficial to the heart when eaten as part of a low-fat diet. They are believed to be helpful in lowering blood cholesterol and are a rich source of essential fatty acids, which are needed for normal tissue growth and development. Here is a delicious recipe for walnuts laced with aromatic spices and roasted in the oven. With their crisp texture, they make a delicious starter or a fabulous snack.

350g/12oz/1⅔ cups shelled walnut halves

2–3 tablespoons light olive oil

3 cloves garlic, crushed to a fine pulp

1 teaspoon hot chilli powder or to taste

½ teaspoon ground cumin

Salt and freshly milled black pepper

1 Preheat the oven to 180°C/350°F/Gas Mark 4.

2 In a mixing bowl, toss the walnuts and oil until the nuts are coated. Add the garlic and mix well. Put the nuts in a roasting tin and place in the centre of the oven for 5–6 minutes.

3 Mix the remaining ingredients together and sprinkle over the nuts. Stir until the nuts are coated with the spices. Return to the oven for 8–10 minutes or until the nuts begin to brown. Remove and allow to cool completely.

Steamed Chickpea Flour Squares

Preparation time: 10 minutes plus resting
Cooking time: 20 minutes

Serves 4

This is a new version of a delicious savoury snack known as *khandvi* from the state of Gujerat in western India. Low in fat and packed with essential nutrients, it can be served with Instant Tamarind Chutney *(page 37)* for a perfect appetizer.

275g/10oz/1¼ cups chickpea flour
   (besan)
125g/4oz/⅔ cup low-fat plain
   yogurt
90ml/3fl oz/⅓ cup water
2 fresh red chilli peppers, finely
   chopped (seeded if wished)
1 teaspoon salt or to taste
½ teaspoon ground turmeric
3 tablespoons olive oil
1 tablespoon desiccated coconut
2 tablespoons chopped coriander
   (cilantro) leaves
½ teaspoon black mustard seeds
6 fresh or 8 dried curry leaves
¼ teaspoon asafoetida

1   Sieve the chickpea flour (besan) into a mixing bowl and add the yogurt, water, half the chilli peppers, salt and turmeric. Mix thoroughly with a wooden spoon and add half the oil. Work the oil well into the mixture. It will be more like a thick paste. Cover and set aside for 30 minutes.

2   Spray or brush a little oil (from the remaining specified amount) on a 30cm/12-inch heat-proof plate and spread half the above mixture (as you would a pancake) on it to cover the entire surface. It is easier to spread the mixture with lightly greased palms or a greased metal spoon. Divide the coconut, the rest of the chilli peppers and coriander (cilantro) equally into two portions. Sprinkle one portion on the surface, set the plate on a steamer and steam for 8 minutes. Set aside for 5 minutes and gently ease away the steamed pancake with a thin spatula or fish slice. Place on a cutting board and cut into 2.5cm/1-inch squares. Cook and cut the second half of the mixture in the same way.

3   In a non-stick wok, heat the remaining oil over a medium heat and add the mustard seeds. As soon as they start popping, switch off the heat, add the curry leaves and asafoetida and let them sizzle for 15–20 seconds. Add the chickpea flour squares and mix gently. Transfer to a serving dish and serve hot or cold.

Steamed Semolina Cakes

Preparation time: 20 minutes plus standing time
Cooking time: 45–50 minutes

Makes 18 Cakes

Hot, soft and fluffy steamed cakes *(idlis)* served with spiced lentils are the signature dish of the state of Tamil Nadu in southern India. This is an easier version of the traditional steamed cake, which is made from a combination of ground and fermented rice and lentils. The cakes are served with a spiced lentil dish known as *sambar,* and together they make a completely balanced and nourishing vegetarian meal. Serve with Cumin and Coriander Scented Lentils with Sautéed Shallots *(page 60)* for a main meal, and with Courgette Chutney *(page 35)* or Sautéed Lentil Chutney *(page 38)* as an appetizer. The cakes freeze extremely well.

275g/10 oz/1½ cups semolina
   (cream of wheat)
1 teaspoon baking powder
½ teaspoon bicarbonate of soda
1 fresh red chilli pepper, finely
   chopped (seeded if wished)
1 tablespoon raw cashew nuts,
   chopped
1 tablespoon coriander (cilantro)
   leaves, finely chopped
½ teaspoon salt or to taste
225g/8oz/1 cup low-fat plain
   yogurt, beaten well
450ml/16fl oz/2 cups soda water

1   Mix all the dry ingredients together and add the yogurt. Blend with a wooden spoon and gradually add the soda water. Continue to mix until you have a thick paste which should be the consistency of a cake mix, but slightly more moist. If the mixture has any lumps, beat it with a wire beater. Cover the bowl and set aside for 30 minutes.

2   Brush the cups from an egg poacher with oil. Prepare a steamer over a saucepan of boiling water. Place 1½ tablespoons of the mix into each poacher and steam for 10 minutes. You will need to do this in batches. Keep the cooked cakes hot by wrapping in a piece of foil and placing in a low oven until you have finished cooking them all.

Stuffed Courgettes

Preparation time: 15 minutes
Cooking time: 10 minutes

Serves 4

This lovely young marrow is full of essential nutrients including vitamin C and betacarotene. As cheese is also included in this recipe, you have the added bonus of protein and calcium.

4 large courgettes (zucchini)
2 tablespoons sunflower or olive oil
3 shallots, finely chopped
2 fresh red or green chilli peppers,
    finely chopped (seeded if liked)
2 tablespoons canned and drained
    sweetcorn
75g/3oz/¾ cup half-fat mild
    Cheddar cheese, grated
2 tablespoons chopped coriander
    (cilantro) leaves
Salt and pepper to taste
Sliced tomatoes and mixed salad
    leaves, to serve

1 Halve the courgettes (zucchini) lengthways and slice off the bottom of each half so that they sit firmly. Scoop out or scrape off the centre of the courgette halves. Chop half the tender flesh finely and discard the remainder.

2 Heat the oil over a medium heat and use some of it to brush the courgette shells inside and out. Place the courgette halves on a grill (broiler) pan.

3 Fry the shallots and chilli peppers in the remaining oil for 3–4 minutes. Stir in the sweetcorn and the chopped courgette flesh. Remove from the heat and cool slightly.

4 Meanwhile, preheat the grill (broiler) to medium. Mix the fried ingredients with the cheese and fresh coriander (cilantro), and season to taste. Divide the mixture equally between the courgette shells and press down to fill the hollows firmly. Grill for 6–8 minutes or until browned. Serve garnished with the sliced tomatoes and lettuce.

Chapter 2

Salads and Chutneys

First, I would like to dispel the general misconception that salads do not exist in Indian cuisine. Indeed, from ancient times, salads have always been extremely interesting in India. Some are served as side dishes and others as main courses, and they can be hot or cold. You will find a great selection in the following pages.

A salad is generally accepted as a dish containing raw vegetables and/or fruits with a simple dressing. Gone are the days, however, when salad was considered boring 'rabbit food'. In recent years, salad dressings have taken on a new dimension. Many different and exotic dressings are commercially available, and the ingredients to make them at home are also sold by retailers.

Indian salads have always been different to their Western counterparts. The dressing is exquisitely flavoured with yogurt, rather than oil or vinegar, as the main ingredient. The *raita* – raw fruits and vegetables served with a spiced yogurt dressing – originated in north India. Others, from south and west India, are simply flavoured with a hot-oil seasoning.

The term 'chutney' is thought to come from the Persian *chasney,* meaning 'relish'. Chutneys originated in rural India during the colonial period. A few chosen ingredients would be ground together and used to liven up an otherwise boring meal of boiled rice and lentils. Somewhat different from the original versions, today's Indian chutneys are made by grinding all the ingredients together to a fine powder or paste.

Chutneys add zest to any meal, and they can be used both as a condiment and a sauce. In the West, Indian chutneys have firmly established themselves as an integral part of a meal. Chutneys and raitas together give Indian meals that unusual and interesting twist.

Carrot Raita

This recipe works best with a thick and creamy yogurt, which gives it a wholesome taste.

½ teaspoon cumin seeds
10 black peppercorns
150g/5oz/¾ cup thick set
   wholemilk natural yogurt
½ teaspoon salt
½ teaspoon sugar
175g/6oz/1 cup grated carrots

1   Preheat a small, heavy-based saucepan or frying pan (skillet) over a medium heat and dry roast the cumin seeds and the peppercorns until they release their aroma (a minute or so). Transfer to a plate and allow to cool.

2   Beat the yogurt with a fork until smooth and add the salt and sugar. Crush the roasted spices with a pestle or place in a plastic bag and crush with a rolling pin. Mix most of the spice mixture with the yogurt and add the grated carrots. Stir and mix thoroughly, then sprinkle the remaining spices on top.

Radish and Carrot Raita

Preparation time: 15 minutes   **Serves 4–6**

White radish *(mooli)* is becoming increasingly available in supermarkets. Combined with carrots, it makes a lovely and colourful relish, perfect with any meal. For a variation, use white cabbage instead of radish.

125g/4oz/⅔ cup low-fat natural yogurt

1 teaspoon salt or to taste

1 teaspoon sugar

1 tablespoon fresh mint leaves, finely chopped

½ red onion (about 50g/2oz), finely chopped

1 white radish (about 225g/8oz/2¼ cups), grated

2 carrots (about 200g/7oz/1 cup), grated

1   Beat the yogurt with a fork until smooth. Add the salt, sugar, mint and onion and mix thoroughly.

2   Stir in the grated radish and carrots; mix and chill.

Cauliflower Raita

Preparation time: 10–15 minutes
Cooking time: 5–6 minutes plus cooling Serves 4

Slightly crunchy florets of cauliflower, flavoured with the warmth of cumin seeds and the nutty taste of mustard seeds, are delicious on their own or combined with plain yogurt as in this recipe.

1 tablespoon sunflower or olive oil
½ teaspoon black mustard seeds
½ teaspoon cumin seeds
1 large garlic clove, crushed
1 dried red chilli pepper, chopped
125g/4oz/1 cup bite-sized
    cauliflower florets
½ teaspoon salt or to taste
175g/6oz/¾ cup set plain yogurt
½ teaspoon sugar

1 Heat the oil over a medium heat. When hot, but not smoking, add the mustard seeds and reduce the heat to low.

2 Add the cumin followed by the garlic and red chilli pepper. Stir-fry for about a minute and add the cauliflower and salt. Increase the heat to medium and stir-fry the cauliflower for 3–4 minutes, sprinkling regularly with a tablespoon of water, until the edges of the florets begin to brown.

3 Remove from the heat and allow to cool.

4 Beat the yogurt and sugar together, add the cooled cauliflower and serve.

Mushroom Raita

Preparation time: 15 minutes
Cooking time: 8–9 minutes

Serves 4

Use only the freshest mushrooms for this recipe. They should be firm to the touch without any bruising or discolouration.

25g/1oz butter
2–3 cloves garlic, crushed
1 green chilli pepper, seeded and chopped
225g/8oz/2½ cups closed-cup mushrooms, chopped
½ teaspoon salt or to taste
½ teaspoon ground cumin
2 tablespoons chopped coriander (cilantro)
225g/8oz/1 cup wholemilk set plain yogurt

1 Melt the butter over a low heat and fry the garlic and chilli pepper until the garlic begins to brown.

2 Add the mushrooms and salt, increase the heat to high and stir-fry for 5 minutes.

3 Add the cumin and fresh coriander (cilantro). Stir-fry for 15–20 seconds. Remove from the heat and cool.

4 Beat the yogurt until smooth and stir in the cooked mushrooms.

Pumpkin Raita

Preparation time: 10–15 minutes
Cooking time: 15 minutes plus cooling

Serves 4

Pumpkin is a good source of vitamin E and betacarotene, and the latter is converted by the body into vitamin A. For this recipe, other varieties of winter squash, such as butternut or acorn, can be used.

~~~~~~

1 tablespoon sunflower or olive oil
½ teaspoon black mustard seeds
2 cloves garlic, crushed
1–2 fresh green chilli peppers, seeded and chopped
1 teaspoon ground cumin
225g/8oz/2 cups pumpkin, peeled and cut into 2.5cm/1-inch cubes
½ teaspoon salt
1 teaspoon sugar
125g/4oz/½ cup low-fat set plain yogurt
50g/2oz/¼ cup low-fat crème fraîche
1 tablespoon coriander (cilantro) leaves, finely chopped
Pinch each of paprika and ground cumin

1   Heat the oil over a medium heat until hot, but not smoking, then add the mustard seeds. As soon as they pop, add the garlic and let it brown a little. Add the fresh chilli peppers, cumin, pumpkin, salt and sugar. Stir and mix thoroughly. Reduce the heat to low and sprinkle 2–3 tablespoons of water over the vegetables. Cover and cook for 10 minutes, stirring once or twice. Remove from the heat and cool.

2   Beat the yogurt and crème fraîche together until well blended, and stir in the cooled pumpkin along with the coriander (cilantro) leaves. Serve sprinkled with the paprika and cumin.

Spinach Raita

Preparation time: 15 minutes
Cooking time: 10 minutes plus cooling   **Serves 4**

Spinach has long been credited with having medicinal properties. In recent years, research has also found spinach to be beneficial in fighting certain types of cancer because of its high concentration of carotenoids, including betacarotene.

1 tablespoon sunflower or olive oil
½ teaspoon black mustard seeds
½ teaspoon cumin seeds
2 cloves garlic, crushed
1–2 green chilli peppers, seeded and chopped
225g/8oz/4 cups fresh spinach, chopped
½ teaspoon salt or to taste
1 tablespoon sunflower seeds
225g/8oz/1 cup wholemilk set plain yogurt

1 Heat the oil over a medium heat. When quite hot, but not smoking, throw in the mustard seeds, followed by the cumin. Reduce the heat to low and let the seeds pop for 5–10 seconds.

2 Add the garlic and chilli peppers and stir-fry briefly (30–40 seconds).

3 Add the spinach and salt. Increase the heat to high, stir and cook till the spinach begins to wilt. Reduce the heat slightly and continue to stir-fry until the natural juices evaporate. Remove from the heat and cool.

4 Meanwhile, preheat a small, heavy pan over a medium heat and dry-roast the sunflower seeds, stirring constantly until they brown a little (35–40 seconds). Remove and let cool.

5 Beat the yogurt until smooth and add the cooked spinach. Mix thoroughly and transfer to a serving dish. Serve sprinkled with the roasted sunflower seeds.

Baby Spinach Salad

Preparation time: 15–20 minutes

Cooking time: 3–4 minutes   Serves 4

Spinach teamed with grated carrots looks stunning. I use baby spinach, but you could use the mature leaves as long as they are absolutely fresh. Make the salad on the day you buy the spinach.

225g/8oz baby spinach, finely chopped

1 small carrot, scraped and grated

25g/1oz/¼ cup desiccated coconut

1 tablespoon olive oil

½ teaspoon black mustard seeds

½ teaspoon cumin seeds

2 teaspoons lime juice

¼ teaspoon sugar

¼ teaspoon salt

1   In a large mixing bowl, mix the spinach, carrot and coconut together.

2   In a small saucepan or steel ladle, heat the oil over a medium heat. When hot, but not smoking, throw in the mustard seeds and switch off the heat source. Add the cumin seeds and let them sizzle for a few seconds. Pour this mixture over the spinach and add the lime juice, sugar and salt. Mix thoroughly and serve.

Baby Corn Raita

Preparation time: 5 minutes
Cooking time: 6–8 minutes plus cooling

Serves 4

Traditionally, only the mature corn is used in Indian cooking, but baby corn is delicious stir-fried on its own or in salads. Lightly spiced and used with a yogurt dressing (raita) as in this recipe, it is the perfect accompaniment to any meal.

∂≈≈ ∂≈≈ ∂≈≈ ∂≈≈ ∂≈≈ ∂≈≈ ∂≈≈ ∂≈≈ ∂≈≈ ∂≈≈

1 tablespoon sunflower or olive oil
½ teaspoon black mustard seeds
1 large clove garlic, crushed
1 tablespoon finely chopped green (bell) pepper
1 tablespoon finely chopped sweet red (bell) pepper
175g/6oz/¾ cup baby corn, finely sliced
½ teaspoon salt or to taste
1 tablespoon coriander (cilantro) leaves, finely chopped
225g/8oz/1 cup wholemilk set plain yogurt

1   Heat the oil over a medium heat until fairly hot, but not smoking. Add the mustard seeds and reduce the heat to low. Add the garlic and stir-fry until lightly browned.

2   Add both types of pepper and stir-fry for about a minute, then add the baby corn and salt. Sprinkle in a tablespoon of water and continue to stir-fry for a further minute or two.

3   Reserve a little coriander (cilantro) and stir in the remainder. Remove from the heat and allow to cool.

4   Beat the yogurt until smooth and stir in the cooked vegetables. Garnish with the reserved coriander and serve.

Tomato and Coconut Raita

Preparation time: 15–20 minutes
Cooking time: 10–12 minutes plus cooling

Serves 4

The tomato is one of the most widely used ingredients the world over. Its flavour and nutritional value are at their best in sun-drenched tomatoes, plucked and eaten immediately. As most of us buy ours from supermarkets, try vine tomatoes for this recipe. Cherry tomatoes are also excellent.

1 tablespoon sunflower or olive oil
½ teaspoon black mustard seeds
½ teaspoon cumin seeds
450g/1lb/2⅔ cups fresh tomatoes, skinned and chopped
1–2 fresh green chilli peppers, seeded and chopped
1 teaspoon salt or to taste
1 teaspoon sugar
25g/1oz/⅓ cup desiccated coconut, ground in a coffee mill
125g/4oz/½ cup low-fat set plain yogurt
1 tablespoon finely chopped coriander (cilantro) leaves

1   Heat the oil over a medium heat until hot but not smoking. Throw in the mustard seeds and, as soon as they pop, add the cumin seeds.

2   Add the tomatoes, fresh chilli peppers, salt, sugar and coconut. Reduce the heat slightly, cover and cook for 8–10 minutes. Stir once or twice. Remove from the heat and cool.

3   Beat the yogurt until smooth. Reserve a little coriander (cilantro) and add the remainder to the yogurt. Stir in the cooked tomato and coconut mixture and serve garnished with the reserved coriander.

Tomato and Cucumber Raita

Preparation time: 10–15 minutes   **Serves 4**

Tomato and cucumber together make a nutritious combination, which is further enhanced by adding plain yogurt.

175g/6oz/¾ cup plain set yogurt
½ teaspoon salt
½ teaspoon sugar
½ teaspoon ground cumin
8–10 fresh mint leaves, finely
    chopped
½ a cucumber, coarsely chopped
2 firm ripe tomatoes, seeded and
    chopped
1 tablespoon roasted salted
    peanuts, lightly crushed

1   Beat the yogurt with a fork until smooth and add the salt, sugar, cumin and mint leaves. Mix thoroughly and stir in the cucumber and tomatoes.

2   Put into a serving bowl and sprinkle the crushed peanuts on top.

Celery and Cucumber Raita

Preparation time: 10–15 minutes

Cooking time: 2–3 minutes

Serves 4–6

Although celery is not a traditional Indian vegetable, it is excellent in a raita. Combined with cucumber and flavoured with a hot-oil seasoning, it tastes superb.

150g/5oz/¾ cup wholemilk set
   plain yogurt

½ teaspoon salt or to taste

1 teaspoon sugar

1 tablespoon finely chopped
   coriander (cilantro) leaves

2 teaspoons sunflower or olive oil

½ teaspoon black mustard seeds

¼ teaspoon ground cumin

¼ teaspoon freshly milled black
   pepper

90g/3oz/½ cup celery, trimmed and
   finely chopped

90g/3oz/½ cup cucumber,
   unpeeled and finely chopped

1   Put the yogurt in a mixing bowl and beat with a fork until smooth.

2   Add the salt, sugar and coriander (cilantro) leaves and mix well.

3   In a small saucepan or a steel ladle, heat the oil over a medium heat. When hot, but not smoking, add the mustard seeds. As soon as they pop, remove pan from heat and add the cumin and pepper. Pour the hot oil and the spices over the salad and mix lightly.

4   Add the celery and cucumber and mix well. Chill before serving.

Cucumber Salad in Mustard and Curry Leaf Dressing

Preparation time: 10 minutes
Cooking time: 2–3 minutes

Serves 4–5

Cucumber is low in calories, cooling and refreshing.

1 large cucumber (400g/14oz approx.), finely chopped
50g/2oz/¼ cup dry roasted peanuts, lightly crushed
1 tablespoon lime juice
Salt to taste
2 tablespoons sunflower or light olive oil
½ teaspoon black mustard seeds
4–5 fresh or 6–7 dried curry leaves
1–2 fresh red chilli peppers, seeded and finely chopped

1   Mix the cucumber, peanuts, lime juice and salt together.
2   In a small saucepan or a steel ladle, heat the oil over a medium heat. When hot, but not smoking, throw in the mustard seeds. As soon as they begin to pop, switch off the heat source and add the curry leaves and chilli peppers. Let them sizzle for 25–30 seconds and pour over the cucumber salad. Mix and serve immediately.

Pear and Cucumber Salad

Preparation time: 10–15 minutes   **Serves 4**

This is a delicious and unusual combination. Use nashi pears when they are in season, as they are wonderful for this salad.

1½ teaspoons cumin seeds
3 firm William or Peckham pears
1 tablespoon lime juice
1 small or ½ large cucumber
150g/5oz/⅔ cup low-fat crème
    fraîche
½ teaspoon salt
1 teaspoon sugar
½ teaspoon chilli powder

1   Preheat a small, heavy-based pan over a medium heat. Add the cumin seeds and stir until they are a shade darker and you can smell the aroma. Transfer the seeds to a plate and allow to cool.

2   Peel and core the pears and cut into bite-sized pieces. Put into a mixing bowl and sprinkle with the lime juice. Chop the cucumber into chunks the same size as the pears and mix together.

3   Crush the roasted cumin seeds with a pestle and mortar or the back of a wooden spoon.

4   Mix the crème fraîche with the salt, sugar, half the chilli powder and half the crushed cumin seeds. Add the mixture to the pear and cucumber and mix well. Transfer to a serving dish and sprinkle the remaining chilli powder and crushed cumin on top. Serve immediately.

Green Bean Salad

Preparation time: 10 minutes
Cooking time: 6–8 minutes   **Serves 4**

Here green beans are combined with finely sliced radish, and the south-Indian tradition of flavouring salads with a hot-oil seasoning is used. Use French beans or dwarf beans for this recipe.

1 tablespoon olive oil
¼ teaspoon black mustard seeds
225g/8oz/1 cup green beans
½ teaspoon salt or to taste
25g/1oz/¼ cup desiccated coconut
140ml/5fl oz/⅔ cup boiling water
Bunch of radishes, trimmed and
    sliced lengthways
3–4 spring onions (scallions), white
    parts only, finely sliced
1 green chilli pepper, seeded and
    finely chopped
1 tablespoon lime juice
1 tablespoon chopped coriander
    (cilantro) leaves

1   Heat the oil to smoking point and add the mustard seeds, followed by the beans and salt. Stir once, reduce the heat to low, cover the pan and let the beans sweat for 6–8 minutes.

2   Meanwhile, soak the coconut in the water for 5 minutes, drain and add to the beans. Mix well, remove from the heat and let cool.

3   Stir in the remaining ingredients and set aside for 30 minutes to allow the flavours to mingle. Serve at room temperature.

Pineapple Salad

Preparation time: 15 minutes
Cooking time: 15–20 minutes   Serves 4

The sweet juicy flesh of pineapple, combined with ripe firm banana and seasoned with mustard and chilli, is totally delicious. You can also serve it at the end of a meal instead of a dessert. Try to buy a small pineapple with a rich, golden colour. Sometimes these are sold as extra-sweet ones.

1 small pineapple
½ teaspoon ground turmeric
1 teaspoon salt or to taste
25g/1oz/¼ cup granulated sugar
25g/1oz/¼ cup desiccated coconut
1 dried red chilli pepper, chopped
2 ripe, firm bananas, thickly sliced
1 tablespoon olive oil
½ teaspoon black mustard seeds
1 green chilli pepper, seeded and
   finely chopped
6 fresh or 8 dried curry leaves

1 Peel the pineapple and remove the 'eyes' with a small sharp knife. Cut into 8 boat-shaped pieces and remove the central core from each piece. Cut into 1cm/½-inch wedges and place in a saucepan with the turmeric, salt and sugar. Add 300ml/½ pint/1⅓ cups water and cook over a medium heat, covered, until the pineapple is tender (about 15 minutes).

2 Meanwhile, grind the coconut and the red chilli pepper in a coffee grinder and add to the cooked pineapple. Stir in the bananas and remove from the heat.

3 In a small saucepan or a steel ladle, heat the oil over medium heat. When hot, switch off the heat source and add the mustard seeds followed by the green chilli pepper and curry leaves. Stir the mixture into the pineapple, allow to cool and serve.

Potato Salad with Roasted Peanut Dressing

Preparation time: 15 minutes
Cooking time: 15–20 minutes

Serves 4

Potato is an excellent vegetable for a low-fat diet as it is 99 per cent fat-free. It is also a source of easy-to-digest carbohydrate. Besides containing a small amount of protein, potato is a good source of iron, vitamin C and B-vitamins.

450g/1lb small new potatoes
2 teaspoons coriander (cilantro) seeds
½ teaspoon cumin seeds
1–2 dried red chilli peppers, broken up
½ teaspoon salt or to taste
1 red onion, finely chopped
1½ tablespoons lime juice
90g/3oz/½ cup dry roasted peanuts

1   Boil the potatoes gently in their jackets and let cool. Peel them if you like, then cut them into bite-sized pieces. Put into a large mixing bowl.

2   In a small, heavy pan, dry-roast the coriander (cilantro), cumin and chilli peppers. Cool and either grind in a coffee grinder or crush finely with a pestle and mortar. Add this to the potatoes with the salt, onion and lime juice. Mix well.

3   Put the peanuts in a plastic food bag and crush coarsely with a rolling pin. Mix into the potato salad and serve.

Potato Salad with Roasted Cumin and Coriander

Preparation time: 20 minutes
Cooking time: 20 minutes

Serves 4

I like new potatoes for this salad as you can taste their wonderful natural flavour through the subtle spices. Coconut enriches the yogurt dressing and the raisins provide a fabulous contrast in taste and appearance.

25g/1oz/¼ cup seedless raisins

680g/1½lb new potatoes, boiled, peeled and cut into 2.5cm/1-inch cubes

1 red onion, finely chopped

1 teaspoon cumin seeds

1½ teaspoons coriander (cilantro) seeds

1–2 long, slim, dried red chilli peppers, chopped

25g/1oz/¼ cup desiccated coconut

½ teaspoon salt or to taste

½ teaspoon sugar

125g/4oz/½ cup low-fat plain yogurt

1 Soak the raisins in boiling water for 10 minutes, then drain.

2 Put the potatoes and onion in a large mixing bowl, add the raisins and set aside.

3 Preheat a small, heavy pan over a medium heat and dry-roast the cumin and coriander (cilantro) seeds for about a minute. Remove from the pan and let cool, then grind with the chilli peppers in a coffee mill. When half-ground, add the coconut and grind until fine. Add this mixture to the potato and onion.

4 Beat the salt, sugar and yogurt together until smooth. Add to the potato mixture and mix well. Let it stand for 30 minutes before serving. Can be served chilled or at room temperature.

Smoked Tofu Salad

Preparation time: 25–30 minutes
Cooking time: 6–8 minutes

Serves 2–4

Hard tofu works well in this salad. It makes a balanced and nutritious main meal for two or a side dish for four people.

255g/9oz/1 cup smoked tofu, cut
  into 2.5cm/1-inch cubes
2 tablespoons olive oil
1 tablespoon lemon juice
½ teaspoon ground aniseed
½ teaspoon chilli powder
2.5cm/1-inch cube root ginger,
  finely grated
2 cloves garlic, crushed to a fine
  pulp
Salt to taste
1 large sweet red (bell) pepper
1 large sweet green (bell) pepper
1 red onion, finely chopped
3–4 tomatoes, seeded and chopped
1 tablespoon lime juice
1 tablespoon chopped coriander
  (cilantro) leaves
1 fresh red or green chilli pepper,
  seeded and chopped

1 Bring a panful of water to the boil and add the tofu. Switch off the heat source and leave the tofu in the hot water for a couple of minutes, then drain and dry with a cloth. This prepares the tofu to absorb the flavours of the spices.

2 In a large mixing bowl, mix the oil, lemon juice, aniseed, chilli powder, ginger, garlic and salt. Add the tofu and mix well. Cover the pan and leave to marinate for an hour or so.

3 Meanwhile, roast or grill (broil) the peppers until the skin is charred. Put them in a plastic bag and set aside for 20–25 minutes. Peel off the skin and seed the peppers. Remove the white pith and cut them into bite-sized pieces.

4 Thread the tofu onto oiled skewers and cook over a hot barbecue or under a pre-heated hot grill (broiler) until browned, basting with any remaining marinade mixed with a little more oil if necessary. Remove and allow to cool.

5 Mix the onion, tomatoes, lime juice, coriander (cilantro) leaves and chilli pepper in a mixing bowl. Add the peppers and mix well. Arrange this salad around a serving plate as a border and place the tofu in the middle. Serve at room temperature.

Apple Chutney

Preparation time: 10 minutes
Cooking time: 10–12 minutes

Serves 6–8

This chutney is traditionally made from raw mangoes. However, as they are difficult to get hold of in the West, I use cooking (baking) apples, which work very well. Stored in a sterilized jar, it will keep for 6–8 weeks in the fridge.

2 large cooking (baking) apples
2 tablespoons sunflower oil or light olive oil
¼ teaspoon black mustard seeds
¼ teaspoon onion seeds (kalonji)
¼ teaspoon fennel seeds
¼ teaspoon cumin seeds
1 teaspoon crushed dried chilli peppers or hot chilli powder
½ teaspoon ground turmeric
½ teaspoon ground cumin
1½ teaspoons salt or to taste
3 tablespoons soft light brown sugar

1   Peel and core the apples and chop them finely.

2   Heat the oil in a small pan over medium heat. When hot, but not smoking, add the mustard seeds. As soon as they start popping, throw in the onion, fennel and cumin seeds. Let them crackle and pop for 15–20 seconds.

3   Add the chilli, turmeric and cumin, stir and immediately follow with the apples. Stir, then add the salt and sugar. Stir over a medium heat until the apples start releasing the natural juices.

4   Reduce the heat to low, cover the pan and cook for 6–7 minutes, stirring regularly. Some of the apple should now turn quite pulpy, coating the remaining pieces. Remove the pan from the heat and allow to cool completely. Transfer to a sterilized jar and refrigerate.

Courgette Chutney

Preparation time: 5 minutes
Cooking time: 6–8 minutes
Suitable for freezing
Serves 4–6

The combination of courgette (zucchini) and coconut is wonderful though, traditionally, tender marrow is used in this chutney.

50g/2oz/⅔ cup desiccated coconut
225g/8oz courgettes (zucchini),
    washed and roughly chopped
300ml/10fl oz/1¼ cups water
½ teaspoon salt or to taste
1 level teaspoon tamarind
    concentrate or 1 tablespoon
    lime juice
1 fresh green chilli pepper, seeded
    and chopped
1cm/½-inch cube root ginger,
    peeled and roughly chopped
1 small clove garlic, peeled
15g/½oz coriander (cilantro) leaves,
    including the tender stalks

1   Put the coconut, courgettes (zucchini) and water in a wok or saucepan and place over a high heat. Bring to the boil, reduce heat to low, cover the pan and simmer for 5 minutes. Add the salt and tamarind and stir until the tamarind is dissolved (if using lime juice, do not add it at this stage). Remove the pan from the heat and allow the ingredients to cool.

2   Purée the courgette mixture with the remaining ingredients in a food processor until smooth. If using lime juice, add this while blending.

Coriander and Coconut Chutney

Preparation time: 6–8 minutes   **Serves 4**

Freshly grated coconut is the traditional choice for this chutney, but it is quite time-consuming to prepare. Desiccated coconut works well, but you will need to grind it first in a coffee grinder; a blender or processor will not grind it finely enough.

25g/1oz/⅓ cup desiccated coconut

25g/1oz chopped fresh coriander (cilantro), including the tender stalks

1cm/½-inch cube root ginger, peeled and roughly chopped

1 large clove garlic, peeled and roughly chopped

1–2 fresh green chilli peppers, chopped (seeded if liked)

½ teaspoon salt

½ teaspoon sugar

125g/4oz/½ cup low-fat set plain yogurt

1   Grind the coconut in a coffee grinder until smooth.

2   Transfer the coconut to a blender and add the remaining ingredients. Blend until smooth. Serve at room temperature.

Instant Tamarind Chutney

Preparation time: a few minutes
Cooking time: 3–4 minutes

Serves 4

Tamarind juice, available from larger supermarkets, makes it easy to put together this delicious chutney.

90ml/3fl oz/⅓ cup tamarind juice
2 tablespoons dark brown sugar
½ teaspoon salt or to taste
1 tablespoon sunflower oil
¼ teaspoon black mustard seeds
¼ teaspoon onion seeds (kalonji)
¼ teaspoon cumin seeds
½ teaspoon ground cumin
½ teaspoon chilli powder

1 Put the tamarind juice in a glass bowl and stir in the sugar and salt.
2 In a small pan or steel ladle, heat the oil over a medium heat and add the mustard seeds. As soon as they pop, add the remaining ingredients except the chilli powder.
3 Switch off the heat source and add the chilli powder. Pour this flavoured oil over the tamarind juice and mix thoroughly.

Mint and Onion Chutney

Preparation time: 10 minutes
Cooking time: 5 minutes

Serves 6–8

If stored in a moisture-free, air-tight container, this will keep for a month in the fridge.

2 tablespoons sunflower or light
    olive oil
225g/8oz/2 cups onions, chopped
15g/½oz fresh mint leaves
1 green chilli pepper, chopped
1½ tablespoons lime juice
½ teaspoon salt
½ teaspoon sugar

1 Heat the oil over a medium heat and fry the onions until soft but not brown (5 minutes). Allow to cool.
2 Purée the onions with the remaining ingredients in a blender or food processor. Transfer to a serving dish.

Sautéed Lentil Chutney

Preparation time: 10 minutes
Cooking time: 5 minutes

Serves 6

Yellow split lentils *(channa dhal),* sautéed with curry leaves and red chilli peppers are the main ingredients in this delicious chutney. Although I have suggested yellow split peas as an alternative to channa dhal in other recipes, it is worth getting the real thing for this recipe for its distinctive, nutty flavour. The chutney also freezes well.

1 tablespoon sunflower or light
    olive oil
1 tablespoon sunflower seeds
125g/4oz/⅔ cup yellow split lentils
    (channa dhal)
1 tablespoon fresh or 2 tablespoons
    dried curry leaves
2–4 dried red chilli peppers,
    chopped
200ml/7fl oz/¾ cup water
Salt to taste
½ teaspoon sugar
1½ tablespoons lime juice

1 In a small sauté pan or saucepan, heat the oil over a medium heat and add the sunflower seeds and lentils. Stir-fry for about a minute and add the curry leaves and red chilli peppers. Continue to stir-fry for 2 minutes, then remove from the heat and let cool. When completely cold, grind the mixture in a coffee grinder, 2–3 tablespoons at a time, until fine.

2 Heat the water and add the salt, sugar and lime juice. Stir until well blended and add to the ground mixture. Mix thoroughly and allow to cool completely before serving.

Mango Dip

Preparation time: a few minutes   **Serves 6–8**

A delicious combination of mango purée, chilli and cumin. I have used natural yogurt and crème fraîche for the base, but you can vary this by using mayonnaise or unflavoured fromage frais instead of the crème fraîche. Buy a ripe fresh mango for a more savoury taste. Once peeled, you can chop it and push through a sieve, or purée it in an electric blender. Sliced canned mangoes can be used if drained thoroughly, but this will produce a savoury taste with a sweet undertone. Alternatively, you can buy canned mango purée from Indian shops.

25g/1oz wholemilk natural yogurt
25g/1oz crème fraîche
40g/1½oz mango purée
½ teaspoon chilli powder
½ teaspoon salt
½ teaspoon ground cumin

1   Mix all the ingredients thoroughly and chill for 1–2 hours before serving.

Minted Yogurt and Coriander Sauce

Preparation time: 10 minutes   **Serves 4**

Mint and coriander (cilantro) make a magical combination. Use all the tender stalks of the coriander for they add as much flavour as the leaves and have plenty of nutritional value.

2 tablespoons fresh mint leaves,
    finely chopped
25g/1oz/½ cup coriander (cilantro)
    leaves and stalks, chopped
1 fresh red chilli pepper, seeded and
    chopped
1 small clove garlic, crushed to a
    fine pulp
1 teaspoon sugar
½ teaspoon salt
2 tablespoons lemon juice
125g/4oz/½ cup low-fat set plain
    yogurt
125g/4oz/½ cup low-fat sour
    cream
1 tablespoon ground almonds

1   Put all the ingredients in a blender and blend until smooth. Transfer to a serving dish and chill for at least 2 hours to allow the different flavours to develop.

Oil-free Cauliflower Pickle

Preparation time: 15–20 minutes
Cooking time: 10 minutes

Makes about 450g/1lb/3¼ cups

Although this pickle can be served straight away, it tastes better after 24 hours. The longer you keep it, the better it tastes, and you can safely store it in the fridge for up to 2 weeks. Try and cut the cauliflower into really small, equal-sized pieces. The cauliflower must be absolutely fresh, so aim to make the pickle on the day you buy it. It is worth getting hold of some asafoetida, not only for its distinctive taste but also for its disinfectant qualities, which help to preserve the pickle. It is sold in blocks or powdered in Indian stores. A small quantity will go a long way.

1 cauliflower

2 teaspoons salt

1 teaspoon sugar

1cm/½ inch cube root ginger, finely grated

1–2 green chilli peppers, seeded and finely chopped

½ teaspoon ground turmeric

¼ teaspoon asafoetida

¼–½ teaspoon chilli powder

1 level tablespoon cornflour (cornstarch)

2 teaspoons prepared English mustard

2 tablespoons lime juice

1. Remove all the outer layers and stems from the cauliflower and cut it into florets of approximately 3mm/⅛ inch.

2. Put the salt and sugar into a medium-sized saucepan and add 230ml/8fl oz/1 cup water. Bring to the boil and let it boil for 5 minutes.

3. Reduce the heat to low and stir in the ginger, green chilli peppers, turmeric, asafoetida and chilli powder.

4. Blend the cornflour (cornstarch) with a little water and add to the pan along with the mustard. Stir until the sauce has thickened, then add the lime juice and remove from the heat.

5. Put the raw cauliflower in a glass bowl and pour over the hot sauce. Mix thoroughly and allow to cool. Leave at room temperature for 24 hours, then refrigerate in an air-tight container.

Chapter 3

Soups

Following a low-fat diet does not mean you have to reduce your food intake. In fact, you can enjoy a three-course meal without having to worry about putting on the pounds. In this section, you will find some delicious soup recipes. They have been carefully devised to be as low in fat as possible, and in some cases, fat-free. During the hot summer months you can enjoy a refreshing Carrot and Orange Soup spiced with cinnamon and coriander (cilantro) *(page 43).* To draw comfort on a cold winter's night there is Roasted Parsnip Soup *(page 45),* spiced with the warm and assertive flavour of cumin, highlighted by the heat of chilli.

Carrot and Orange Soup

Preparation time: 20 minutes
Cooking time: 25 minutes

Serves 4

This wonderfully refreshing and satisfying soup is low in calories and high in vitamins and other nutrients. I love the combination of citrus fruit and chilli, but you can omit the chilli if you wish.

2 tablespoons sunflower or light olive oil

2 × 2.5cm/1-inch pieces cinnamon stick

1 green chilli pepper, seeded and chopped (optional)

1 teaspoon ground coriander (cilantro)

300g/10½oz/1⅓ cups carrots, grated

Grated zest of 1 large orange

1 teaspoon salt or to taste

50g/2oz/¼ cup sugar

700ml/1¼ pints/2¾ cups water

230ml/8fl oz/1 cup freshly squeezed orange juice

1　Heat the oil over a low heat and sauté the cinnamon, chilli pepper and coriander (cilantro) for 30–40 seconds.

2　Add the carrots and orange zest and sauté for a further 2 minutes.

3　Add the salt, sugar and water. Bring to the boil, reduce the heat to low, cover the pan and simmer for 15–20 minutes. Cool slightly and purée in a blender until smooth.

4　Return to the heat and add the orange juice. Simmer gently for 1–2 minutes, remove and serve hot or cold.

Pumpkin Soup

Preparation time: 25 minutes
Cooking time: 10 minutes   Serves 4

Pumpkins are more easily available in the autumn (fall) in time for Halloween. As this is a cold summer soup, you could use a summer squash such as marrow or courgette (zucchini) instead. However, Oriental and Caribbean stores have pumpkin throughout the year.

275g/10oz/1¾ cups pumpkin, peeled and roughly chopped

2 green chilli peppers, seeded and chopped

8 fresh or 10 dried curry leaves

2 teaspoons root ginger, peeled and roughly chopped

125ml/4fl oz/½ cup reduced-fat coconut milk

225g/8oz/1 cup low-fat plain yogurt

1 teaspoon salt or to taste

2 teaspoons sugar

1 tablespoon lime juice

1 tablespoon coriander (cilantro) leaves, finely chopped

1 Put the pumpkin, chilli peppers, curry leaves, ginger and coconut milk into a saucepan and add 300ml/½ pint/1⅓ cups hot water. Bring to the boil, cover the pan, reduce the heat to low and cook for 10 minutes or until the pumpkin is tender. Remove from the heat and let it cool for 5–6 minutes.

2 Purée the pumpkin and add 300ml/½ pint/1⅓ cups cold water and the yogurt, salt and sugar. Mix until well blended.

3 Add the lime juice and fresh coriander (cilantro), blend for a few seconds and serve chilled or at room temperature.

Roasted Parsnip Soup

Preparation time: 15 minutes

Cooking time: 30–35 minutes

Serves 4

One of the best winter root vegetables, parsnips are a good source of vitamins C and E as well as starch and fibre. They also contain folate, which is necessary for maintaining healthy blood cells.

2 tablespoons sunflower or light olive oil

300g/10½oz/1⅓ cups parsnips, peeled and evenly cut

1 large onion, peeled and coarsely chopped

6 large garlic cloves, peeled

1 small green chilli pepper, chopped

1 teaspoon ground cumin

1 teaspoon salt or to taste

Freshly milled black pepper

425ml/¾ pint/2 cups skimmed or semi-skimmed milk

300ml/½ pint/1⅓ cups vegetable stock

1 Preheat the oven to 190°C/375°F/Gas Mark 5. In a roasting tin, heat the oil on the stove top and add the parsnips, onions, garlic and chilli pepper. Stir over medium-high heat for a couple of minutes and add the cumin, salt and pepper. Place the roasting tin in the centre of the oven and roast for 20–25 minutes until the vegetables are browned and tender.

2 Purée the roasted vegetables with the milk and put into a saucepan. Add the stock and simmer gently for 6–8 minutes. Season with more pepper if desired and serve hot.

Spiced Lentil Broth

Preparation time: 10 minutes
Cooking time: 35 minutes

Serves 4–5

This spicy lentil broth from southern India is traditionally served with meals. It is also wonderful to drink as an appetizer in small cups.

90g/3oz/½ cup red split lentils
½ teaspoon ground turmeric
4–5 large garlic cloves, crushed
4–5 shallots, chopped
25g/1oz/⅓ cup unsweetened
 desiccated coconut
3–4 dried red chilli peppers, torn
 into pieces
1 tablespoon coriander (cilantro)
 seeds
1 teaspoon cumin seeds
10–12 black peppercorns
8–10 curry leaves
1½ teaspoons salt or to taste
¾ teaspoon tamarind concentrate
1 tablespoon finely chopped
 coriander (cilantro) leaves

1   Wash the lentils in several changes of water and put into a saucepan with the turmeric, garlic, shallots and 1.2 litres/2 pints hot water. Place over a medium heat and let it come to a rolling boil.

2   Meanwhile, grind the coconut, chilli peppers, coriander (cilantro) seeds, cumin seeds and peppercorns in a coffee grinder and add to the lentils. When the liquid has come to the boil, reduce the heat to low, partially cover the pan and simmer for 20 minutes. Add the curry leaves, salt and tamarind and simmer for a further 5–6 minutes. Check that the tamarind has dissolved completely.

3   Remove from the heat, purée the mixture in a blender until smooth then return to the pan. Heat gently and stir in the coriander leaves. Serve hot.

Tomato and Coriander Soup

Preparation time: 10 minutes
Cooking time: 20 minutes   **Serves 4**

Based on a recipe from southern India, this soup is traditionally served in a cup to accompany a meal. Fresh curry leaves provide the main flavour here, but if you cannot get them, use the dried ones sold in larger supermarkets.

2 tablespoons sunflower or plain
  olive oil
2 cloves garlic, crushed
1cm/½-inch cube root ginger,
  peeled and grated
2 dried red chilli peppers, chopped
½ teaspoon black peppercorns,
  crushed
6–8 fresh or 8–10 dried curry leaves
565g/1¼lb chopped fresh or canned
  tomatoes
1 teaspoon salt
1 teaspoon sugar
2 tablespoons chopped coriander
  (cilantro) leaves

1   Heat the oil and fry the garlic, ginger, chilli peppers, peppercorns and curry leaves until the garlic and ginger have browned and the chilli peppers have blackened a little.

2   Add the tomatoes and pour in 300ml/10fl oz/1¼ cups hot water.

3   Add the salt and sugar and bring to the boil. Cover and simmer for 15–20 minutes. Cool slightly and liquidize, then strain.

4   Return the soup to the saucepan and reheat gently. Stir in the coriander (cilantro) leaves and serve.

Chapter 4

Protein Dishes – the Body Builders

The recipes in this chapter are based on protein, a fundamental requirement in everyone's diet. Protein forms approximately one sixth of our body. It is made up of chemical units known as amino acids, the building blocks that grow, repair and replace body tissues.

In a vegetarian diet, most of the protein comes from plant sources such as nuts, peas and beans. A combination of these ingredients should be included in a daily diet as a single protein ingredient derived from plant sources cannot provide all the amino acids required by the body. Good combinations would be whole-wheat bread or rice with a dish containing legumes, or rice with a dish containing nuts.

In the following pages you will find exciting recipes containing all the essential nutrients to help maintain a healthy lifestyle.

Spiced Chickpeas with Sun-dried Mango

Preparation time: 20 minutes
Cooking time: 15 minutes

Chickpeas (garbanzos) have a wonderful nutty flavour and are loaded with protein, fibre and essential minerals. Asian grocers and some larger supermarkets stock sun-dried mango (amchoor). If you cannot get it, use lime juice to taste.

🌀🌀🌀🌀🌀🌀🌀🌀🌀🌀🌀🌀

275g/10oz/2 cups potatoes, peeled and cut into 2.5cm/1-inch dice

400g/14oz can of chickpeas (garbanzos), drained and well rinsed

250ml/9fl oz/1¼ cups reduced-fat canned coconut milk

5–6 cloves garlic, peeled and roughly chopped

1 teaspoon salt or to taste

2 tablespoons sunflower or plain olive oil

1½ teaspoons ground coriander (cilantro)

½ teaspoon ground turmeric

½ teaspoon chilli powder

2 teaspoons sun-dried mango powder (amchoor)

1 Put 250ml/9fl oz/1¼ cups hot water in a saucepan and add the potatoes. Bring to the boil, reduce the heat to low and cook, covered, for 6–7 minutes. Add the chickpeas (garbanzos) and cook, uncovered, for 3–4 minutes or until the potatoes are tender.

2 Add the coconut milk and bring to a slow simmer.

3 Meanwhile, crush the garlic and salt together to a smooth pulp. This is easy with a pestle and mortar, the back of a wooden spoon or the blade of a large knife.

4 Heat the oil in a small saucepan over a medium heat and fry the garlic until lightly browned. Add the coriander (cilantro), turmeric and chilli powder and stir-fry for 30 seconds. Add this mixture to the potato and chickpeas.

5 Blend the sun-dried mango powder with a little water and add to the chickpeas. Stir and mix well and simmer for 2–3 minutes without a lid, then remove from the heat. If using lime juice, stir in just before removing from the heat. Serve with boiled basmati rice or any bread.

Potatoes and Chickpeas with Sun-dried Mango

Preparation time: 20–25 minutes

Cooking time: 20 minutes   **Serves 4**

In this well-known delicacy from the state of Punjab in northern India, sun-dried mango *(amchoor)* lends a tangy taste with an exotic touch. If you cannot get it, use lime juice, although this will alter the taste.

3 tablespoons sunflower or plain
  olive oil
1 × 5cm/1-inch cube root ginger,
  peeled and cut into julienne
  strips
1–2 fresh green chilli peppers,
  seeded and cut into julienne
  strips
6 cloves garlic, peeled and crushed
  to a fine pulp
1 red onion, finely sliced
1 teaspoon salt or to taste
1 teaspoon ground cumin
1 teaspoon ground coriander
  (cilantro)
½ teaspoon ground turmeric
½ teaspoon chilli powder
125ml/4fl oz/½ cup passata (Italian
  sieved tomato)
400g/14oz can of chickpeas
  (garbanzos), drained and well
  rinsed
175g/6oz/1¼ cups boiled potatoes,
  peeled and cut into 2.5cm/1-
  inch cubes
140ml/5fl oz/⅔ cup warm water
1 teaspoon sun-dried mango
  powder (amchoor)
½ teaspoon garam masala
2 tablespoons coriander (cilantro)
  leaves, chopped
1 tablespoon fresh mint leaves,
  chopped
1–2 sprigs fresh mint
1 small tomato, seeded and cut into
  strips

1 Heat the oil over a medium heat in a heavy based saucepan
   and add half the ginger, the fresh chilli peppers and garlic;
   stir-fry for 30 seconds.
2 Add the onion and salt and stir-fry for 4–5 minutes or until
   the onion is soft and just beginning to colour.
3 Add the cumin, coriander (cilantro), turmeric and chilli
   powder; stir-fry for 1 minute, then add the passata. Cook for
   2–3 minutes or until the oil begins to separate from the
   spiced tomato paste.
4 Add the chickpeas (garbanzos), potatoes and water. Bring to
   the boil and reduce the heat to low. Cover the pan and
   simmer for 10–12 minutes.
5 Blend the sun-dried mango with a little water and add to the
   chickpeas.
6 Stir in the garam masala, coriander and mint leaves and
   remove from the heat. Transfer to a serving plate and
   garnish with the reserved ginger, sprigs of mint and strips of
   tomato. Serve with naan or any other bread.

Spinach and Chickpeas in Chilli and Garlic Sauce

Preparation time: 20–25 minutes
Cooking time: 25 minutes

Serves 4–6

The combination of spinach and chickpeas (garbanzos) is visually pleasing as well as highly nutritious. I have used fresh spinach but you can use frozen if you wish. Do make sure it is frozen leaf spinach and not the purée, and thaw and drain it first. This recipe is suitable for freezing as long as fresh spinach is used.

1 large onion, roughly chopped
2.5cm/1-inch cube root ginger, peeled and roughly chopped
1 green chilli pepper, roughly chopped
3 tablespoons sunflower or olive oil
1 teaspoon fennel seeds
6–8 cloves garlic, peeled and crushed
1 teaspoon ground cumin
1 teaspoon ground coriander (cilantro)
½ teaspoon ground turmeric
1–1½ teaspoons hot chilli powder
1 tablespoon tomato purée (paste)
400g/14oz can chickpeas (garbanzos), drained and rinsed
140ml/¼ pint/⅔ cup warm water
225g/8oz spinach, finely chopped
1 teaspoon salt or to taste
125g/4oz/½ cup canned chopped tomatoes, including juice
½ teaspoon garam masala

1. Purée the onion, ginger and green chilli in a food processor until smooth.
2. In a wok or non-stick saucepan, heat the oil over a medium heat. When the oil is hot but not smoking, add the fennel seeds followed by the garlic. Stir-fry for 30 seconds.
3. Add the cumin and coriander (cilantro), stir-fry for 30 seconds, then add the puréed ingredients. Stir-fry for 4–5 minutes or until the oil surfaces the spice paste.
4. Add the turmeric, chilli powder and tomato purée (paste) and stir-fry for 1 minute.
5. Add the chickpeas (garbanzos) and water, bring to the boil then reduce the heat to low. Cover the pan and simmer for 10 minutes.
6. Add the spinach and salt and increase the heat to medium-high. Stir-fry for 1 minute when the spinach will shrink and release its natural juices.
7. Add the tomatoes and stir-fry for 6–8 minutes, reducing the heat slightly if necessary. Sprinkle with the garam masala, stir-fry for 1 minute, then remove from the heat and serve with any bread.

Black-eyed Beans in Chilli and Tamarind Sauce

Preparation time: 10 minutes
Cooking time: 10 minutes

Serves 4

Black-eyed beans are an excellent source of nutrients, including protein, zinc, iron and thiamin. This simple recipe takes little effort and produces a superb flavour. I have used canned beans here. You can, of course, use the dried beans, which will need soaking and pre-cooking.

680/1½lb/2⅓ cups canned black-eyed beans, drained and rinsed
400ml/14fl oz/1¾ cups reduced-fat coconut milk
1 teaspoon salt or to taste
1 level teaspoon tamarind concentrate or 1½ tablespoons lemon juice
1 teaspoon chickpea flour (besan)
2 tablespoons sunflower or light olive oil
4–5 large garlic cloves, crushed
2 teaspoons ground coriander (cilantro)
1 teaspoon ground turmeric
½–1 teaspoon hot chilli powder

1   Put the black-eyed beans in a saucepan and pour in the coconut milk, salt and tamarind (if using lemon juice, do not add it yet).

2   Blend the chickpea flour (besan) with a little water, making sure there are no lumps, and add it to the beans. Stir over a low heat and let it simmer for 5–6 minutes.

3   In a small saucepan or a steel ladle, heat the oil gently and add the garlic. Let it brown a little and add the remaining ingredients. Cook for about a minute and pour everything over the beans. If using lemon juice, add it now. Stir well, remove from the heat and serve with boiled basmati rice.

Aubergines Stuffed with Spicy Soya Mince

Preparation time: 20 minutes
Cooking time: 15 minutes plus 55 minutes baking time   Serves 4–6

Aubergines (eggplants) are rich in vitamins and iron. Here they are combined with soya mince, which is high in protein and free from cholesterol. Soya mince is available from supermarkets and health-food stores.

3 tablespoons sunflower or light
    olive oil

5–6 shallots, finely chopped

4 cloves garlic, crushed

2.5cm/1-inch cube root ginger,
    finely grated

1 green chilli pepper, finely
    chopped (seeded if wished)

½ teaspoon ground turmeric

2 teaspoons ground cumin

1½ teaspoons ground coriander
    (cilantro)

¼ teaspoon chilli powder or to taste

175g/6oz/1 cup chopped canned
    tomatoes with juice

90g/3oz/¼ cup soya mince

1 teaspoon salt or to taste

300ml/½ pint/1⅓ cups hot water

15g/½oz/⅛ cup coriander (cilantro)
    leaves, chopped

15g/½oz/⅛ cup mint leaves,
    chopped

2–3 aubergines (eggplants) (about
    700g/1½lb)

1   Heat two tablespoons of the oil in a wok over a medium heat and fry the shallots for 3–4 minutes. Add the garlic, ginger and chilli pepper and fry for a further minute.

2   Reduce the heat to low and add the turmeric, cumin, coriander (cilantro) and chilli powder. Stir-fry for about 2 minutes and add the tomatoes. Increase the heat to medium-high and cook for 2–3 minutes until the mixture resembles a thick paste.

3   Add the soya mince and stir-fry for a minute or two. Add the salt and water, bring to the boil, cover the pan and reduce the heat to low. Cook for 5–6 minutes.

4   Stir in the coriander and mint and remove from the heat. Set aside until cool enough to handle. Meanwhile, preheat the oven to 200°C/400°F/Gas Mark 6.

5   Wash and wipe the aubergines (eggplants). Lay them horizontally on a chopping (cutting) board. Starting at one end, slit across to the other end at 2.5cm/1-inch intervals. Take care not to cut them right down to the bottom; the aubergines should remain whole.

6   Gently pull a slice of the aubergine away at one end and hold it apart. Fill this gap generously with some of the soya mixture, bringing it right up to the top. Continue doing this until you have filled up all the slits right across the aubergine. Fill the remaining aubergines the same way and smear the reserved oil on the skin. Any remaining filling can be spread on each aubergine.

7   Wrap the aubergines tightly in foil and place them in a baking tray. Bake in the centre of the oven for 30 minutes. Reduce the temperature to 190°C/375°F/Gas Mark 5 and bake for a further 20–25 minutes or until they give a little when pressed. Remove and serve with Toasted Sesame Rice (page 107) and a salad if liked.

Butterbeans, Carrots and Green Beans with Hot-oil Seasoning

Preparation time: 10–12 minutes
Cooking time: 15 minutes

Serves 4

Butterbeans have a delicious buttery texture and they are full of protein and fibre. In this recipe, combined with green beans and carrots, they will provide plenty of vitamins and minerals.

225g/8oz/1½ cups carrots, cut into thick (1cm/1½-inch) coins
225g/8oz/2 cups green beans, cut into 2.5cm/1-inch pieces
1 tablespoon coriander (cilantro) seeds
2–3 long, slim, dried red chilli peppers, chopped
25g/1oz/⅓ cup desiccated coconut
225g/8oz/1½ cups canned, drained butterbeans
1 teaspoon salt or to taste
1 tablespoon olive oil
4–5 large garlic cloves, crushed
½ teaspoon ground turmeric

1 Put the carrots and beans in a saucepan. Add 450ml/16fl oz/ 2 cups hot water. Bring to the boil, reduce the heat to low, cover and simmer for 6–7 minutes.

2 Meanwhile, preheat a small, heavy based pan over a medium heat and dry-roast the coriander (cilantro) seeds and chilli peppers for a minute or so. Transfer the spices to a plate to prevent them overheating, allow to cool then grind in a coffee grinder. When they are half-ground, add the desiccated coconut and grind until fine. Add the mixture to the vegetables in the pan and stir to distribute well.

3 Rinse the beans in cold water and add to the vegetables. Add the salt, stir and simmer gently, uncovered, for 5–6 minutes.

4 Heat the oil in a small pan over a low heat and fry the garlic until just beginning to brown. Stir in the turmeric and pour the spiced oil over the vegetables and beans. Stir and remove from the heat. Serve with boiled basmati rice or any bread.

Stir-fried Mung Beans

Preparation time: 25 minutes, plus time for soaking beans
Cooking time: 25 minutes

Serves 4

This recipe is suitable for freezing.

⊱⊰⊱⊰⊱⊰⊱⊰⊱⊰⊱⊰⊱⊰⊱⊰⊱⊰⊱⊰

150g/5oz/¾ cup mung beans

300ml/½ pint/1⅓ cups water

2 tablespoons sunflower or olive oil

½ teaspoon black mustard seeds

½ teaspoon cumin seeds

2.5cm/1-inch cube root ginger, peeled and grated

1–2 green chilli peppers, finely chopped (seeded if wished)

50g/2oz/½ cup red pepper, cut into 2.5cm/1-inch dice

1 bunch spring onions (scallions), finely chopped

125g/4oz/1 cup carrots, halved lengthways and thinly sliced

125g/4oz cauliflower, divided into 5mm/¼-inch florets

1 teaspoon salt or to taste

2 tablespoons chopped coriander (cilantro) leaves

1 Pick over the mung beans, wash and soak in plenty of cold water overnight. Drain and rinse several times.

2 Put the beans and water in a saucepan and place over a high heat. Bring to the boil, partially cover the pan and cook over a medium heat for 5–6 minutes or until it stops being frothy. Reduce the heat to low, cover and simmer for 10–12 minutes or until the beans are tender and the liquid reduces to about 2–3 tablespoons.

3 In a wok or non-stick saucepan, heat the oil over a medium heat. When the oil is hot but not smoking, add the mustard seeds followed by the cumin seeds. As soon as the seeds pop, add the ginger, red pepper and spring onions (scallions). Stir-fry for 1 minute.

4 Add the carrots and cauliflower, stir-fry for a further minute, then add the salt. Stir-fry for 1–2 minutes.

5 Add the cooked beans, along with the cooking liquid left in the pan. Stir-fry for 2–3 minutes or until the beans and vegetables are well blended.

6 Stir in the coriander (cilantro) leaves, remove from the heat and serve with Griddle-cooked Fenugreek Flat Bread *(page 85)* accompanied by Mushroom Do-Piaza *(page 150)*, if liked.

Spiced Red Kidney Beans

Preparation time: 10 minutes
Cooking time: 15 minutes

Serves 4

Red kidney beans are wonderful to cook with spices. The dried beans are normally soaked and boiled until tender before being cooked. If you use dried beans, boil the beans for 10–15 minutes, drain, rinse and then cook them in fresh water. This process is necessary to remove the toxins present in red kidney beans. To make things easier, I have used canned beans for this recipe. As an alternative, you could use black-eyed beans or butterbeans.

1 onion, roughly chopped

2.5cm/1-inch cube root ginger, peeled and roughly chopped

4 cloves garlic, peeled and roughly chopped

3 tablespoons sunflower or olive oil

2 teaspoons ground cumin

2 teaspoons ground coriander (cilantro)

½ teaspoon ground turmeric

¼–½ teaspoon chilli powder

1 tablespoon tomato purée (paste)

450g/1lb/2⅓ cups canned red kidney beans, drained and rinsed

1 teaspoon salt or to taste

230ml/8fl oz/1 cup warm water

3–4 green chilli peppers (preferably the long slim ones)

½ teaspoon garam masala

2 tablespoons chopped coriander (cilantro) leaves

1   Purée the onion, ginger and garlic in a food processor.

2   In a wok or medium saucepan, heat the oil over a medium-high heat and add the puréed ingredients. Stir-fry for 4–5 minutes.

3   Reduce the heat to low, add the ground cumin and coriander (cilantro), and stir-fry for 1 minute. Add the turmeric, chilli powder and tomato purée (paste), and stir-fry for another minute.

4   Add the beans and salt, increase the heat to medium and stir-fry for 1 minute.

5   Add the water and chilli peppers and simmer gently for 5 minutes, stirring frequently.

6   Sprinkle with garam masala, stir in the coriander leaves, remove from the heat and serve.

Lentils with Cumin and Coriander

Preparation time: 15 minutes
Cooking time: 30 minutes

Serves 4

Lentils are one of my favourite ingredients. A steaming hot bowl of freshly cooked basmati rice and a dish of lentils enlivened with spices is a meal I often enjoy at home.

∽ЮᏇ∽ЮᏇ∽ЮᏇ∽ЮᏇ∽ЮᏇ∽ЮᏇ∽ЮᏇ∽ЮᏇ∽ЮᏇ∽ЮᏇ∽ЮᏇ∽ЮᏇ

225g/8oz/1 cup red split lentils (masoor dhal)
2 tablespoons olive oil
5–6 shallots, finely chopped
1–2 fresh green chilli peppers, chopped (seeded if wished)
1 teaspoon ground turmeric
2 teaspoons ground coriander (cilantro)
2 teaspoons ground cumin
1½ teaspoons garam masala
1¼ teaspoons salt or to taste
2 tablespoons chopped coriander (cilantro) leaves

1 Wash and rinse the lentils 2–3 times and set aside in a colander.

2 Using a non-stick saucepan, heat the oil over a medium heat and add the shallots and chilli peppers. Fry until the shallots are lightly browned (5–6 minutes).

3 Add the spices, stir-fry for 30 seconds and add the lentils. Stir-fry over a medium-low heat until the lentils are dry and the grains look quite separate from each other (3–4 minutes). Pour in 850ml/1½ pints/3¾ cups hot water and bring to the boil. Reduce the heat to low, cover and simmer for 25 minutes. Stir in the salt and coriander (cilantro) leaves, remove from the heat and serve.

Cumin and Coriander Scented Lentils with Sautéed Shallots

Preparation time: 20 minutes
Cooking time: 30 minutes

Serves 4

This recipe is based on a well-known and much-loved south-Indian dish known as *sambhar*. In spite of the use of specially prepared spices, it is relatively easy to make. The traditional lentils used here are a special variety known as *tuvar* or *toor dhal,* available from Asian grocers. Alternatively, try red split lentils.

175g/6oz/1 cup yellow split gram (tuvar dhal)
1 tablespoon coriander (cilantro) seeds
1 teaspoon cumin seeds
2–3 dried red chilli peppers
10–12 whole black peppercorns
½ teaspoon black mustard seeds
2 teaspoons Bengal gram (channa dhal) or yellow split peas
3 tablespoons sunflower or light olive oil
225g/8oz/2 cups shallots, quartered
1 teaspoon ground turmeric
1 tablespoon tamarind juice or 1½ tablespoons lime juice
2 tablespoons fresh coriander (cilantro), chopped

1   Put the lentils in a saucepan and add 850ml/1½ pints/ 3¾ cups hot water. Bring to the boil and let it boil, uncovered, for 6–7 minutes, then reduce the heat to low. Cover the pan and cook for 20 minutes.

2   Meanwhile, preheat a heavy based pan and dry-roast the spices and Bengal gram or yellow split peas until they are just a shade darker. Stir constantly. Remove from the heat, allow to cool then grind in a coffee grinder.

3   Heat the oil gently and fry the shallots until lightly browned. Add the turmeric and the ground spices. Stir and cook for 30 seconds, then fold the entire mixture into the lentils.

4   Add the tamarind or lime juice and coriander (cilantro) leaves. Remove from the heat and keep the pan tightly covered until required. This keeps the flavours locked in. Serve with boiled basmati rice and a raita.

Garlic-infused Lentils with Butter and Cream

Preparation time: 15–20 minutes plus soaking time for the lentils
Cooking time: 45 minutes   Serves 4

Known as *dhal makhani,* this is probably the most famous and well-loved lentil delicacy in India after *Tarka Dhal.* The lentils used here are whole brown lentils *(sabut masoor dhal).* When skinned and split, they are known as red split lentils or *masoor dhal.* Whole masoor dhal is available in Asian stores and health-food shops.

175g/6oz/¾ cup whole brown
  lentils (whole masoor dhal)

2 tablespoons sunflower or olive oil

1 tablespoon tomato purée (paste)

10 cloves garlic, peeled and minced

2.5cm/1-inch cube root ginger,
  peeled and finely grated

1 teaspoon ground turmeric

1 teaspoon ground cumin

½ teaspoon chilli powder

570ml/1 pint/2½ cups hot water

2 small fresh tomatoes, skinned
  and chopped

3–4 fresh whole green chilli
  peppers

1 teaspoon salt or to taste

1 tablespoon half-fat butter or
  margarine

200ml/7fl oz/¾ cup half-fat single
  (half and half) cream

2 teaspoons lime juice

2 tablespoons chopped coriander
  (cilantro) leaves

1 Pick over the lentils and wash in several changes of water. Soak for 3–4 hours or overnight if you wish. Drain well.

2 Heat the oil in a non-stick saucepan over a medium heat. When hot, add the lentils and stir-fry for 2 minutes. Reduce the heat slightly and stir-fry for a further 2 minutes.

3 Add the tomato purée (paste) and stir-fry for 1 minute, then add the garlic, ginger, turmeric, ground cumin and chilli powder. Stir-fry for 2 minutes then add the water. Increase the heat, bring to the boil and allow to boil for 1 minute. Reduce the heat to low, cover the pan and simmer for 30–35 minutes, stirring half-way through.

4 Mash some of the lentil mixture with a wooden spoon (only about a quarter of the entire quantity) and add the tomatoes, chilli peppers, salt, butter or margarine and cream. Cook gently for 5 minutes, uncovered.

5 Add the lime juice and coriander (cilantro) leaves; stir and remove from the heat. Serve with plain rice or chappatis.

Ginger and Curry Leaf Flavoured Lentils with Baby Spinach

Preparation time: 15–20 minutes
Cooking time: 30 minutes   Serves 4

You can choose from a variety of lentils for this dish. I have used yellow split lentils (split *moong dhal*) because they are the fastest-cooking variety. If you like, you could use yellow split peas, but you will need to soak them first and the cooking time will be longer. Canned chickpeas (garbanzos) can also be used instead of lentils.

225g/8oz/1 cup yellow split lentils (moong dhal), washed and drained
1 teaspoon salt or to taste
175g/6oz/3 cups baby spinach
3 tablespoons sunflower or plain olive oil
3–4 shallots, finely chopped
2.5cm/1-inch cube root ginger, peeled and grated
1–2 green chilli peppers, chopped
8 fresh or 10–12 dried curry leaves
1 teaspoon ground turmeric
125g/4oz/½ cup chopped fresh tomatoes

1   Put the lentils into a saucepan with 570ml/1 pint/2½ cups hot water and bring to the boil. Reduce the heat to medium and cook, uncovered, for 15 minutes, stirring to ensure that the thickened lentils do not stick to the bottom of the pan.

2   Add the salt and the baby spinach. Cook until the spinach has wilted and reduce the heat to low. Cover the pan and cook for 5–7 minutes or until the lentils and spinach are tender.

3   Meanwhile, heat the oil over a medium heat and fry the shallots for 4–5 minutes. Add the ginger, chilli peppers and curry leaves and fry for a further minute or two.

4   Add the turmeric and stir, then add the mixture to the lentils. Add the tomatoes and cook for 2–3 minutes. Remove from the heat and serve with Coconut Rice *(page 101)*.

Lentil Squares with Coconut and Coriander Dressing

Preparation time: 10 minutes plus soaking time for the lentils
Cooking time: 25–30 minutes

Serves 4–6

In India, where afternoon tea is still a strong tradition, these are enjoyed as a snack. Known as *amiri khaman,* this recipe originated in the state of Gujerat in western India. Serve this simple, delicious and highly nutritious dish with a vegetable curry and boiled basmati rice for a completely balanced meal.

350g/12oz/1⅔ cups yellow split lentils (channa dhal)

3 tablespoons sunflower or light olive oil

½ teaspoon black mustard seeds

¼ teaspoon asafoetida

2.5cm/1-inch cube root ginger, peeled and grated

6 cloves garlic, peeled and crushed to a fine pulp

2–4 green chilli peppers, finely chopped (seeded if wished)

½ teaspoon ground turmeric

1 teaspoon salt or to taste

1 teaspoon sugar

425ml/¾ pint/2 cups skimmed or semi-skimmed milk

2 tablespoons lemon juice

1 tablespoon coriander (cilantro) leaves, finely chopped

1 tablespoon desiccated coconut

1 Wash the lentils and soak in cold water for 5–6 hours or overnight. Drain and process in a food processor until a fine paste is formed.

2 In a wok or non-stick pan, heat the oil over a medium heat. When the oil is hot, but not smoking, add the mustard seeds and reduce the heat to low.

3 Add the asafoetida followed by the ginger, garlic, chilli peppers and turmeric. Fry gently for about 2 minutes and add the lentil paste, salt and sugar. Cook over a medium-low heat, stirring constantly, until the mixture is completely dry and looks crumbly.

4 Add a third of the milk and continue to cook, stirring, for 3–4 minutes. Repeat the process with the remaining milk.

5 Add the lemon juice and stir until well blended. On a lightly greased plate, spread the mixture into a 30cm/12-inch rectangle and garnish with the coconut and coriander (cilantro). Cut into squares or diamonds and serve hot or cold.

Lentil Cakes in Tomato, Mint and Coriander Sauce

Preparation time: 20 minutes plus time for soaking the lentils
Cooking time: 25 minutes   Makes 14–16

This is a two-in-one recipe: the lentil cakes can be served without the sauce as an appetizer; and with the glorious tomato, mint and coriander (cilantro) sauce, this is a dish that will grace any dinner party table.

For the cakes:

225g/8oz/1 cup red split lentils (masoor dhal)

2.5cm/1-inch cube root ginger, peeled and coarsely chopped

1 green chilli pepper, chopped (seeded if wished)

1 dried red chilli pepper, chopped

15g/½oz/⅛ cup coriander (cilantro) leaves and stalks, coarsely chopped

1 teaspoon salt or to taste

1 red onion, finely chopped

2 tablespoons sunflower or light olive oil

A little flour for dusting

For the sauce:

175g/6oz/1 cup chopped canned tomatoes with juice

140ml/¼ pint/⅔ cup water

5cm/2-inch piece cinnamon stick, halved

2 bay leaves, crumpled

1 green chilli pepper, chopped (seeded if liked)

1 tablespoon sunflower or plain olive oil

4 large garlic cloves, crushed

½ teaspoon ground turmeric

½ teaspoon ground cumin

1 teaspoon ground coriander (cilantro)

90ml/3fl oz/⅓ cup water

½ teaspoon salt or to taste

2 tablespoons coriander (cilantro) leaves, chopped

1 tablespoon fresh mint leaves, chopped

1 Wash the lentils several times and soak in cold water for 2–3 hours. Drain well and place them in a food processor along with the remaining ingredients for the cakes, except the onion, oil and flour. Blend the ingredients until smooth, transfer to a mixing bowl and add the onion. Mix well.

2 Pour half the oil into a non-stick frying pan (skillet), brushing it across the entire surface. Heat the oil over a medium heat. Mould the lentil mixture into flat cakes approximately 2.5cm/1 inch in diameter and about 1cm/½-inch thick. Use two tablespoons to mould the cakes if you find it difficult to do this between your palms. Dust each cake lightly with the flour, brown on both sides and drain on absorbent paper. You will need to do this in two batches.

3 To make the sauce, put the tomatoes, water, cinnamon, bay leaves and chilli pepper into a saucepan and bring to the boil. Cover and simmer for 15 minutes. Remove from the heat and sieve the mixture, discarding what's left in the sieve.

4 In a small pan, heat the oil gently and fry the garlic until browned. Add the turmeric, cumin and coriander (cilantro) and fry for about a minute. Sprinkle with two tablespoons of water and continue to cook for a further minute or two, then remove from the heat and set aside.

5 In a frying pan (skillet) large enough to hold the lentil cakes in a single layer, heat the spiced and sieved tomatoes, the cooked spice mixture, salt, coriander leaves and mint. Mix well and remove half the tomato mixture. Arrange the lentil cakes in the pan and spoon the other half of the sauce over. Cover the pan and simmer gently for 7–8 minutes. Remove from the heat and serve with Lemon Rice *(page 104)* or chapattis and a salad.

Lentils with Courgettes

Preparation time: 15 minutes
Cooking time: 30–35 minutes

Serves 4

The deliciously light flavour of courgettes (zucchini) is perfectly compatible with the nutty taste of the lentils. Courgettes are low in calories and a good source of vitamin C and betacarotene.

225g/8oz/1 cup yellow split lentils
(moong dhal)
2 tablespoons sunflower or plain
olive oil
4 green cardamom pods
1 teaspoon royal cumin (shahi
zeera or kala zeera)
4 whole cloves
1 red onion, finely sliced
4 large cloves garlic, crushed
2.5cm/1-inch cube root ginger,
grated
1–2 fresh red chilli peppers, sliced
(seeded if wished)
1 teaspoon ground turmeric
½ teaspoon ground cumin
1 teaspoon salt or to taste
225g/8oz/2 cups courgettes
(zucchini), cut into bite-sized
pieces
½ teaspoon garam masala
2 tablespoons chopped coriander
(cilantro) leaves
2 fresh tomatoes, skinned, seeded
and chopped

1   Wash the lentils thoroughly and leave to drain in a colander.
2   Heat the oil over a medium heat. Peel back each cardamom pod very slightly and add to the oil, along with the royal cumin and cloves. Let them sizzle for 15–20 seconds.
3   Add the onions, garlic, ginger and chilli peppers. Stir-fry until the onions are caramel brown (7–8 minutes).
4   Add the lentils, turmeric and cumin; stir-fry for 2 minutes then pour in 570ml/1 pint/2½ cups hot water. Bring to the boil, reduce the heat to low, cover the pan and cook for 15–20 minutes. Stir once or twice.
5   Add the salt, courgettes (zucchini) and garam masala, stir, re-cover and cook for 2–3 minutes.
6   Stir in the coriander (cilantro) leaves and tomatoes, remove from the heat and serve with boiled basmati rice or chapattis.

Lentils in Fenugreek and Chilli-infused Coconut Milk

Preparation time: 15 minutes
Cooking time: 25 minutes   Serves 4

This delicious combination provides protein and vitamins in one dish.

~~~

225g/8oz/1 cup yellow split lentils (moong dhal)

225g/8oz/1½ cups green beans, cut into 2.5cm/1-inch pieces

1 teaspoon ground turmeric

2 teaspoons sunflower or plain olive oil

2–4 dried red chilli peppers, chopped

¾ teaspoon fenugreek seeds

230ml/8fl oz/1 cup reduced-fat coconut milk

1 teaspoon salt or to taste

1½ tablespoons lime juice

1   Wash and drain the lentils and put into a saucepan with the beans.

2   Add the turmeric and 570ml/1 pint/2½ cups hot water. Place over a high heat and bring to the boil. Let it boil for 2–3 minutes, then reduce the heat to medium and cook, uncovered, for 10 minutes.

3   Meanwhile, heat the oil in a small saucepan over a low heat and fry the chilli peppers and fenugreek seeds until they are a shade darker. Remove from the heat and cool, then crush them with the oil into a paste. You can do this in the pan itself, using a wooden pestle or the back of a wooden spoon.

4   Add the coconut milk and salt to the lentils. Bring back to a slow simmer and cook, uncovered, for 5 minutes.

5   Add the chilli and fenugreek paste and lime juice. Stir once and simmer for 2–3 minutes. Remove from the heat and serve with Cumin Rice *(page 102)* or any bread.

Mixed Lentils with Five-spice Seasoning

Preparation time: 10 minutes
Cooking time: 25–30 minutes

Serves 4

Five-spice seasoning *(panch phoran)* is a typical combination of whole spices used in east and northeast India. Just the aroma of the finished dish will bring your taste buds alive!

125g/4oz/½ cup red split lentils (masoor dhal)

125g/4oz/½ cup yellow split lentils (moong dhal)

1 teaspoon salt or to taste

1 tablespoon lemon juice

2 tablespoons fresh coriander (cilantro), chopped

1 tablespoon plain olive oil

¼ teaspoon black mustard seeds

¼ teaspoon cumin seeds

¼ teaspoon onion seeds

¼ teaspoon fennel seeds

8–10 fenugreek seeds

4 small dried red chilli peppers

½ teaspoon ground turmeric

1 small tomato, seeded and cut into strips, to garnish

Fresh chives, to garnish

1 Mix both types of dhal together and wash thoroughly, then drain. Put into a saucepan with 850ml/1½ pints/3¾ cups hot water. Bring to the boil and reduce the heat slightly. Let it boil for 5–6 minutes, then reduce the heat to low, cover and cook for 20 minutes. Add the salt and lemon juice and beat the dhal with a wire whisk, adding a little more hot water if the dhal is too thick. Add the fresh coriander (cilantro) and leave the saucepan over a very low heat while you prepare the seasoning.

2 Heat the oil in a small saucepan over a medium heat. When the oil is quite hot, but not smoking, add the mustard seeds. As soon as they begin to pop, reduce the heat to low and add the remaining ingredients, except the turmeric. Let the spices sizzle until the seeds begin to pop and the chilli peppers have blackened. Stir in the turmeric and pour the entire contents over the lentils, scraping off every bit from the saucepan.

3 Turn off the heat and keep the saucepan covered until you are ready to eat. Transfer to a serving dish and garnish with the tomato and chives. Serve with boiled basmati rice and Cauliflower and Potato with Toasted Sesame Seeds and Coconut *(page 145)* or a raita.

Spicy Green Lentils

Preparation time: 10–15 minutes
Cooking time: 30–35 minutes   **Serves 4**

Although green lentils are not produced in India, spices have a magical influence on them. You can buy them from supermarkets.

225g/8oz/1 cup green lentils

3 tablespoons sunflower or plain olive oil

1 teaspoon cumin seeds

2 bay leaves, crumpled

1 medium onion, chopped

1–2 green chilli peppers, chopped

1–2 dried red chilli peppers, chopped

3–4 large cloves garlic, crushed

½ teaspoon ground turmeric

125g/4oz/½ cup chopped fresh tomatoes

1 teaspoon salt or to taste

2 tablespoons fresh coriander (cilantro), chopped

1   Wash the lentils and put into a saucepan with 850ml/1½ pints/3¾ cups hot water. Bring to the boil, reduce the heat to low, cover and cook for 20–25 minutes.

2   Heat the oil over a medium heat and add the cumin and bay leaves. Let them sizzle gently for 15–20 seconds.

3   Add the onions and both types of chilli pepper. Fry them for 5–6 minutes and add the garlic. Continue to fry, stirring, until the onions are caramel brown.

4   Add the turmeric and tomatoes. Cook for a minute or so and stir the mixture into the lentils, along with the salt. Bring to the boil, add the fresh coriander (cilantro) and remove from the heat. Serve with Coconut Rice (*page 101*) or Lemon Rice (*page 104*) and a raita.

Lentils in the Royal Style

Preparation time: 10–12 minutes plus soaking time for the lentils
Cooking time: 40–45 minutes   Serves 4–6

This is not an ordinary lentil dish, but one that originated in the courtly kitchens of Lucknow in north-ern India. The recipe has been adapted for low-fat cooking. In addition, the original recipe uses *urad dhal* (black split gram), but as *channa dhal* and yellow split peas are more easily available in the West, I have opted for these. You can, however, buy urad dhal from health-food shops and Indian stores.

225g/8oz/1 cup channa dhal or
    yellow split peas
½ teaspoon ground turmeric
Pinch of saffron strands, pounded
1 tablespoon hot milk
140ml/5fl oz/⅔ cup half-fat single
    (half and half) cream
1 teaspoon salt or to taste
½ teaspoon sugar
50g/2oz/¼ cup low-fat plain yogurt
2 tablespoons sunflower or olive oil
1 tablespoon blanched and slivered
    almonds
1 tablespoon raw unsalted
    pistachio nuts
1 tablespoon seedless raisins
2.5cm/1-inch cube root ginger,
    grated
1–2 green chilli peppers, seeded
    and chopped
½ teaspoon ground coriander
    (cilantro)
½ teaspoon garam masala
½ teaspoon chilli powder
2 small fresh tomatoes, skinned
    and chopped
1 tablespoon fresh mint leaves,
    chopped or ½ teaspoon dried
    mint
2 tablespoons coriander (cilantro)
    leaves, chopped

1 Clean and wash the lentils and soak for 1 hour. Drain well and put into a saucepan with 850ml/1½ pints/3¾ cups water and the turmeric. Bring to the boil, reduce the heat to medium and cook, uncovered, for 10–15 minutes. Reduce the heat slightly, cover the pan and cook until the lentils are tender (25–30 minutes). Stir occasionally to discourage foam rising to the top.

2 Meanwhile, infuse the pounded saffron in the hot milk and set aside.

3 Add the cream, saffron and milk, salt and sugar to the lentils. If using dried mint, add it now. Continue to cook on a low heat for 2–3 minutes.

4 Beat the yogurt with a fork and fold into the lentils, then switch off the stove.

5 In a small non-stick pan, heat half the oil gently and fry the nuts and raisins together until the nuts are lightly browned and the raisins puffed. Remove with a slotted spoon and set aside.

6 Add the remaining oil to the same pan. Fry the ginger, green chilli peppers and the spices for 1 minute, then add the chopped tomatoes. Continue to cook for 2 minutes, then fold the entire contents into the lentils.

7 Stir in the fresh mint and coriander (cilantro) and remove from the heat. Transfer the lentils to a serving dish and garnish with the fried nuts and raisins.

Tarka Dhal

Preparation time: 10 minutes
Cooking time: 30 minutes

Serves 4

Tarka or *tadka* means seasoning. When preparing the seasoning for Tarka Dhal, the ingredients can vary quite a lot. This recipe is one of the simplest.

225g/8oz/1½ cups red split lentils (masoor dhal)
1 teaspoon salt or to taste
2 teaspoons unsalted butter
1 tablespoon sunflower or plain olive oil
½ teaspoon black mustard seeds
2 large cloves garlic, crushed
½–1 teaspoon crushed dried chilli peppers
1 teaspoon ground turmeric
1 teaspoon cumin seeds
2 tablespoons coriander (cilantro) leaves, chopped
1 tablespoon lemon juice

1 Wash the dhal and put into a saucepan with 570ml/ 1 pint/2½ cups hot water. Place over a high heat and bring to the boil. Let it boil for 5 minutes, then reduce the heat to low. Cover the pan and simmer for 25–30 minutes, then stir in the salt.

2 Heat the butter and oil together over a medium heat until quite hot, but not smoking. Add the mustard seeds. As soon as they pop, add the garlic and allow it to brown slightly.

3 Add the chilli peppers, turmeric and cumin. Stir for 10–15 seconds and pour into the lentils.

4 Stir in the coriander (cilantro) leaves and lemon juice. Remove from the heat and keep the saucepan tightly covered until required, to keep the flavours locked in. Serve with any bread or Garlic Rice *(page 103)* and a side dish of your choice.

Fennel-flavoured Lentils

Preparation time: 30 minutes plus soaking time for the lentils
Cooking time: 40 minutes   Serves 4

A superb lentil delicacy with the distinctive flavour of fennel. The lentils used here are Bengal gram (*channa dhal*), but you can use yellow split peas instead, though they do not have the same flavour. This recipe is suitable for freezing.

175g/6oz Bengal gram (channa dhal) or yellow split peas
570ml/1 pint/2½ cups water
3 tablespoons sunflower or olive oil
2 × 2.5cm/1-inch pieces cinnamon stick
1 teaspoon fennel seeds
6–8 cloves garlic, peeled and crushed
½ teaspoon crushed dried chilli peppers
1 red onion, finely sliced
1–2 green chilli peppers, seeded and cut into juliennes
1 teaspoon salt or to taste
1 teaspoon ground fennel
1 teaspoon ground cumin
225g/8oz/1 cup canned chopped tomatoes, including juice
1 teaspoon garam masala
2 tablespoons chopped coriander (cilantro) leaves

1. Pick over the lentils and wash in several changes of water. Soak in plenty of cold water for 2 hours (longer would not matter). Drain thoroughly.

2. Put the lentils and water in a saucepan and place over a high heat. Bring to the boil and boil steadily for 8–10 minutes. Reduce the heat to low, cover and simmer for 30–35 minutes until the lentils are tender and have absorbed nearly all the water. The lentils at this stage should have the consistency of baked beans. Remove from the heat and set aside.

3. In a wok or non-stick pan, heat the oil over a medium heat. When the oil is hot but not smoking, add the cinnamon and fennel seeds, and let them sizzle for 15–20 seconds. Add the garlic and stir-fry for 1 minute.

4. Add the crushed chilli peppers followed by the onion and fresh chilli peppers. Stir-fry for 2 minutes, then add the salt and stir-fry for a further 2–3 minutes.

5. Add the ground fennel, cumin and half the tomatoes. Stir-fry for 2–3 minutes or until you can see oil floating on the surface.

6. Add the cooked lentils, increase the heat slightly and stir-fry for 4–5 minutes. Add the remaining tomatoes and garam masala. Stir-fry for 1 minute. Stir in the coriander (cilantro) leaves, remove from the heat and serve with any bread or boiled basmati rice and a raita.

The Five Jewels

Preparation time: 20–25 minutes plus time to soak lentils
Cooking time: 45–50 minutes

Serves 4

This delicacy from the Punjab uses five types of lentils. It is known as *dhal panchrattan* – 'panch' meaning 'five' and 'rattan' meaning 'jewels'. Try other combinations too. This recipe is suitable for freezing.

40g/1½oz/⅕ cup red split lentils (masoor dhal)

40g/1½oz/⅕ cup yellow split lentils (moong dhal)

40g/1½oz/⅕ cup channa dhal or yellow split peas

40g/1½oz/⅕ cup whole brown lentils (whole masoor dhal)

40g/1½oz/⅕ cup mung beans (whole moong dhal)

850ml/1½ pints/3¾ cups water

2 teaspoons ground cumin

1 teaspoon ground turmeric

2 × 2.5cm/1-inch pieces cinnamon stick

1 teaspoon salt or to taste

3 tablespoons sunflower or olive oil

1 onion, finely chopped

1–2 green chilli peppers, seeded and cut into juliennes

2.5cm/½-inch cube root ginger, peeled and cut into juliennes

¼ teaspoon crushed dried chilli peppers

90g/3oz/½ cup canned chopped tomatoes, including juice

½ teaspoon garam masala

2 tablespoons chopped coriander (cilantro) leaves

1. Pick over each variety of lentil, mix together and wash in several changes of water. Soak for 4–5 hours or overnight.

2. Put the lentils and water in a saucepan over a high heat. Bring to the boil and cook for 10 minutes, skimming off scum as necessary.

3. Add the cumin, turmeric and cinnamon, stir and reduce the heat to low. Cover and simmer for 20–25 minutes, stirring occasionally. Stir in the salt and mash some of the lentils (about a quarter) with a spoon. Remove from the heat and set aside.

4. In a wok or saucepan, heat the oil over a medium heat. When the oil is hot, add the onion, fresh chilli peppers and ginger and fry for 5–6 minutes, then add the dried chilli peppers. Stir-fry for a further 30 seconds and add the tomatoes. Stir-fry for 2 minutes, then stir in the garam masala and coriander (cilantro) leaves. Add this mixture to the cooked lentils, stir well and return the pan to the heat. Let the lentils bubble for 1 minute, remove from the heat and serve with Lemon Rice *(page 104)* or any bread.

Quorn in a Rich Tomato and Onion Sauce

Preparation time: 10 minutes
Cooking time: 30 minutes

Serves 4

Quorn, a vegetable protein, is high in protein and dietary fibre and free from cholesterol and animal fat, which makes it ideal for a vegan diet. Delicious as well as nutritious, it is widely available in supermarkets. It has a succulent taste and readily absorbs the flavours of other ingredients. If you prefer, you can use firm or extra-firm tofu instead.

2 tablespoons sunflower or olive oil

4–5 shallots, finely chopped

3–4 cloves garlic, crushed

2.5cm/1-inch cube root ginger, grated

1–2 green chilli peppers, chopped (seeded if wished)

350g/12oz/2 cups Quorn, diced

½ teaspoon ground turmeric

1½ teaspoons ground coriander (cilantro)

½ teaspoon ground cumin

225g/8oz/1 cup canned chopped tomatoes with their juice

1 teaspoon salt or to taste

125g/4oz/1 cup frozen garden peas

½ teaspoon garam masala

1 tablespoon chopped fresh mint or 1 teaspoon dried mint

2 tablespoons chopped fresh coriander (cilantro)

3 tablespoons half-fat single (half and half) cream

1   In a medium-sized saucepan, heat the oil over a medium heat and fry the shallots, garlic, ginger and green chilli peppers for 4–5 minutes.

2   Add the Quorn, stir-fry for 3–4 minutes and add the spices. Cook for 1–2 minutes and add the tomatoes. Stir and cook for 2–3 minutes.

3   Pour in 230ml/8fl oz/1 cup hot water and add the salt. Stir, bring to the boil, reduce the heat to low and cover the pan. Cook for 15 minutes.

4   Add the remaining ingredients, stir, increase the heat slightly and cook gently for 3–4 minutes. Remove from the heat and serve with Lemon Rice *(page 104)* or any bread and a raita.

Quorn Korma

Preparation time: 15 minutes
Cooking time: 35 minutes

Serves 4

If you cannot get Quorn, hard tofu works very well.

50g/2oz/¼ cup raw cashew nut pieces

Pinch of saffron threads, pounded

2 tablespoons rosewater

3 tablespoons sunflower or light olive oil

5–6 shallots, finely chopped

4 cloves garlic, crushed

2.5cm/1-inch cube root ginger, finely grated

2 teaspoons ground coriander (cilantro)

300ml/½ pint/1⅓ cups warm skimmed or semi-skimmed milk

230ml/8fl oz/1 cup warm water

255g/9oz packet of Quorn, cut into 2.5cm/1-inch cubes

90g/3oz/½ cup frozen garden peas

1 teaspoon salt or to taste

½ teaspoon freshly milled white pepper

½ teaspoon garam masala

4 glacé cherries, quartered and rinsed

1 Soak the cashews in 140ml/¼ pint/⅔ cup boiling water and set aside for 15 minutes.

2 Soak the pounded saffron in the rosewater and set aside.

3 In a wok, heat the oil over a medium heat and fry the shallots for 3–4 minutes until softened. Add the garlic and ginger and cook for a minute.

4 Add the coriander (cilantro) and cook for about 30 seconds. Stir in two tablespoons of the warm milk and cook for a minute or two. Repeat this process twice more and add the remaining milk. Bring to a slow simmer and cook, uncovered, for 5–6 minutes.

5 Add the warm water and the Quorn, peas and salt. Let it come to a rolling boil, reduce the heat to low and cover the pan. Simmer for 10 minutes.

6 Add the pepper, garam masala, half the cherries and the saffron-infused rosewater. Simmer for 2–3 minutes, transfer to a serving dish and serve garnished with the remaining cherries.

Smoked Tofu in Saffron-cream Sauce

Preparation time: 25–30 minutes
Cooking time: 30–35 minutes

Serves 4

The smoky flavour of tofu, the silky-smooth cream sauce and the toasted poppy seeds combine to produce a delicious dish, good enough to serve when you want to impress someone special. Tofu is readily available in large supermarkets and health-food stores.

255g/9oz/1⅓ cups smoked tofu
255g/9oz old potatoes
1 tablespoon white poppy seeds
2 tablespoons sunflower or light
   olive oil
4–5 shallots, finely chopped
3 cloves garlic, crushed
2 teaspoons ground coriander
   (cilantro)
½ teaspoon chilli powder or to taste
200ml/7fl oz/¾ cup skimmed or
   semi-skimmed milk, warmed
Pinch of saffron threads, pounded
½ teaspoon salt or to taste
2–3 tablespoons half-fat single (half
   and half) cream
½ teaspoon garam masala
2 tablespoons coriander (cilantro)
   leaves, finely chopped

1 Remove tofu from packaging and leave to drain thoroughly on absorbent paper. Cut into 2.5cm/1-inch cubes.

2 Peel and cut the potatoes into 2.5cm/1-inch cubes, boil for 6–8 minutes until tender but firm then rinse in cold water to stop further cooking. Leave to drain in a colander.

3 Grind the poppy seeds in a coffee grinder until fine and set aside.

4 In a wok, heat the oil over a medium heat and fry the shallots for 3–4 minutes until softened. Add the garlic and cook for about a minute.

5 Reduce the heat to low and add the coriander (cilantro) and chilli powder. Cook for a minute and add the ground poppy seeds. Stir-fry for a minute.

6 Add the warm milk, pounded saffron and salt. Bring to a slow simmer, add the tofu, cover and simmer for 10 minutes.

7 Add the boiled potatoes and cook, uncovered, for 5–6 minutes.

8 Add the cream, garam masala and coriander (cilantro) leaves. Stir, simmer for 2–3 minutes, remove from the heat and serve with boiled basmati rice or chapattis.

Eastern Vegetarian Burgers

Preparation time: 20 minutes
Cooking time: 8–10 minutes

Makes 8

These burgers with soya mince are delicious and filling. If you like, you can use Quorn or hard tofu instead of soya mince.

125g/4oz/1 cup soya mince
1 small onion, finely chopped
1–2 fresh green chilli peppers, seeded and chopped
1 teaspoon ground coriander (cilantro)
1 teaspoon ground cumin
1 teaspoon garam masala
2 tablespoons coriander (cilantro) leaves, chopped
1 tablespoon tomato purée (paste)
1 teaspoon salt or to taste
25g/1oz cornmeal (polenta)
2 large (extra large) eggs, beaten
Olive oil for brushing
25g/1oz plain (all purpose) flour

1 Put the soya mince in a large mixing bowl with the onions and chilli peppers and pour in 230ml/8fl oz/1 cup hot water. Mix thoroughly and add the remaining ingredients, except the oil and flour.

2 Halve the mixture and make 4 equal-sized balls out of each portion. Flatten them into burger shapes and set aside for 10 minutes. It is difficult to shape the burgers when the mixture is cold, so make sure you do this while it is hot. If the mixture sticks to your hands, grease them lightly.

3 Brush a non-stick frying pan (skillet) with olive oil and heat over a medium heat. Dust each burger in the flour and fry gently until well-browned (3–4 minutes on each side). Brush or spray a little more oil over the burgers, if necessary. Drain on absorbent paper and serve with a salad and Baby Vegetable Pilau *(page 113)*. Alternatively, serve sandwiched with soft buns, tomato ketchup and crisp lettuce leaves.

Chickpea Pilau shown with Baby Vegetable Pilau, pages 116, 113

Baby Vegetable Pilau, page 113

Tomato and Coriander Rice, shown with Lemon Rice, pages 109, 104

Mixed Lentils with Five-spice Seasoning, page 68

Eastern Vegetarian Burgers, page 78

Polenta Pancakes with Ginger, Chilli and Cumin, page 89

Okra in Sesame and Poppy Seeds with Peppers, page 153

Pear and Cucumber Salad, page 28

Chapter 5

The Bread Basket

In northern India, wheat and barley have been staple foods since ancient times. Grains of wild grasses have been transformed to what we know as wheat today through decades of cultivation and the use of natural organic fertilizers.

While southern India thrives on rice, northerners eat bread as their daily staple. There is a wide range of leavened and unleavened breads. Some are made very simply within the farming community, some are adapted to suit the modern family and others grace banqueting tables. In spite of this huge variety, the daily bread is unleavened flat bread (chapattis). These are made fresh every day. They are very nutritious as the wheat is ground together with the entire kernel to produce a flour naturally rich in wheat germ, thereby providing plenty of dietary fibre.

As well as making your own bread, to save time you can also choose from the wide variety available in our supermarkets. With one or two clever twists you can transform plain breads into something special. For instance, buy wholemeal pitta and brush over with a little beaten egg white or beaten plain yogurt. Sprinkle with some seeds such as sesame, poppy or onion, or with minced garlic, chilli peppers and finely chopped coriander (cilantro). Pop them under the grill (broiler) for 2–3 minutes and you have a completely different product.

Bought chapattis can make a quick and nutritious meal if you wrap dry-spiced lentils, beans or vegetables in them and serve them as rolls. Use your imagination and make life easier!

Dry-roasted Flat Bread

Preparation time: 10–15 minutes plus resting the dough (batter)

Cooking time: 30 minutes   Makes 16

These dry-roasted flat breads *(chapattis)* are the everyday bread in India. They are simple and virtually fat-free. They are also extremely nutritious as they are made of whole-wheat flour, known as chapatti flour or *atta,* which has a higher fibre content than other flours.

400g/14oz/2½ cups chapatti flour
   (atta)

1 teaspoon salt

½ teaspoon sugar

2 tablespoons sunflower or
   vegetable oil

250ml/9fl oz/1¼ cups lukewarm
   water

A little extra flour for dusting

1   In a large mixing bowl, mix the flour, salt and sugar together.

2   Add the oil and work well into the flour with your fingertips. Gradually add the water, mixing at the same time. When the dough (batter) is formed, transfer to a pastry board and knead it for 4–5 minutes. The dough is ready when all excess moisture has been absorbed by the flour. Alternatively, make the dough in a food processor. Cover the dough with a damp cloth and leave to rest for 30 minutes.

3   Divide the dough into 2 parts and make 8 balls out of each. Rotate each ball between your palms and flatten them into round cakes. Dust each cake lightly in the flour and roll it out to a 15cm/6-inch disc. Keep the cakes covered with a damp cloth at all times. The chapattis will cook better when freshly rolled out; so roll out one at a time and cook.

4   Preheat a heavy cast iron griddle (tawa) over a medium high heat. Place a chapatti on it, cook for about 30 seconds and turn over using a thin spatula or a fish slice. Cook until bubbles begin to appear on the surface and turn it over again. Press the edges down gently to encourage the chapatti to puff up. Cook until brown patches appear on the underside. The chapattis should have brown spots or patches rather than black, so keep an eye on the heat and turn it down if necessary. Keep the cooked chapattis hot by wrapping them in a piece of foil lined with kitchen paper.

Variations

You can transform basic chapattis into something special whenever you want. Make delicious Mint Chapattis by adding approximately 25g/1oz/¼ cup finely chopped fresh mint leaves to the dough.

To make Onion Chapattis, add 1 medium-sized grated onion, preferably red, to the dough. Watch the amount of water used as grated onion will add moisture to the dough.

To make Cumin and Coriander Chapattis, add 1 teaspoon crushed cumin seeds and 2 tablespoons finely chopped fresh coriander (cilantro) leaves to the dough.

Goan Rice Flat Bread

Preparation time: 10 minutes
Cooking time: 30–35 minutes

Makes 8

These fabulously flavoured rice flat breads *(apa de arroz)* were introduced to India by the Portuguese when they colonized Goa and established themselves there for four centuries. They are so good that you can often eat them without any accompaniments! With soup, they will make a nutritious and satisfying meal. They can, of course, be served with anything from lentils and beans to vegetables and raitas.

150g/5oz/¾ cup ground rice

90g/3oz/½ cup plain (all purpose) flour

40g/1½oz/¼ cup desiccated coconut, ground in a coffee grinder until fine

1–2 green chilli peppers, seeded and finely chopped

3 tablespoons finely chopped coriander (cilantro) leaves

½ teaspoon salt or to taste

300ml/½ pint/1⅓ cups water

3 tablespoons sunflower or light olive oil

1   Place all the ingredients, except water and oil, into a large mixing bowl and mix well. Gradually add the water and mix with a wooden spoon until a thick batter is formed. This should be of spreading consistency.

2   Place a cast-iron griddle or other heavy-based pan over a medium heat, add about a teaspoon of the oil then spread it quickly over the entire surface.

3   Add 2 tablespoons of the batter to the hot griddle and spread it to form a disc of approximately 15cm/6 inches in diameter. Cook for 3–4 minutes until the top is well set and the underside has brown patches. Spread a little oil on the top and turn it over carefully, easing it away all around the edge with a thin spatula or fish slice. Cook for 2–3 minutes until browned.

4   Line a large tray with absorbent paper and arrange the cooked breads in a single layer on top. Do not stack them up or they will turn soggy. They can be kept hot in a low oven for 15–20 minutes or reheated under a low grill (broiler). They can be frozen when cold.

Mint and Coriander Flat Bread

Preparation time: 10 minutes plus resting the dough (batter)
Cooking time: 40 minutes   Makes 16

Mint and coriander (cilantro) is a combination I find hard to resist. The flat breads are delicious and take no more effort than the basic flat breads (chapattis). Instead of water, I have used milk to make the dough (batter), which will produce moister and softer breads.

450g/1lb/3¼ cups chapatti flour (atta), plus a little extra for dusting
1 teaspoon salt
Freshly milled black pepper
2 tablespoons sunflower or light olive oil
2 tablespoons fresh mint leaves, finely chopped or 1 tablespoon dried mint
2 tablespoons coriander (cilantro) leaves, finely chopped
250ml/9fl oz/1¼ cups skimmed or semi-skimmed milk

1 Mix all the ingredients together except the milk. Gradually add the milk and mix until a dough (batter) is formed. Transfer to a pastry board and knead until smooth. Alternatively, make the dough in a food processor. Wrap with plastic food film and set aside for 30 minutes.

2 Divide the dough into two parts and form 8 equal-sized balls out of each. Flatten them into round cakes. Dust each cake lightly in the extra flour and roll it out to a 15cm/5-inch disc. Keep the remaining cakes covered while you work on one.

3 Preheat a heavy cast-iron griddle or other suitable shallow pan over a medium-high heat. Place a disc on it and cook until bubbles begin to appear on the surface. Using a fish slice, turn it over and cook until the underside has brown patches. Turn it over again and press the edges down to encourage the bread to puff up. Cook until brown patches appear on the other side. Once the pan is well heated, you may need to turn the heat down slightly.

4 Wrap the cooked breads in a sheet of foil lined with absorbent paper until you have finished cooking all of them.

Kashmiri Flat Bread

Preparation time: 15–20 minutes
Cooking time: 20–25 minutes

Makes 8

Barley and wheat have been staple foods of northern India since ancient times. Indeed, archaeologists have found brick-built ovens and the remains of wooden pestles, used to grind wheat into flour. Kashmiris still follow this practice today. The modern *tava* (iron griddle) for cooking bread must have developed over time from the clay and metal-plate models found in the Indus Valley.

450g/1lb/3¼ cups atta or chapatti flour

1 teaspoon salt

2 teaspoons sugar

1 teaspoon royal cumin (shahi jeera)

1 teaspoon onion seeds (kalonji)

250ml/9fl oz/1¼ cups warm milk

3 tablespoons olive oil

Olive oil for frying

1 Put the flour, salt, sugar, royal cumin and onion seeds in a large mixing bowl and mix thoroughly.

2 Gradually add the warm milk and knead until a dough (batter) is formed. Alternatively, use a food processor with a dough hook. For both methods, now add the oil and knead for 2–3 minutes or until the oil is absorbed by the dough. If using a food processor, knead the dough until it stops sticking to the bowl and dough hook. For the hand method, transfer the dough to a pastry board and knead until it is soft and pliable and stops sticking to the board.

3 Divide the dough into 2 equal parts and make 4 equal portions out of each. Rotate each portion between your palms to make a ball, then flatten by pressing down. Cover the flattened cakes with a damp cloth and set aside for 20 minutes. Longer would not matter.

4 Preheat a cast-iron griddle or other heavy-based frying pan (skillet) over a medium heat. Roll out a flattened cake to a 20.5cm/8-inch disc and place on the griddle. Allow to cook for 1 minute, then turn over and cook the other side for 1 minute. Meanwhile, spread a little oil (about ½ teaspoon) on the cooked side. Cook the first oiled side until brown patches appear (you can check this by lifting gently). Turn it over and cook the second oiled side until brown patches appear.

5 Place the cooked flat bread on one end of a long piece of foil lined with absorbent paper. Cover with the other end to keep hot while you cook the remaining flat breads.

Griddle-cooked Fenugreek Flat Bread

Preparation time: 15–20 minutes
Cooking time: 25 minutes

Makes 8

Fenugreek (*methi*) leaves are sold fresh or dried in Indian stores. This recipe uses *Kasoori methi* (dried fenugreek leaves). It grows abundantly in Kasoor in Pakistan and is considered to be the best. The fresh leaves are dried and chopped with their stalks, which you need to remove.

450g/1lb/3¼ cups atta or chappati flour

1 teaspoon salt

2 teaspoons sugar

2 tablespoons Kasoori methi, stalks removed

2–3 cloves garlic, peeled and crushed

3 tablespoons sunflower or olive oil

250ml/9fl oz/1¼ cups warm water

Extra flour for dusting

Sunflower or olive oil for frying

1 Put the flour in a large mixing bowl. Add the salt, sugar, Kasoori methi and garlic, and mix thoroughly with your fingertips.

2 Add the oil and work it well into the flour. Gradually add the warm water and knead until you have a soft dough (batter). Transfer the dough to a pastry board and knead with your hands until it is soft and smooth and does not stick to your fingers or the board. Now cover the dough with a damp cloth and leave to rest for 20–30 minutes.

3 Divide the dough into 2 equal parts and either break off or cut 4 equal portions from each. Flatten each portion by rotating it between your palms and pressing it down to a flat cake. Cover again with a damp cloth. Preheat a cast-iron griddle or other heavy-based frying pan (skillet) over a medium heat for 2–3 minutes.

4 Dust one flat cake in flour and roll out to an 18cm/7-inch disc. Carefully lift from the board and place on the griddle. Cook for 1 minute, then turn over and cook the other side for 30–40 seconds. Meanwhile, spread the entire surface of the side you cooked first with 1 teaspoon oil. Turn over and cook until brown patches appear (you can lift it to check using a thin, flat spatula). Now oil the second side, turn over and cook until brown patches appear. Each flat bread will take 2–3 minutes. Transfer the cooked flat breads to a plate lined with absorbent paper.

Chilli Pancakes with Yogurt and Coriander

Preparation time: 10–15 minutes
Cooking time: 18–20 minutes

Makes 6

These egg-free pancakes have the wholesome taste of chapatti flour (atta). You could use wholemeal bread flour, but not the strong kind. They are easy to make and delicious with dry or semi-dry dishes.

175g/6oz/1 cup chapatti flour
    (atta)
50g/2oz/¼ cup cornmeal (polenta)
½ teaspoon salt
½ teaspoon onion seeds (kalonji)
2 tablespoons low-fat plain yogurt
500ml/18fl oz/2¼ cups water
2 fresh red chilli peppers, seeded
    and finely chopped
2 tablespoons coriander (cilantro)
    leaves, finely chopped
3 tablespoons sunflower or light
    olive oil for shallow frying

1. In a mixing bowl, combine the flour, cornmeal, salt and onion seeds. Beat the yogurt and water together and add to the flour mixture. Add the chilli peppers and coriander (cilantro) leaves and mix well.

2. Preheat a cast-iron or other heavy griddle, preferably non-stick, over a medium heat and add about a teaspoon of oil. Spread it quickly over the entire surface and wait until it reaches smoking point.

3. Measure 125ml/4fl oz/½ cup of the batter in a jug and pour it on the pan, then spread it with the back of the spoon to close any gaps and holes. Cook for 30–40 seconds and sprinkle about a tablespoon of water round the edges. Cook for a further 30–40 seconds, spread a teaspoon of oil on the uncooked side and turn it over. Do this carefully by loosening the pancakes all the way around with a thin spatula or fish slice. Cook until both sides are browned (2½–3 minutes per pancake). If the first one is not successful, don't worry (it often looks like scrambled eggs in my case!). Once the pan is well heated and seasoned, the subsequent pancakes will be perfect.

4. Place the cooked pancakes on a wire rack in a single layer or they will turn soggy. Serve immediately.

Easy Rice and Lentil Pancakes

Preparation time: 10 minutes plus resting
Cooking time: 30–35 minutes

Makes 10 × 23cm/9-inch pancakes

These pancakes, known as *dosas,* are the classic snacks from south India. They are made of a mixture of rice and lentils. The lentils are soaked, ground and left to ferment. This recipe is an easy version that you can make instantly. The traditional version is also included *(page 88)* for those who do not mind the extra time and effort involved. The pancakes can be served with a chutney or filled with spicy potatoes *(masala dosas).* Use the recipe on page 143 to fill the pancakes.

90g/3oz/½ cup semolina (cream of wheat) or fine cornmeal
90g/3oz/½ cup ground rice
50g/2oz/¼ cup plain (all purpose) flour
½ teaspoon salt or to taste
1 teaspoon cumin seeds, crushed
150g/5oz/⅔ cup low-fat plain yogurt
350ml/12fl oz/1½ cups cold water
2–3 tablespoons sunflower or light olive oil

1   In a large mixing bowl, mix the dry ingredients thoroughly.

2   Blend the yogurt and the cold water together and gradually add it to the bowl. Stir with a wooden spoon until the mixture is well blended and looks thinner than a coating consistency. Cover the bowl and set aside for 10 minutes.

3   Place a large, heavy-based griddle or skillet, preferably non-stick, over a medium heat and spread about a teaspoon of oil over the entire surface.

4   Pour 125ml/4fl oz/½ cup batter into a measuring jug, then pour into the griddle, spreading it quickly and evenly to a disc of approximately 17cm/9 inches. Allow the mixture to set and cook for 3–4 minutes. Carefully turn it over with a thin spatula or fish slice and cook the other side for 3–4 minutes. Place the cooked pancakes on a wire rack in a single layer and keep them hot in a low oven until you have finished cooking them all.

Traditional Rice and Lentil Pancakes

Preparation time: 20 minutes plus soaking and fermentation
Cooking time: 30–35 minutes

Makes 10 × 9-inch pancakes

❧❧❧❧❧❧❧❧❧❧❧❧❧❧❧❧❧❧❧❧❧❧❧❧❧❧

225g/8oz/½ **cup any white rice**
150g/5oz/¾ **cup skinless black gram (urid dhal)**
1 **tablespoon yellow split lentils (channa dhal)**
1 **teaspoon fenugreek seeds**
½ **teaspoon salt or to taste**
2–3 **tablespoons sunflower or light olive oil**

1　Wash the rice and soak it in cold water for 4–6 hours or overnight. Drain well.

2　Mix the black gram and the yellow split lentils together and wash them. Add the fenugreek seeds and soak them all together in cold water for 4–6 hours or overnight. Drain.

3　Blend the rice in an electric blender with 60ml/2fl oz/¼ cup water until very smooth and pour it into a large mixing bowl.

4　Blend the gram mixture with 170ml/6fl oz/⅔ cup cold water until smooth and add to the puréed rice. Add the salt then mix with a wooden spoon and pour in 350ml/12fl oz/1½ cups cold water. Stir until the batter is slightly thinner than a coating consistency.

5　Cover the bowl and leave in a warm place for the mixture to ferment. This will normally take 6–8 hours – you could leave it overnight on top of a boiler or airing cupboard and at room temperature during hot weather.

6　Use the batter the same way as for Easy Rice and Lentil Pancakes *(page 87)* and either serve with a chutney or fill the pancakes with the spiced potatoes on page 139.

Polenta Pancakes with Ginger, Chilli and Cumin

Preparation time: 15 minutes
Cooking time: 40–45 minutes

Makes 12

These delicious savoury pancakes are very nutritious and sustaining. Keep the cooked pancakes in a low oven on an open tray until you finish cooking all of them. Avoid piling them up to retain their crisp texture.

150g/5oz/¾ cup fine polenta
150g/5oz/¾ cup semolina (cream of wheat)
1 teaspoon salt or to taste
½ teaspoon bicarbonate of soda
1 red onion, finely chopped
1 teaspoon finely grated root ginger
2 fresh red chilli peppers, finely chopped (seeded if wished)
1 teaspoon cumin seeds
2 tablespoons chopped coriander (cilantro) leaves
150g/5oz/¾ cup plain yogurt
Sunflower or olive oil for shallow frying

1   In a large mixing bowl, mix the polenta and semolina (cream of wheat) with the salt and soda. Add the remaining ingredients, except the yogurt and oil. Stir and mix thoroughly.

2   Blend the yogurt with 300ml/½ pint/1⅓ cups cold water and gradually add to the semolina mixture. Mix until a thick paste is formed which is of spreading consistency.

3   Spread 2 teaspoons of oil in an iron griddle or small, non-stick, heavy-based frying pan (skillet) and heat over a medium-low heat. Pour in 1 heaped tablespoon of the pancake mix and gently spread it around to make a 7.5cm/3-inch disc. Cover with a lid and let it cook for about 2 minutes.

4   Spread a teaspoon of oil on the uncooked side and turn it over. Cook, uncovered, for 2 minutes or until the pancake is set. Cook, tossing and turning, for a further 2–3 minutes or until well-browned on both sides.

Quick and Easy Plain Naan

Preparation time: 10 minutes
Cooking time: 15–18 minutes

Makes 8

This is a simplified recipe for making naan at home. Because ghee (clarified butter) or butter has not been used, milk has been added to the dough (batter) to make the naans soft and moist. Once they are cooked, you could brush them lightly with a little melted butter if you wish, but they are delicious without. For a variation, add a teaspoon of onion seeds (kalonji) or crushed cumin seeds to the dough.

450g/1lb/3¼ cups self-raising flour
2 teaspoons sugar
1 teaspoon salt
1 teaspoon baking powder
4 tablespoons sunflower or olive oil
250ml/9fl oz/1¼ cups semi-skimmed milk, warmed

1   In a large mixing bowl, sift the flour, sugar, salt and baking powder together. Add the oil and rub in well with your fingertips. Gradually add the warmed milk and mix until a soft dough (batter) is formed. Transfer it to a pastry board and knead for 5–6 minutes until smooth, soft and pliable. Cover the bowl with plastic food wrap or a damp cloth and set aside for 20–25 minutes.

2   Divide the dough into 8 equal-sized portions and flatten them into thick cakes by rotating them between your palms. Cover them again and set aside for 10–15 minutes.

3   Preheat the grill (broiler) to high for 8–10 minutes. Line a grill pan with a piece of foil and brush well with some oil.

4   Roll each flattened cake into discs of about 13cm/5 inches and pull the lower end gently to form a teardrop if you wish to make the traditional shape. Roll them carefully again, maintaining the teardrop shape, to about 23cm/9 inches. Alternatively, roll them out to 23cm/9-inch circles.

5   Place the prepared naan on the lined grill pan and grill (broil) about 13cm/5 inches below the heat source for about 1½ minutes until puffed. Watch carefully and as soon as brown spots appear on the surface, turn it over and grill the other side until browned lightly. Place the cooked naan on a clean tea towel and wrap it up while you finish cooking the rest.

Chilli and Garlic Naan

Preparation time: 10 minutes

Serves 4

This is a quick way to transform plain naan, which can be home-made or shop-bought.

4 plain naan

2 large cloves garlic, finely chopped
or minced

1–2 green chilli peppers, finely
chopped (seeded if wished)

1 tablespoon snipped fresh chives

1 tablespoons coriander (cilantro)
leaves, finely chopped

The white of a small egg, beaten

1 Preheat the grill (broiler) to medium for 5–6 minutes.

2 Moisten each naan under running cold water and shake off excess water. Place in a grill pan and place the pan about 18cm/3 inches below the heat source. Grill (broil) until the surface water dries up. Repeat on the other side. Remove the pan from the grill.

3 Mix all the remaining ingredients together, except the egg white. Brush the egg white generously on each naan and spread equally with the chilli and garlic mixture. Grill for 1–2 minutes, remove and serve.

Stuffed Wholemeal Bread

Preparation time: 30–35 minutes plus resting time
Cooking time: 15–20 minutes   Makes 8

This rich, unleavened bread, known as *paratha,* can be served plain or with a stuffing. This version is stuffed with spiced potatoes. Instead of using ghee (Indian clarified butter) I have used olive oil. In my opinion, the wholesome taste of chapatti flour (atta) used in Indian breads more than makes up for the absence of ghee or butter.

450g/1lb/3¼ cups atta or chapatti
  flour
½ teaspoon salt
2 tablespoons olive oil
250ml/9fl oz/1¼ cups warm water
Extra flour for dusting
Sunflower or olive oil for shallow
  frying

For the filling:

225g/8oz/1½ cups potatoes, boiled
  in their jackets and peeled
2 shallots, very finely chopped
1 green chilli pepper, seeded and
  finely chopped
15g/½oz coriander (cilantro) leaves,
  finely chopped
½ teaspoon salt or to taste

1 Put the flour and salt in a large mixing bowl and work in the oil with your fingertips. Gradually add the water and mix until a soft dough (batter) is formed. Transfer the dough to a pastry board and knead for 3–4 minutes or until all traces of stickiness disappear. Alternatively, put all the ingredients into a food processor with a dough hook and run the machine until the dough feels soft and there is no stickiness. Cover the dough with a damp cloth and set aside for 30 minutes.

2 Meanwhile, mash the potato and add the onion, green chilli pepper, coriander (cilantro) and salt. Divide the mixture into 8 equal portions and shape each into a ball.

3 Now divide the dough into two equal parts and make four portions out of each. Shape each portion into a ball by rotating between your palms and flatten into a cake. Shape the flattened cake into a saucer shape, large enough to encase the potato ball. Place a potato ball in the centre of the saucer shape and seal the edges by pressing them together firmly, then press it gently to form a flat cake.

4 Preheat a cast-iron griddle or other heavy-based frying pan (skillet) over a medium heat. Dust a potato-filled cake with flour and, with very gentle pressure, roll it out to form a disc of approximately 15cm/6 inches. Place on the hot griddle and cook for 1 minute, then turn it over and cook the other side for 1 minute. Meanwhile, spread 1 teaspoon oil on the cooked side, turn it over and spread oil on the second side. Cook the first greased side till brown patches appear (you can lift the paratha slightly to check this). Turn it over and cook the second greased side until brown patches appear. Place the cooked paratha on one end of a long piece of foil lined with absorbent paper. Cover with the other end to keep hot while you cook the remaining parathas.

Tandoori Bread

Preparation time: 15 minutes plus proving
Cooking time: 20–25 minutes

Makes 8

Tandoori bread (or chapatti) is the basic bread baked in the *tandoor,* the clay oven. Traditionally, nothing other than plain water is used in the dough (batter), but you must eat this bread straight away as cold tandoori chapatti loses its appeal quickly. In order to overcome this problem I have modified the recipe so that the bread stays moist, soft and delicious even when cold.

450g/1lb/2¾ cups wholemeal (whole-wheat) self-raising flour plus 1–2 tablespoons extra for dusting

½ teaspoon salt

1 teaspoon sugar

1 sachet easy-blend yeast

1 tablespoon sunflower or vegetable oil

150g/5oz/¾ cup low-fat plain yogurt

230–300ml/8–10fl oz/1–1⅓ cups soda water

1   Put the flour, salt, sugar and yeast into a large mixing bowl and mix well.

2   Beat the oil and yogurt together and rub into the flour with your fingertips.

3   Gradually add the soda water and mix until a sticky dough (batter) is formed. Transfer the dough to a pastry board and knead until the excess moisture has been absorbed by the flour and the dough feels soft and springy. As long as you mix the dry ingredients well first, the dough can be made in a food processor.

4   Put the dough in a large, warmed metal bowl and cover with plastic wrap. Leave the dough to prove in a warm place for 1–1½ hours.

5   Preheat the oven to 230°C/450°F/Gas Mark 8. Line a baking sheet with greased greaseproof (wax) paper or baking parchment.

6   Divide the dough into 8 equal-sized portions and shape each one into a smooth, round ball, then flatten to a round cake. Dust in a little flour and roll it out to a 10cm/4-inch disc. Place on the prepared baking sheet and bake on the top shelf of the oven for 9–10 minutes or until puffed and browned in patches.

Variations

To make delicious Tandoori Garlic Bread, add 4 large garlic cloves, crushed to a fine pulp, to the dough. When the bread is still hot, brush over with a little virgin olive oil.

For an extra-special taste, add ½ teaspoon onion seeds (kalonji) and ½ teaspoon carum seeds (ajowan) to the dough.

Chapter 6

The Rice Bowl

Mogul Emperor Jahangir once described rice as 'the most wonderful gift of nature'. Today, India grows at least 10,000 different varieties of rice. Basmati rice, which is the most popular long-grain variety, grows abundantly in the foothills of the Himalayas. Indian cuisine has a huge repertoire of rice dishes, some of which are very simple while others are quite exotic and exciting.

Rice is also used as a religious offering in Hindu temples all over India. It is believed that the Aryan civilization discovered rice growing in northern India and cooked it with milk to offer to their god.

Rice is an easily digestible, gluten-free carbohydrate, which also provides some protein. More than half the population in India eats rice every day. A traditional Indian meal begins with wholewheat flat breads (chapattis) with several curries and a salad with yogurt dressing (raita) followed by rice, which is eaten with the same accompaniments. This is a healthy and balanced meal, providing protein, carbohydrate, vitamins and minerals all at once.

Cooking rice perfectly is not as difficult as some people imagine. Following these few simple steps will enable you to cook rice to perfection every time:

1 Always wash rice thoroughly before cooking. It is important to remove as much of the milling starch as possible. Make sure you wash the rice in several changes of water until the water becomes less cloudy.

2 Soaking the washed rice briefly helps to remove further milling starch. This stage also prepares the grains to absorb the cooking liquid more efficiently resulting in long, fluffy grains.

3 Once the lid goes on the cooking pot, it is most important not to lift it. Just allow it to cook for the specified time and once cooked, let the rice stand for a few minutes in the covered cooking pot. This helps the grains absorb any fresh starch back into themselves, which in turn stops them being sticky.

4 Always use a metal spoon to serve rice, especially basmati, as the grains can be fragile. As freshly cooked basmati rice is extra fragile, it is a good idea to cook it at least 20 minutes before serving. Cooked rice, left in its cooking pot with a lid, will stay hot for 30–35 minutes.

Plain Boiled Basmati Rice

Preparation time: A few minutes plus soaking time for the rice
Cooking time: 15 minutes   Serves 4–6

The wonderful natural aroma and flavour of basmati rice seems to have the power to complement any accompanying dish. In India, basmati is known as 'the king of rice'. Unlike other long-grain rice, basmati is not packed for the market just after it is harvested. It is matured for two to four years before it is ready for commercial purposes. It is during this maturing time that the rice develops that wonderful, distinctive flavour, a bit like good wine!

275g/10oz/1½ cups basmati rice
500ml/18fl oz/2¼ cups water
½ teaspoon salt
Knob of butter

1   Wash the rice in several changes of water and soak for at least 20 minutes. Drain thoroughly.

2   Put the water in a heavy-based saucepan and bring to the boil over a high heat. Add the rice, salt and butter, bring back to the boil and cook for 1 minute. Reduce the heat to low and cover the pan tightly. Cook for 10 minutes without lifting the lid. Remove from the heat and set aside, undisturbed, for 8–10 minutes.

3   Fork through the rice and transfer it to a serving dish using a flat metal or plastic spoon.

Basmati Rice with Coconut and Coriander Pesto

Preparation time: 30 minutes plus soaking time for the rice
Cooking time: 25 minutes

Serves 4

This dish is equally at home in the family dining room and on a banqueting table. It is my all-time favourite rice recipe as it is a complete meal in itself with an unusually adorable flavour. All you need is a raita to accompany it, but some grilled pappadums wouldn't go amiss.

225g/8oz/1 cup basmati rice

25g/1oz/¼ cup desiccated coconut

140ml/¼ pint/⅔ cup boiling water

4 cloves garlic, peeled and chopped

2.5cm/1-inch cube root ginger, peeled and roughly chopped

15g/½oz/¼ cup coriander (cilantro) leaves and stalks, roughly chopped

1–2 green chilli peppers, chopped (seeded if wished)

3 tablespoons sunflower or light olive oil

2 × 2.5cm/1-inch pieces of cinnamon stick

4 cloves

8–10 black peppercorns

1 medium onion, finely sliced

90g/3oz/½ cup whole green beans, cut into 2.5cm/1-inch pieces

90g/3oz/½ cup frozen garden peas or fresh cooked peas

1 teaspoon salt or to taste

450ml/16fl oz/2 cups hot water

50g/2oz/¼ cup raw cashew nuts

1 Wash the rice in several changes of cold water until the water runs clear. Soak in cold water for 20 minutes.

2 Soak the coconut in the boiling water for 10 minutes and put it in a blender along with the water. Add the garlic, ginger, coriander (cilantro) and chilli peppers and blend until you have a smooth purée (paste).

3 Heat the oil in a heavy-based saucepan over a low heat and sauté the cinnamon, cloves and peppercorns for 25–30 seconds. Add the onion and increase the heat to medium. Fry, stirring regularly, until the onion turns a light golden colour (7–8 minutes).

4 Drain the rice and add to the pan. Stir-fry for 2–3 minutes and add the puréed ingredients. Cook for a further 2–3 minutes, stirring, and add the beans, peas and salt. Pour in the hot water and bring it to the boil. Reduce the heat to low, cover the pan and cook for 8–9 minutes. Remove from the heat and leave it undisturbed for 6–8 minutes.

5 Meanwhile, brown the cashews under the grill (broiler) or in a heavy pan on the stove top over a medium heat. Reserving a little for decoration, add them to the rice and mix gently with a fork. Transfer to a serving dish, garnish with the reserved cashews and serve.

Saffron Rice

Preparation time: 15 minutes plus soaking time for the rice
Cooking time: 25–30 minutes   Serves 4–6

The best varieties of saffron come from India (Kashmir) and La Mancha in Spain.

275g/10oz/1½ cups basmati rice
500ml/18fl oz/2¼ cups water
3 × 2.5cm/1-inch pieces cinnamon
   stick
6 whole cloves
6 green cardamom pods, bruised
½ teaspoon black peppercorns
2 bay leaves, crumpled
1 teaspoon salt
½ teaspoon saffron strands,
   pounded
2 tablespoons hot milk
2 tablespoons sunflower or olive oil
3–4 shallots, finely sliced
15g/½oz toasted flaked almonds, to
   garnish
Few sprigs of fresh coriander
   (cilantro), to garnish

1 Wash the rice in several changes of water and soak for at least 20 minutes. Drain well.

2 Put the water, cinnamon, cloves, cardamom, peppercorns, bay leaves and salt into a saucepan. Bring to the boil, cover and simmer for 15 minutes. Strain and set aside.

3 Soak the saffron in the hot milk and set aside for 10–15 minutes.

4 Heat the oil over a medium heat in a heavy saucepan. Add the shallots and stir-fry until a pale golden colour, about 5–6 minutes. Add the rice, reduce the heat to low and stir-fry for 2–3 minutes.

5 Add the spiced liquid and saffron milk with all the strands and increase the heat to high. Bring to the boil, cover the pan and reduce the heat to very low. Cook for 10 minutes. Remove from the heat and leave undisturbed for 8–10 minutes.

6 Fork through the rice, then transfer to a serving dish using a metal spoon. Serve garnished with toasted almonds and sprigs of coriander (cilantro).

Coconut Rice

Preparation time: A few minutes plus soaking time for the rice
Cooking time: 12–14 minutes   **Serves 4**

Coconut rice is a speciality from southern India. The snow-white basmati rice, speckled with black mustard seeds and dotted with red chilli pieces, looks quite stunning. It is best served with a simple lentil dish or a vegetable curry.

225g/8oz/1 cup basmati rice
2 tablespoons sunflower or plain olive oil
1 teaspoon black mustard seeds
1 teaspoon cumin seeds
1–2 dried red chilli peppers, chopped
6 fresh or 8–10 dried curry leaves
1 teaspoon salt or to taste
225ml/8fl oz/1 cup reduced-fat coconut milk

1   Wash the rice at least twice in cold water, soak for 15 minutes and drain thoroughly.

2   Heat the oil in a non-stick saucepan over a medium heat. When the oil is quite hot, but not smoking, add the mustard seeds followed by the cumin seeds, chilli peppers and curry leaves. Let them all sizzle for 10–15 seconds.

3   Drain the rice and add to the pan along with the salt. Stir-fry for 1–2 minutes.

4   Add the coconut milk and pour in 225ml/8fl oz/1 cup hot water. Bring to the boil and allow to boil for about a minute, then reduce the heat to very low, cover the pan and cook for 6–8 minutes. Remove from the heat and leave undisturbed for 6–7 minutes. If the rice looks soggy, just leave it a little longer. This will be because of the coconut milk which the rice will absorb more slowly than plain water.

Cumin Rice

Preparation time: 5–10 minutes plus soaking time for the rice
Cooking time: 15 minutes   Serves 4

Cumin-flavoured fried basmati rice is perfect even with the simplest curry.

2 tablespoons sunflower or olive oil
1 teaspoon cumin seeds
2 bay leaves, crumpled
225g/8oz/1 cup basmati rice,
    washed and soaked for 15
    minutes
1 teaspoon salt or to taste

1   Heat the oil in a non-stick saucepan over a low heat and fry
    the cumin seeds and bay leaves for about a minute.
2   Drain the rice thoroughly and add to the pan. Stir-fry for 3–4
    minutes.
3   Add the salt and pour in 450ml/16fl oz/2 cups of hot water.
    Bring to the boil, reduce the heat to low, cover the pan and
    cook for 10 minutes without lifting the lid. Remove from the
    heat and leave undisturbed for 6–7 minutes, then fork
    through and serve.

Garlic Rice

Preparation time: 5 minutes plus soaking time for the rice
Cooking time: 15–18 minutes   Serves 4

This simple but delicious garlic rice is an ideal accompaniment to a korma as it is not as rich as Pilau Rice.

40g/1½oz unsalted butter

4–5 garlic cloves, peeled and finely sliced

225g/8oz/1 cup basmati rice, soaked for 30 minutes and drained

½ teaspoon salt

¼ teaspoon ground turmeric

450ml/16fl oz/2¼ cups hot water

Sprigs of fresh coriander (cilantro), to garnish

1   Melt the butter gently over a low heat and fry the garlic until lightly browned.

2   Add the rice, salt and turmeric. Stir-fry the rice for 2–3 minutes.

3   Add the water, bring to the boil and allow to boil for 1 minute. Reduce the heat to very low and cover the pan. Cook for 8–9 minutes. Remove the pan from the heat and let it stand undisturbed for 10–12 minutes. Fork through the rice and transfer to a serving dish. Serve garnished with the coriander (cilantro).

Lemon Rice

The flavour of fresh curry leaves adds a distinctive taste to this simple rice dish. They are available in Indian stores and can be frozen, but if you cannot get them, use dried ones, which can be bought from larger supermarkets.

225g/8oz/1 cup basmati rice
2 tablespoons sunflower or olive oil
1 teaspoon black mustard seeds
6–8 fresh or 10 dried curry leaves
25g/1oz broken cashew pieces
¼ teaspoon ground turmeric
1 teaspoon salt or to taste
2 tablespoons lemon juice

1 Wash the rice in cold water at least twice and soak for 15–20 minutes, then drain well.

2 Heat the oil in a non-stick saucepan over a medium heat. When the oil is quite hot, but not smoking, add the mustard seeds, curry leaves and cashews and let them sizzle for 15–20 seconds.

3 Remove a few pieces of cashew nut and add the rice, turmeric and salt to the pan. Stir-fry the rice for 2–3 minutes and add 450ml/16fl oz/2 cups hot water, followed by the lemon juice. Stir once and bring to the boil. Let it boil steadily for 2 minutes.

4 Cover the pan tightly and reduce the heat to low. Cook for 10 minutes, remove from the heat and let it stand undisturbed for 6–7 minutes. Fork through the rice and serve garnished with the reserved cashews.

Orange Rice

Preparation time: 15 minutes plus soaking time for the rice
Cooking time: 10–12 minutes

Serves 4–6

A unique flavour is created here with the fabulous natural aroma of basmati rice and the refreshing taste of zest and juice of oranges. For a real treat, serve it with Spiced Chickpeas with Sun-dried Mango *(page 49)* or Lentils with Courgettes *(page 66)*.

275g/10oz/1½ cups basmati rice
1 large orange
2 tablespoons sunflower or olive oil
1 × 5cm/2-inch piece of cinnamon stick, halved
4 green cardamom pods, bruised
1 teaspoon salt or to taste
450ml/16fl oz/2 cups hot water
1 tablespoon seedless raisins
25g/1oz/¼ cup flaked almonds

1 Wash the rice until the water runs clear and soak it in cold water for 20 minutes. Drain thoroughly.

2 Grate the orange rind finely and squeeze out the juice (you need about 60ml/2fl oz/¼ cup).

3 In a heavy-based saucepan, heat the oil gently over a low heat and add the cinnamon and cardamom. Let them sizzle until the cardamom pods have puffed up.

4 Add the rice and salt and sauté for 2–3 minutes, then add the hot water, raisins, orange juice and zest. Bring to the boil and allow to boil steadily for 2–3 minutes. Reduce the heat to low, cover the pan tightly and cook for 7–8 minutes. Remove from the heat and keep the pan undisturbed for 5–6 minutes.

5 Meanwhile, grill (broil) or roast the almonds until browned. Fluff up the rice with a fork and transfer to a serving dish. Gently mix in half the toasted almonds and scatter the remainder on top. Serve immediately.

Saffron and Rose-scented Rice

Preparation time: A few minutes plus soaking time for the rice
Cooking time: 10 minutes   Serves 4

Full of exotic flavours and garnished with fresh rose petals, this recipe has the hallmark of the Mogul era. Rather than colouring all the grains with saffron, I have gone for an attractive two-tone look. It is simple to make and perfect for special occasions, even a romantic dinner for two!

225g/8oz/1 cup basmati rice
¼ teaspoon saffron strands, pounded
2 tablespoons rose water
4 green cardamom pods, bruised
½ teaspoon salt
1½ tablespoons rose water
25g/1oz shelled roasted pistachio nuts, crushed
A few fresh rose petals, washed

1   Wash the rice in several changes of water and soak in cold water for 20 minutes.
2   Soak the pounded saffron in the first quantity of rose water and set aside.
3   Drain the rice and put into a saucepan. Add the remaining ingredients, except the pistachio nuts and rose petals. Stir and mix well. Pour in 450ml/16fl oz/2 cups of hot water and bring to the boil. Let it boil for a minute or two then reduce the heat to low, cover the pan and cook for 7–8 minutes. Remove from the heat, sprinkle the saffron-infused rose water over the top, then cover the pan again and let it stand for 10 minutes.
4   Fluff up the rice with a fork and transfer to a serving dish using a metal spoon. Sprinkle the crushed pistachio nuts on top, garnish with the rose petals and serve.

Toasted Sesame Rice

Preparation time: 10 minutes plus soaking time for the rice
Cooking time: 10–12 minutes

Serves 4–6

Like any other seeds, sesame seeds are high in calories and should be used sparingly, but they are also an excellent source of nutrients such as protein, vitamin E, the B-vitamins, calcium and fibre. Toasted Sesame Rice is easy to make and has a delightful flavour. It is a perfect accompaniment to any vegetable, lentil, bean or pea dish.

275g/10oz/1½ cups basmati rice
500ml/18fl oz/2¼ cups hot water
1 teaspoon salt or to taste
25g/1oz/¼ cup raw split cashew nuts
1½ tablespoons sunflower or olive oil
1½ tablespoons sesame seeds
2 dried red chilli peppers, chopped
6 fresh or 8 dried curry leaves

1 Wash the rice until the water runs clear. Soak in cold water for 20 minutes and drain. Put it into a heavy-based saucepan and add the water and salt. Bring to the boil and allow to boil steadily for 2–3 minutes, then reduce the heat to minimum setting. Cover the pan tightly and cook for 7–8 minutes, then remove from the heat and set aside.

2 Meanwhile, preheat the grill (broiler) to medium and grill (broil) the cashews until they brown, turning them regularly. Remove and set aside.

3 Heat the oil in a non-stick wok over a low heat and fry the sesame seeds and chilli peppers until they begin to brown. Add the curry leaves and fry for a further 25–30 seconds. Switch off the heat source and carefully add the cooked rice to the wok. Add the browned cashews, mix gently with a fork and transfer to a serving dish.

Mustard-flavoured Mango Rice

Preparation time: 15 minutes plus soaking time for the rice
Cooking time: 12–15 minutes   Serves 4–6

In India, raw mango is the natural choice for this rice, but as this is difficult to get in the West, I have used dried, ready-to-eat mango. This is not only convenient, but also produces an extremely satisfying dish. You could, however, try a fresh mango which is not fully ripe.

275g/10oz/1½ cups basmati rice
500ml/18fl oz/2¼ cups hot water
1 teaspoon salt or to taste
2 tablespoons sunflower or olive oil
½ teaspoon black mustard seeds
1–2 green chilli peppers, seeded and finely chopped
1–2 dried red chilli peppers, seeded and chopped
1cm/½-inch cube root ginger, peeled and cut into julienne strips
¼ teaspoon ground turmeric
225g/8oz/1 cup dried, ready-to-eat mango, chopped
Sprigs of fresh mint, to garnish

1 Wash the rice in several changes of cold water and soak it for 20 minutes. Drain thoroughly.

2 Put the drained rice into a heavy-based saucepan and add the hot water and salt. Bring to the boil and allow to boil vigorously for 1–2 minutes. Reduce the heat to low, cover the pan tightly and cook for 7–8 minutes. Remove from the heat and leave the pan undisturbed for 6–8 minutes.

3 Meanwhile, in a non-stick wok or a small saucepan, heat the oil over a medium heat. When the oil reaches smoking point, switch off the heat source and add the mustard seeds, followed by both types of chilli pepper and ginger. Let them all sizzle for 25–30 seconds and return the pan to low heat. Add the turmeric and the mango, increase the heat to medium and stir-fry the ingredients for 1–2 minutes. Pour over the cooked rice, mix gently with a fork, transfer to a serving dish and serve garnished with the mint.

Tomato and Coriander Rice

Preparation time: A few minutes plus soaking time for the rice
Cooking time: 12–14 minutes

Serves 4

This tasty and attractive dish is also easy to cook. Serve it with any lentil or chickpea (garbanzo) dish.

225g/8oz/1 cup basmati rice

2 tablespoons sunflower or olive oil

1 teaspoon royal cumin (shahi zeera or kala zeera)

1 tablespoon tomato purée (paste)

1 teaspoon salt or to taste

25g/1oz/½ cup chopped coriander (cilantro) leaves

1 tablespoon pine nut kernels, toasted

1 Wash the rice at least twice in cold water and soak for 15 minutes. Drain.

2 In a heavy-based saucepan, heat the oil over a medium heat and fry the royal cumin for 15–20 seconds.

3 Add the rice, tomato purée (paste) and salt. Stir fry for 2–3 minutes and pour in 450ml/16fl oz/2 cups hot water. Bring to the boil, stir in the coriander (cilantro) leaves, reduce the heat to low and cover the pan. Cook for 10 minutes. Remove from the heat and leave undisturbed for 6–7 minutes, then fork through the rice and serve garnished with the toasted pine nuts.

Yogurt Rice with Chilli and Curry Leaf Seasoning

Preparation time: 10 minutes plus soaking time for the rice
Cooking time: 10–12 minutes   Serves 4–6

Yogurt rice is very popular in southern India. Served cold, it is especially enjoyable during the summer as yogurt has a cooling effect.

275g/10oz/1½ cups basmati rice
500ml/18fl oz/2¼ cups hot water
1 teaspoon salt or to taste
1 tablespoon sunflower or olive oil
1 dried red chilli pepper, seeded
   and chopped
1 fresh green chilli pepper, seeded
   and chopped
6 fresh or 8 dried curry leaves
225g/8oz/1 cup low-fat plain
   yogurt
½ teaspoon sugar
1 tablespoon finely chopped
   coriander (cilantro) leaves

1   Wash the rice until the water runs clear and soak it in cold water for 20 minutes. Drain the rice well and put into a heavy saucepan with the hot water and salt. Bring to the boil and allow to boil steadily for 2–3 minutes. Reduce the heat to minimum setting, cover the pan tightly and cook for 7–8 minutes. Switch off the heat source and tip the cooked rice into a large tray. Spread it gently with a fork and let it cool.

2   Meanwhile, heat the oil over a low heat in a small saucepan or a wok and fry both types of chilli pepper and the curry leaves for about a minute.

3   In a mixing bowl, whisk the yogurt and sugar together and add the fried ingredients and the coriander (cilantro) leaves. Pour the mixture over the rice and mix gently but thoroughly. Transfer to a serving dish.

Fried Rice with Spring Onions

Preparation time: 10 minutes plus soaking time for the rice
Cooking time: 17–18 minutes

Serves 4

This is a quick and easy way to present a wonderfully flavoured rice which is perfect with any main course.

~~~

225g/8oz/1 cup basmati rice
2 tablespoons sunflower or olive oil
2 cloves garlic, crushed
1 bunch spring onions (scallions),
    both green and white parts,
    chopped
2 vegetable stock cubes
450ml/16fl oz/2 cups hot water
Salt to taste (optional)

1   Wash the rice at least twice in cold water and soak for 15–20 minutes then leave to drain in a colander.
2   Gently heat the oil in a non-stick pan and fry the garlic and spring onions (scallions) for 2–3 minutes.
3   Add the rice, stir and fry for 4–5 minutes.
4   Crumble the stock cubes and sprinkle over the rice, then pour in the hot water. Add salt to taste if liked. Bring to the boil, reduce the heat to low and cover the pan tightly. Cook for 10 minutes. Remove from the heat and leave undisturbed for 5–10 minutes. Fork through the rice and serve.

Kedgeree

Preparation time: 10 minutes plus soaking time for the rice
Cooking time: 12–15 minutes

Serves 4

Kedgeree, with hard-boiled eggs and cooked smoked fish, was created as a breakfast dish during the British Raj and is based on an Indian vegetarian dish known as *khichri*. This is the original vegetarian version with a few modifications.

125g/4oz/½ cup yellow split lentils
   (moong dhal)
225g/8oz/1 cup basmati rice
3 tablespoons sunflower or light
   olive oil
1 × 5cm/2-inch piece cinnamon
   stick, halved
4 cloves
4 green cardamom pods, bruised
2 bay leaves, crumpled
4–5 shallots, peeled and quartered
1 green chilli pepper, finely
   chopped
1 teaspoon salt or to taste
450ml/16fl oz/2 cups vegetable
   stock
1 small tomato, seeded and finely
   chopped, to garnish
Sprigs of fresh coriander (cilantro),
   to garnish

1 Wash the lentils several times in cold water and drain.

2 Wash the rice until the water runs clear and soak in cold water for 20 minutes. Drain.

3 In a heavy-based saucepan, heat the oil over a medium heat and add the cinnamon, cloves, cardamom and bay leaves. Sauté them for about a minute and add the shallots and green chilli pepper. Fry for 3–4 minutes.

4 Add the lentils and rice, reduce the heat slightly and cook, stirring, for 2–3 minutes.

5 Pour in the stock, bring to the boil and reduce the heat to low. Cover the pan tightly and cook for 10 minutes. Remove from the heat and leave undisturbed for 6–8 minutes. Using a metal spoon, transfer the kedgeree to a serving dish and serve garnished with the chopped tomatoes and sprigs of coriander (cilantro).

Baby Vegetable Pilau

Preparation time: 20–25 minutes plus soaking time for the rice
Cooking time: 30 minutes

Serves 4

Pilau is traditionally cooked in ghee (Indian clarified butter), which gives it a rich and nutty taste. I have used ordinary cooking olive oil and find the taste just as delicious.

225g/8oz/1 cup basmati rice
1 red onion, finely sliced
2 tablespoons plain olive oil, plus a
    little extra for drizzling
4 green cardamom pods, split at the
    top of each pod
2 × 5cm/2-inch pieces of cinnamon
    stick, halved
3 large cloves garlic, crushed
2.5cm/½-inch cube root ginger,
    peeled and grated
4 cloves
1–2 green chilli peppers, chopped
    (seeded if wished)
2 bay leaves
½ teaspoon ground turmeric
90g/3oz baby carrots, halved
125g/4oz baby corn, halved
90g/3oz baby green beans, halved
1 teaspoon salt or to taste
60ml/2fl oz/¼ cup semi-skimmed
    milk

1 Wash the rice 2–3 times in cold water and soak for 20 minutes.

2 Meanwhile, preheat the oven to 190°C/375°F/Gas Mark 5. Place the sliced onion on a baking sheet and drizzle over a little oil. Mix with your fingertips and bake in the centre of the oven until browned, stirring and repositioning at regular intervals to ensure even browning. Remove and set aside.

3 Heat the 2 tablespoons of oil over a low heat, add the cardamom, cinnamon, garlic, ginger, cloves, chilli peppers and bay leaves and cook for about a minute.

4 Add the turmeric, the vegetables and the salt. Stir-fry for 2–3 minutes.

5 Drain the rice and add to the vegetables. Stir-fry for 2–3 minutes.

6 Add the milk and 450ml/16fl oz/2 cups of hot water and bring to the boil. Add half the browned onions and allow to boil steadily for 2 minutes. Reduce the heat to low, cover the pan and cook for 12–15 minutes. Remove from the heat and leave the pan undisturbed for 6–7 minutes. Fork through the pilau and serve garnished with the remaining onions. A raita is all you will need to accompany this pilau.

Broccoli Pilau

Preparation time: 20 minutes plus soaking time for the rice
Cooking time: 18–20 minutes

Serves 4

Although broccoli is not a traditional Indian vegetable, I find it an excellent ingredient to cook with as long as you are light-handed with the spices.

225g/8oz/1 cup basmati rice
3 tablespoons sunflower or olive oil
1 teaspoon fennel seeds
6 green cardamom pods, bruised
5cm/2-inch piece of cinnamon
    stick, halved
½ teaspoon black peppercorns
2 bay leaves, crumbled
1 red onion, finely sliced
2 green chilli peppers, seeded and
    sliced lengthways
½ teaspoon ground turmeric
350g/12oz/3 cups broccoli florets
    (approximately 2.5cm/1 inch)
1 teaspoon salt or to taste
450ml/16fl oz/2 cups boiling water
1 firm, ripe tomato, seeded and cut
    into strips, to garnish

1   Wash the rice in several changes of water and soak it in cold water for 20 minutes, then leave to drain in a colander.

2   Heat the oil in a heavy-based saucepan over a medium-low heat and add the fennel seeds, cardamom, cinnamon, peppercorns and bay leaves. Sauté them for 15–20 seconds.

3   Add the onion and green chilli peppers and increase the heat to medium-high. Fry the onions for 5–6 minutes or until browned lightly.

4   Add the turmeric followed by the rice. Stir-fry the rice for 2–3 minutes and add the broccoli and salt. Stir and cook for 30 seconds.

5   Add the hot water, allow to boil for about 2 minutes and reduce the heat to very low. Cover the pan and cook for 7–8 minutes. Remove the pan from the heat and let it stand undisturbed for 5–6 minutes.

6   Fluff up the pilau with a fork and transfer to a serving dish with a metal spoon.

7   Garnish with the tomatoes and serve with a raita and some grilled pappadums.

Butterbean Pilau

Preparation time: 20–25 minutes plus soaking time for the rice
Cooking time: 25 minutes

Serves 4–6

The ways to make vegetarian pilau dishes are limited only by one's imagination. Butterbean Pilau is delightful as the buttery flavour of the beans complements the exquisite basmati rice beautifully.

275g/10oz/1½ cups basmati rice

3 tablespoons coriander (cilantro) leaves, including the tender stalks, roughly chopped

2 tablespoons fresh mint leaves

1 fresh green chilli pepper, seeded and chopped

2 cloves garlic, peeled and roughly chopped

2.5cm/1-inch cube root ginger, peeled and roughly chopped

2 tablespoons sunflower or olive oil

1 teaspoon royal cumin (shahi zeera or kala zeera)

2 bay leaves, crumpled

4 green cardamom pods, split at the top of each pod

1 × 2.5cm/1-inch piece cinnamon stick

4 whole cloves

1 red onion, finely sliced

½ teaspoon ground turmeric

400g/14oz can of butterbeans, drained and rinsed

1 teaspoon salt or to taste

570ml/1 pint/2½ cups warm water

1 Wash the rice in several changes of water and soak for 15–20 minutes in cold water. Drain well.

2 Purée the fresh coriander (cilantro), mint, fresh chilli pepper, garlic and ginger in a blender or food processor until fine, adding a little water if necessary.

3 In a heavy-based saucepan, heat the oil over a medium heat for 1–2 minutes and add the royal cumin and bay leaves. Stir-fry for 15–20 seconds and add the cardamom, cinnamon and cloves. Let them sizzle for 15–20 seconds and add the onion. Fry until lightly browned (7–8 minutes), stirring regularly.

4 Add the turmeric and stir-fry for 30 seconds, then add the puréed ingredients and cook for 2–3 minutes.

5 Add the butterbeans and salt. Stir-fry for 2 minutes then add the rice and fry for 1 minute.

6 Add the warm water, bring to the boil and let it boil for 5 minutes. Stir and reposition the rice twice.

7 Reduce the heat to low, cover the pan tightly and cook for 6–7 minutes. Remove from the heat and allow the pilau to rest for 5–7 minutes. Remove the whole spices if desired and fork through the rice before serving. Serve with a raita and some pappadums.

Chickpea Pilau

Preparation time: 15–20 minutes
Cooking time: 30 minutes

Serves 4

Chickpeas (garbanzos) are used extensively in Asian and Middle-Eastern cooking. They have a nutty taste and combine extremely well with the exquisite aroma of basmati rice. They also contain iron and vitamin E. In order to enhance the overall flavour of this dish, I have used a combination of olive oil and unsalted butter, but you can use just oil if you wish.

☙☙☙☙☙☙☙☙☙☙☙☙☙☙☙

3 tablespoons olive oil

6 green cardamom pods

2 × 5cm/2-inch pieces cinnamon stick, halved

6 cloves

1 red onion, finely sliced

2 fresh red or green chilli peppers, finely chopped (seeded if wished)

2.5cm/½-inch cube root ginger, peeled and grated

2 large cloves garlic, crushed

1 teaspoon ground coriander (cilantro)

½ teaspoon ground cumin

½ teaspoon ground turmeric

225g/8oz/1 cup basmati rice, washed and soaked in cold water for 30 minutes

225g/8oz/1¼ cups canned, drained and rinsed chickpeas (garbanzos)

1¼ teaspoons salt or to taste

15g/½oz/¼ cup chopped coriander (cilantro) leaves

1　Heat the oil over a medium heat in a heavy-based saucepan. Peel the top of each cardamom pod very slightly and add to the oil along with the cinnamon and cloves. Let them sizzle for 15–20 seconds.

2　Add the onions, chilli peppers, ginger and garlic. Stir-fry until the onions are lightly browned.

3　Add the spices and fry for a minute, then add the rice, chickpeas (garbanzos) and salt. Stir-fry for 2–3 minutes and add 450ml/16fl oz/2 cups hot water and the fresh coriander (cilantro). Bring to the boil, reduce the heat to low, cover the pan and cook for 10 minutes. Remove from the heat and leave undisturbed for 6–7 minutes. Fork through the pilau and serve with a raita and grilled or fried pappadums.

Mushroom Pilau

Preparation time: 20–25 minutes plus soaking time for the rice
Cooking time: 20 minutes   Serves 4

Shitake mushrooms are the best for this pilau, although you could use other wild varieties, such as chanterelle. Among the cultivated range, chestnut mushrooms work very well.

225g/8oz/1 cup basmati rice

2 tablespoons sunflower or plain olive oil

1 red onion, finely sliced

4 green cardamom pods, bruised

1 × 2.5cm/1-inch piece of cinnamon stick, halved

3 cloves

1 bay leaf

4 cloves garlic, crushed

1cm/½-inch cube root ginger, peeled and grated

1–2 fresh green or red chilli peppers, cut into julienne strips (seeded if wished)

¼ teaspoon ground turmeric

225g/8oz/2 cups shitake mushrooms, thickly sliced

1 teaspoon salt or to taste

1   Wash the rice in cold water at least twice and soak for 15–20 minutes. Drain thoroughly.

2   Heat half the oil over a medium heat and fry the onion until lightly browned. Remove with a slotted spoon and drain on absorbent paper.

3   Add the remaining oil to the pan and reduce the heat to low. Add the cardamom, cinnamon, cloves and bay leaf. Fry them gently for about a minute.

4   Add the garlic, ginger and chilli peppers and fry them for a further minute or until browned.

5   Add the turmeric, rice, mushrooms and salt. Stir-fry for 2–3 minutes and pour in 425ml/15fl oz/2 cups hot water. Bring to the boil and let it cook, uncovered, for about a minute. Reduce the heat to low and cover the pan tightly. Cook for 10 minutes. Remove from the heat and leave undisturbed for 6–7 minutes. Fork through the rice and transfer to a serving dish. Serve garnished with the fried onion.

Mushroom Pilau with Leftover Boiled Rice

Preparation time: 15 minutes
Cooking time: 5–7 minutes

Serves 2

Leftover boiled rice can be transformed into delicious dishes in numerous ways. Here is one example, but use your imagination and vary the taste and flavour. Be extra careful when storing cooked rice in the fridge. Make sure the rice has cooled thoroughly and reheat it until piping hot in order to destroy any bacteria.

2 tablespoons sunflower or olive oil
2 green cardamom pods, split at the top
1 × 5cm/2-inch piece cinnamon stick, halved
2 whole cloves
2 cloves garlic, crushed
1 green chilli pepper, seeded and cut into diagonal strips
25g/1oz/¼ cup sweet red (bell) pepper strips
125g/4oz/⅔ cup button mushrooms, sliced
½ teaspoon salt or to taste
¼ teaspoon ground turmeric
1 tablespoon fresh coriander (cilantro), chopped
300g/10½oz/2 cups cold boiled basmati rice

1 Heat the oil in a non-stick wok or frying pan (skillet) over a low heat and fry the cardamom, cinnamon and cloves for 15–20 seconds. Add the garlic, green chilli pepper and red pepper strips. Stir-fry until the garlic is lightly browned.

2 Add the mushrooms and salt. Increase the heat to high and stir-fry for 2 minutes or until the mushrooms start releasing their juices.

3 Stir in the turmeric and coriander (cilantro) leaves, followed by the cooked rice. Reduce the heat to low and stir to mix and blend all the ingredients together. Sprinkle a tablespoon of water over the rice and stir-fry for 2–3 minutes. Cover with a lid and let it sweat for 1–2 minutes or until the rice is heated through. Alternatively, once the rice is mixed with all the other ingredients, transfer it to a microwave-proof dish and reheat until piping hot. Serve immediately and do not reheat.

Nut Pilau

Preparation time: 15 minutes plus soaking time for the rice
Cooking time: 12–15 minutes

Serves 4–6

Nuts provide plenty of essential nutrients and are a good source of protein in a vegetarian diet. Research has shown that walnuts may reduce the risk of heart disease. Consumed in small quantities and combined with other food varieties, nuts are essential in a balanced diet. Served with a raita and grilled pappadums, this pilau will make a complete meal.

275g/10oz/1½ cups basmati rice
**Small pinch of saffron threads,
   pounded**
2 tablespoons hot milk
2 tablespoons sunflower or olive oil
**1 × 5cm/2-inch piece of cinnamon
   stick, halved**
4 green cardamom pods, bruised
2 cloves
2 bay leaves, crumpled
1 tablespoon seedless raisins
1 teaspoon salt or to taste
500ml/18fl oz/2¼ cups hot water
25g/1oz/¼ cup walnut halves
**25g/1oz/¼ cup blanched slivered
   almonds**

1 Wash the rice until the water runs clear and soak it in cold water for 20 minutes. Drain thoroughly.

2 Soak the saffron in the hot milk and set aside.

3 In a heavy-based saucepan, heat the oil over a low heat and add the cinnamon, cardamom, cloves and bay leaves. Let them sizzle for 15–20 seconds and add the drained rice, raisins and salt. Sauté the rice for 2–3 minutes and pour in the hot water. Bring it to the boil and allow to boil for 2–3 minutes, then reduce the heat to minimum setting, cover the pan tightly and cook for 7–8 minutes.

4 Pour the saffron-infused milk randomly over the surface of the cooked rice, re-cover the pan and remove from the heat. Set aside, undisturbed, for 6–8 minutes.

5 Meanwhile, grill (broil) or roast the nuts until lightly browned. Let cool.

6 Fluff up the rice with a fork and lightly mix in most of the roasted nuts, leaving a few behind to garnish. Transfer the pilau to a serving dish and serve garnished with the remaining nuts.

Tofu Pilau

Preparation time: 15–20 minutes plus soaking time for the rice
Cooking time: 35 minutes

Serves 4–6

Tofu is a natural food made from soya milk using a process similar to cheese making. High in protein and a good source of calcium, tofu is low in fat and absolutely free from cholesterol.

275g/10oz/1½ cups basmati rice

225g/8oz/1 cup hard tofu

1 large onion, finely sliced

3 tablespoons sunflower or olive oil

25g/1oz/¼ cup walnut pieces

25g/1oz/¼ cup shelled pistachio nuts

6 green cardamom pods, bruised

6 cloves

1 × 2.5cm/1-inch piece of cinnamon stick, halved

2 bay leaves, crumpled

½ teaspoon ground turmeric

1 teaspoon salt or to taste

500ml/18fl oz/2¼ cups hot water

1 tablespoon chopped coriander (cilantro) leaves, to garnish

1 Wash the rice in several changes of cold water and soak for 20 minutes. Leave to drain in a colander.

2 Drain the tofu on absorbent paper and dry well. Cut into 2.5cm/1-inch cubes.

3 Preheat the oven to 190°C/375°F/Gas Mark 5. Place the sliced onion in a roasting tin, drizzle with one tablespoon of the oil and mix thoroughly with your fingertips. Place in the centre of the oven and bake until lightly browned. Stir regularly to encourage even browning, remove and set aside.

4 Put the nuts into an ovenproof dish and roast at the same time as the onions until the nuts are browned. Remove and set aside.

5 In a heavy pan, heat the remaining oil over a medium heat and brown the tofu. Remove with a slotted spoon and drain on absorbent paper.

6 To the remaining oil in the pan, add the cardamom, cloves, cinnamon and bay leaves. Let them sizzle for a few minutes and add the rice. Stir-fry gently for 2–3 minutes and add the turmeric, salt, browned tofu and the onion. Add the water and bring to the boil. Allow to boil for about a minute then reduce the heat to low. Cover the pan and cook for 9–10 minutes. Remove from the heat and keep the pan undisturbed for 6–8 minutes.

7 Fluff up the rice with a fork and transfer to a serving dish. Serve garnished with the coriander (cilantro) leaves and roasted nuts and accompanied by a raita.

Tomato Pilau

Preparation time: 20 minutes plus soaking time for the rice
Cooking time: 20 minutes

Serves 4–6

Tomato Pilau looks stunning and its simple, uncluttered taste is equally at home with curries and dry dishes. Use firm tomatoes, preferably the vine-ripened ones, as their flavour has a pleasant, sweet undertone.

275g/10oz/1½ cups basmati rice
1 large onion, finely sliced
3 tablespoons sunflower or olive oil
450g/1lb firm ripe tomatoes, skinned, seeded and chopped
2 tablespoons chopped coriander (cilantro) leaves
3–4 shallots, finely chopped
3 cloves garlic, crushed
1–2 green chilli peppers, seeded and finely chopped
500ml/18fl oz/2¼ cups hot water
1 teaspoon salt or to taste

1   Wash the rice in several changes of water and soak it in cold water for 20 minutes.

2   Meanwhile, preheat the grill (broiler) to medium for 6–7 minutes. Place the sliced onions in a grill pan and drizzle 1 tablespoon of the oil over them. Season with salt and pepper and grill (broil) the onions until they are light brown (6–8 minutes). Stir and reposition the onions several times to encourage even browning. Add the tomatoes and coriander (cilantro), mix well, remove and set aside.

3   In a heavy-based saucepan, heat the 2 tablespoons oil over a low heat and fry the shallots, garlic and chilli peppers for 4–5 minutes.

4   Drain the rice and add to the pan. Fry gently for 3–4 minutes and pour in the hot water and the salt. Bring it to the boil, reduce the heat to low and cover the pan tightly. Cook for 7–8 minutes, remove from the heat and leave the pan undisturbed for 5–6 minutes.

5   Transfer the rice to a serving dish and add the onions, tomatoes and coriander. Mix gently but thoroughly with a fork and serve.

Kashmiri Vegetable Pilau

Preparation time: 10–15 minutes plus soaking time for the rice
Cooking time: 25 minutes

Serves 4

Kashmir is renowned for its exotic fruits and vegetables, and the local people have used them most imaginatively to create wonderful dishes.

175g/6oz/2 cups large flat
   mushrooms
3 tablespoons sunflower or olive oil
1 onion, finely sliced
4 × 2.5cm/1-inch cinnamon sticks
4 whole cloves
4 green cardamom pods, split at the
   top of each pod
2 bay leaves, crumpled
4–5 dried, ready-to-eat apricots,
   sliced
90g/3oz/¼ cup canned pineapple
   cubes, well drained
50g/2oz/½ cup glacé cherries,
   halved and rinsed
225g/8oz/1 cup basmati rice,
   washed, soaked in cold water
   for 30 minutes, well drained
1 teaspoon salt or to taste
½ teaspoon chilli powder
450ml/16fl oz/2 cups warm water
1 tablespoon coriander (cilantro)
   leaves, chopped

1 Quarter the mushrooms and halve each quarter.
2 Heat the oil in a heavy saucepan over a medium heat and add the onion, cinnamon, cloves, cardamom and bay leaves. Stir-fry for 5–6 minutes.
3 Add the mushrooms and stir-fry for 2 minutes.
4 Add all the fruits, with the rice, salt and chilli powder, and stir-fry for 2–3 minutes.
5 Add the water, bring to the boil and cook for 5 minutes. Add the coriander (cilantro) leaves and stir well.
6 Reduce the heat to very low, cover the pan tightly and cook for 6–7 minutes. Remove from the heat and leave to rest for 5–7 minutes. Use a metal or thin plastic spatula to stir and serve the rice.

Chapter 7

The Vegetable Basket

Vegetables provide creative cooks with a palette of colour and texture to create visually striking dishes. Just imagine a dish containing snow-white cauliflower, emerald-green peas and carrots in shades of coral! With these varied colours, together with their nutritional value and stunning flavours, it is easy to make a vegetable dish the central attraction.

An Indian meal is unimaginable without at least two vegetable dishes, each providing equal amounts of nutrients. Add to this a dish of lentils or peas, a chutney, wholewheat flat breads, rice and yogurt, and you have a totally balanced and healthy meal.

Whether or not you are a vegetarian, vegetables are an essential part of a healthy diet. Now, more than ever before, it is easy to include simple as well as exotic vegetables in our daily diet as we have a fabulous array of them displayed on supermarket shelves and market stalls.

Recent research has shown that vegetables contain beneficial substances known as 'antioxidants'. These are thought to fight 'free radicals' in the body, the agents that cause cancer and heart disease. Good vegetable sources of antioxidants include red (bell) peppers, tomatoes, carrots, cabbage, spinach and yellow-fleshed squashes.

Eating raw vegetables ensures that no food value is lost. Although cooking can destroy some of the nutrients in vegetables, in some cases it actually increases their nutritional value. The best way to cook vegetables is to steam them. In Indian cooking, vegetables are not boiled but allowed to cook gently in their own juices, together with the spices used. This method ensures the retention of all nutrients, including some of the vitamin C, which is sensitive to heat. During the slow cooking process, the vegetables secrete their natural juices, which mingle with the flavours of spices, such as earthy ginger and nutty mustard seeds, to produce an exotic taste sensation.

Indian spices can transform the simple, everyday vegetable into a culinary masterpiece. The enticing aroma of cardamom and coriander (cilantro), the gentle but assertive scent produced by onion seeds and fennel seeds and a sprinkling of freshly chopped coriander leaves will have you drooling over a dish using the humble potato. Cooking vegetables with Indian spices will always produce a melange of flavours highlighted by the contrasts in taste and aroma of each spice used. It is hardly surprising that the vast majority of the Indian population thrives on a vegetarian diet.

The recipes in this chapter are true vegetarian delights.

Aubergine in Coconut Milk

Preparation time: 15–20 minutes
Cooking time: 25 minutes

Serves 4

Aubergines (eggplants) are low in calories, provided they are not fried. The raw vegetable contains only 15 calories per 100g. When buying aubergines, choose ones that are firm to the touch with a glossy, smooth skin. Reduced-fat coconut milk is thinner than the full-fat version. Gentle simmering without a lid will thicken it to the consistency of your choice. Another important point to remember is that coconut milk (both reduced and full-fat) thickens in cooling, so avoid prolonged simmering.

3 tablespoons sunflower or plain olive oil

1 red onion, finely chopped

2.5cm/1-inch cube root ginger, peeled and finely grated

4 large cloves garlic, crushed

1 teaspoon ground cumin

2 teaspoons ground coriander (cilantro)

½ teaspoon ground turmeric

½ teaspoon chilli powder

1 teaspoon garam masala

225g/8oz/1½ cups potatoes, cut into 2.5cm/1-inch dice

1 teaspoon salt or to taste

400ml/14fl oz/1¾ cups reduced-fat coconut milk

225g/8oz/2 cups aubergines (eggplants), cut into 2.5cm/1 inch dice

4 whole green chilli peppers

2 tablespoons fresh coriander (cilantro), chopped

125g/4oz/½ cup fresh tomatoes, skinned and chopped

1   Heat the oil over a medium heat and fry the onion, ginger and garlic until the onions are soft, but not brown (5–6 minutes).

2   Mix together the five spices. Add enough water to the spice mix to make a paste of pouring consistency and add to the onions. Fry for 2–3 minutes, stirring frequently and add 2 tablespoons of water. Continue to fry for a minute or two.

3   Add the potatoes, salt and coconut milk. Bring to a slow simmer, cover and cook for 5–6 minutes.

4   Add the aubergines (eggplants), stir once, re-cover and simmer gently for a further 5–6 minutes.

5   Add the fresh chilli peppers and coriander (cilantro) leaves. Simmer, uncovered, for 2–3 minutes.

6   Stir in the tomatoes, remove from the heat and serve with any bread or boiled basmati rice.

Aubergine in Spiced Tomato Sauce

Preparation time: 15 minutes
Cooking time: 30 minutes

Serves 4–6

Choose tender aubergines (eggplants) with a glossy, unblemished skin. The lighter the aubergine the better because this means it has fewer seeds and more of the wonderful tender flesh.

‿‿‿‿‿‿‿‿‿‿‿‿‿‿‿‿‿‿‿‿‿‿‿

2 large aubergines (eggplants)
   (about 550g/1¼lb)
1 large onion, roughly chopped
2.5cm/1-inch cube root ginger,
   peeled and roughly chopped
6 cloves garlic, peeled and roughly
   chopped
1–2 long, slim, dried red chilli
   peppers, roughly chopped
3–4 tablespoons water
3 tablespoons sunflower or olive oil
½ teaspoon black mustard seeds
½ teaspoon cumin seeds
½ teaspoon ground fennel
1 teaspoon ground coriander
   (cilantro)
½ teaspoon ground cumin
1 teaspoon ground turmeric
15g/5oz/1⅓ cups chopped canned
   tomatoes, including juice
1 teaspoon salt or to taste
1 tablespoon tomato purée (paste)
450ml/16fl oz/2 cups warm water
¼ teaspoon garam masala
2 tablespoons coriander (cilantro)
   leaves, finely chopped

1. Quarter the aubergines (eggplants) lengthways and cut each quarter in half lengthways. Now cut them into 2.5cm/1-inch chunks. Soak them in salted water if you wish. Drain and rinse well.

2. Purée the onions, ginger, garlic and red chilli peppers with the water in a blender.

3. Heat the oil over a medium heat. When the oil is hot, but not smoking, throw in the mustard seeds. As soon as they pop, add the cumin seeds and stir-fry for 15 seconds.

4. Add the puréed ingredients and cook for 3–4 minutes. Reduce the heat to low, cooking for a further 2–3 minutes.

5. Add the fennel, coriander (cilantro), cumin and turmeric. Cook for about 2 minutes and add half the tomatoes. Increase the heat to medium and cook for a further 2–3 minutes. Add the remaining tomatoes and cook for 2–3 minutes or until the oil separates from the spice paste.

6. Add the salt, tomato purée (paste), water and aubergine; stir once and bring to the boil. Reduce the heat to medium and cook for 10 minutes, uncovered. Stir and reposition the aubergine to ensure even cooking. The aubergine will float on the surface during this time. When it begins to soak up the liquid, it will sink; when this happens, reduce heat to low and simmer for 5 minutes. Stir and reposition the aubergine 2–3 times.

7. Sprinkle with the garam masala and add the coriander (cilantro) leaves. Remove from the heat and serve with bread.

Minted Aubergine with Garlic and Fresh Coriander

Preparation time: 10–15 minutes
Cooking time: 20 minutes

Serves 4

Soft and succulent pieces of aubergine (eggplant) with fresh herbs make a real treat. Serve as a side dish or on hot toast as a snack.

⊱⊰⊱⊰⊱⊰⊱⊰⊱⊰⊱⊰⊱⊰⊱⊰⊱⊰⊱⊰

680g/1½lb aubergines (eggplants)
2 tablespoons sunflower or plain olive oil
1 teaspoon cumin seeds
4 cloves garlic, crushed
1–2 fresh red chilli peppers, cut into rings
½ teaspoon ground turmeric
1 teaspoon salt or to taste
3 tablespoons fresh coriander (cilantro), chopped
3 tablespoons fresh mint leaves, chopped

1　Slice through the aubergines (eggplants) lengthways, making 4 slices. Cut the slices into 5cm/2-inch strips and soak in salted water while you get the other ingredients ready, then drain and rinse them.

2　Heat the oil over a medium heat and add the cumin, garlic and chilli peppers. Fry until the garlic begins to brown.

3　Stir in the turmeric followed by the aubergine and salt. Stir-fry for 1–2 minutes then reduce the heat to low. Sprinkle with 2 tablespoons water, cover the pan and cook for 8–10 minutes, stirring and repositioning at least twice.

4　Add the fresh coriander (cilantro) and mint, stir and re-cover. Cook gently for 5–8 minutes, stirring halfway through. Remove from the heat and serve.

Spiced Smoked Aubergines

Preparation time: 20 minutes
Cooking time: 15 minutes

Serves 4

This simple and delicious dish will complement any Indian meal. Serve it with rice and curry or chapattis. The aubergine (eggplant) is traditionally cooked in the burnt-down ashes of wood fire before it is skinned, mashed and spiced. For this recipe I have grilled (broiled) the aubergines. If your oven is in use, pop the aubergines in to cook. In the summer, cook them on a barbecue for a wonderful smoky flavour. Once cooked and skinned, they can be frozen whole or mashed.

2 large aubergines (eggplants) (about 600g/1lb 5oz)
3 tablespoons sunflower or olive oil
½ teaspoon fennel seeds
1 red onion, finely chopped
2.5cm/1-inch cube root ginger, peeled and grated
2–3 large cloves garlic, peeled and crushed
1–2 fresh green chilli peppers, seeded and finely chopped
½ teaspoon ground turmeric
2 small, fresh tomatoes, skinned and chopped
1 teaspoon salt or to taste
2 tablespoons coriander (cilantro) leaves, chopped
1 tablespoon low-fat plain yogurt

1   Preheat the grill (broiler) to high and make two slits lengthways on each aubergine (eggplant) without cutting through it. Rub a little oil on the skin, place on a grill pan and grill (broil) about 15cm/6 inches from the heat source for 15–20 minutes or until the aubergines are tender and the skin is slightly charred. Turn them over frequently during cooking. Remove from the grill and allow them to cool. Cut them lengthways and scrape off the flesh with a knife, then mash it lightly with a fork. Discard the skin.

2   In a medium-sized saucepan, heat the oil gently over a low heat and fry the fennel seeds until browned.

3   Increase the heat to medium and add the onion, ginger, garlic and chilli peppers. Fry for 5–6 minutes, stirring regularly, then stir in the turmeric.

4   Reserve a little tomato and add the rest to the onion mixture. Cook, stirring frequently, until the tomatoes have softened (3–4 minutes).

5   Add the mashed aubergine and salt. Continue to cook, stirring regularly, for 2–3 minutes.

6   Stir in the coriander (cilantro) leaves and remove from the heat.

7   Transfer the aubergine to a serving dish and gently stir in the yogurt, creating a marbled effect. Serve garnished with the reserved tomatoes.

Dry-spiced Cabbage

Preparation time: 20 minutes
Cooking time: 20–25 minutes

Serves 4–6

Cabbage is low in calories and rich in vitamins, especially vitamin C, and iron. As well as fibre, cabbage provides betacarotene, which may help to prevent certain types of cancer. In this recipe, the spicing is subtle and the cabbage is cooked in its own juices to retain maximum nutritional value. For a variation, use 2.5cm/1-inch cauliflower florets instead of cabbage. This recipe is suitable for freezing.

2 tablespoons sunflower or corn oil
1 teaspoon cumin seeds
1 red onion, finely sliced
6 cloves garlic, peeled and crushed
**1 green chilli pepper, seeded and
    cut into juliennes**
¼ teaspoon ground turmeric
**565g/1¼lb/9 cups green cabbage,
    finely shredded**
1 teaspoon salt or to taste
**1 tablespoon chopped coriander
    (cilantro) leaves**

1 In a wok, heat the oil over a medium heat. When the oil is hot but not smoking, add the cumin seeds and allow to sizzle for 15 seconds.

2 Add the onion, garlic and chilli pepper. Stir-fry for 4 minutes then add the turmeric. Stir-fry for 30 seconds.

3 Add the cabbage and salt, stir-fry for 2 minutes then reduce the heat to low. Cover the wok with a piece of foil or lid, and cook the cabbage in its own juices for 10–12 minutes. If you like the cabbage really soft, cook for 15 minutes. Stir in the coriander (cilantro) leaves, remove from the heat and serve with chapattis accompanied by any lentil dish and a raita.

Cabbage Braised with Garden Peas

Preparation time: 15–20 minutes
Cooking time: 20 minutes

Serves 4

Here you can enjoy the fresh, natural taste of crisp, green cabbage through the subtle flavours used to create a simple but superb dish.

2 tablespoons sunflower or plain olive oil
1 red onion, finely sliced
2 green chilli peppers, finely chopped (seeded if wished)
3–4 large cloves garlic, crushed
½ teaspoon ground turmeric
680g/1½lb green cabbage, finely chopped
1 teaspoon salt or to taste
125g/4oz/1 cup frozen garden peas
2 tablespoons coriander (cilantro) leaves, chopped

1 In a non-stick wok, heat the oil over a medium heat. Add the onions and fry until they soften (5 minutes) and add the fresh chilli peppers and garlic. Stir-fry for 4–5 minutes or until the onions turn a shade darker.

2 Stir in the turmeric, then add the cabbage and salt. Increase the heat slightly and stir the cabbage until the turmeric colours it evenly. Reduce the heat to low, cover and cook for 5 minutes. Remove the lid and sprinkle the water collected on it over the vegetables.

3 Add the peas, stir and mix thoroughly. Re-cover and cook for 7–8 minutes. Stir in the coriander (cilantro) leaves, remove from the heat and serve with any curry and rice or bread.

Stir-fried Cabbage with Lentils

Preparation time: 15–20 minutes plus soaking
Cooking time: 20 minutes   Serves 4–6

Yellow split lentils *(moong dhal)* are one of the fastest cooking varieties and have a delicious earthy flavour. All Asian stores and some health-food shops stock them. This recipe is suitable for freezing.

2 tablespoons sunflower or corn oil

1 teaspoon royal cumin (shahi jeera)

4–5 shallots, finely chopped

6 cloves garlic, peeled and crushed

1cm/½-inch cube root ginger, peeled and grated

1 green chilli pepper, seeded and chopped

¼ teaspoon crushed dried chilli peppers (optional)

125g/4oz/½ cup moong dhal, picked over, washed and soaked for one hour, drained

½ teaspoon ground turmeric

300ml/½ pint/1⅓ cups warm water

350g/12oz/6 cups green cabbage, finely shredded

1 teaspoon salt or to taste

1½ teaspoons ground cumin

2 tablespoons chopped coriander (cilantro) leaves

1   In a wok, heat the oil over a medium heat and fry the royal cumin for 15–20 seconds. Add the shallots and stir-fry for 4–5 minutes until golden brown.

2   Add the garlic, ginger, fresh chilli pepper and crushed chilli peppers (if using). Stir-fry for 30 seconds and add the drained lentils. Stir-fry for 1½ minutes, reduce the heat to low and stir-fry for a further 1½ minutes.

3   Add the ground turmeric, stir-fry for 30 seconds, then add the water. Increase the heat to medium and cook for 5 minutes, stirring frequently.

4   Add the cabbage and salt and stir-fry for 5 minutes.

5   Add the cumin, stir-fry for 2 minutes then add half the coriander (cilantro). Stir-fry for 1 minute and remove from the heat. Serve garnished with the remaining coriander.

Oven-roasted Potatoes with Mixed Peppers

Preparation time: 15 minutes
Cooking time: 20–25 minutes

Serves 4

In this simple recipe, roasted poppy and sesame seeds provide a delicious nuttiness. Char-grilled (bell) peppers accentuate both their depth of flavour and visual appeal.

680g/1½lb roasting potatoes
1 small sweet red (bell) pepper
1 small green (bell) pepper
3 tablespoons sunflower or light olive oil
½ teaspoon black mustard seeds
½ teaspoon cumin seeds
1 teaspoon salt or to taste
1½ tablespoons white poppy seeds
1 tablespoon sesame seeds
3–4 dried red chilli peppers, roughly chopped

1 Preheat the oven to 230°C/450°F/Gas Mark 8.

2 Peel and cut the potatoes into 2.5cm/1-inch cubes. Leave them to soak for 10 minutes, then drain and dry off.

3 Meanwhile, grill (broil) the peppers until the skin is charred. You can do this either under a grill preheated to high or on the hob. If using the hob, place a wire rack directly on the burner and grill the peppers. For both methods, turn the peppers around regularly. It will take 5–6 minutes to achieve a charred look. Put the peppers in a plastic bag for 15–20 minutes.

4 Heat the oil in a roasting tin on the hob over medium heat. Add the mustard seeds, and when they pop, add the cumin seeds, potatoes and salt. Increase the heat to medium-high and fry the potatoes for 3–4 minutes until browned. Place the tin in the centre of the oven and cook for 12–15 minutes.

5 Remove the peppers from the bag and peel away the skin. Remove the pith and seeds and cut the peppers into 2.5cm/1-inch cubes.

6 Preheat a small pan over a medium heat. Reduce the heat to low and dry-roast the poppy and sesame seeds and chillis for 50 seconds until they begin to release the roasted aroma. Do not let them brown. Cool the seeds and grind them in a coffee or spice mill or with a pestle and mortar.

7 When the potatoes are ready, add the peppers and the ground ingredients. Mix thoroughly and return to the oven for 3–4 minutes. Remove and serve immediately. They are equally delicious with bread and any main course dish.

Golden Potato Cubes with Green Chilli Peppers and Coriander

Preparation time: 10–15 minutes
Cooking time: 25 minutes

Serves 4–6

A quick and delicious way to cook potatoes. Serve with chapattis and a protein-rich dish.

◈◈◈◈◈◈◈◈◈◈◈◈◈◈◈◈◈◈◈◈◈◈

680g/1½lb new potatoes, cut into small, bite-sized cubes

3 tablespoons sunflower or olive oil

1 teaspoon salt or to taste

1 red onion, finely chopped

1–3 green chilli peppers, seeded if liked, finely chopped

25g/1oz/¼ cup coriander (cilantro) leaves and stalks, finely chopped

1 Wash the potato cubes, drain and dry thoroughly with a cloth.

2 In a sauté or frying pan (skillet) with a non-stick surface, heat the oil over medium-high heat and add the potatoes and salt. Stir for a couple of minutes, then cover the pan and cook for 8–10 minutes. Stir occasionally. Remove the lid and continue to cook for a further 3–4 minutes until browned.

3 Add the onion and chilli peppers and fry for 4–5 minutes, stirring regularly.

4 Add the coriander (cilantro) leaves, cook for 2–3 minutes, remove from the heat and serve immediately.

Green Beans and Potatoes with Poppy Seeds

Preparation time: 15–20 minutes
Cooking time: 25 minutes

Serves 4

Poppy seeds are used frequently in north-Indian cooking. They lend a superb nutty flavour to any dish and act as a thickening agent in sauces.

1½ tablespoons white poppy seeds

2 tablespoons sunflower or olive oil

½ teaspoon black mustard seeds

1–2 dried red chilli peppers, chopped

2.5cm/½-inch cube root ginger, grated

½ teaspoon ground turmeric

350g/12oz/1⅔ cups fresh green beans, cut into 5cm/2-inch pieces

350g/12oz/1⅔ cups potatoes, peeled and cut into 5cm/2-inch strips (like French fries)

¾ teaspoon salt or to taste

1 Preheat a heavy-based saucepan or frying pan (skillet) and roast the poppy seeds until lightly browned, stirring constantly. Transfer to a plate and allow to cool, then grind in a coffee grinder until smooth.

2 In a heavy saucepan, heat the oil over a medium heat. When the oil is hot, but not smoking, add the mustard seeds. As soon as they pop, add the chilli peppers and ginger. Stir-fry for 1 minute.

3 Stir in the turmeric, followed by the vegetables and salt. Stir well and add 125ml/4fl oz/½ cup lukewarm water. Cover the pan and reduce the heat slightly. Cook for 15–20 minutes or until the vegetables are tender. Stir occasionally to ensure the vegetables do not stick to the bottom of the pan. Add a little more water if necessary, but make sure no liquid is left in the pan when the vegetables are tender.

4 Stir in the ground poppy seeds and remove from the heat. Serve as a side dish.

Kashmiri Spiced Potatoes

Preparation time: 20 minutes

Cooking time: 15–20 minutes   **Serves 4**

In this speciality from Kashmir, whole potatoes are traditionally deep-fried before being cooked with yogurt and spices. Small new potatoes are excellent for this dish. In keeping with Kashmiri tradition, they are cooked in mustard oil, which you can buy from Indian stores. You can use sunflower or olive oil, but the distinctive mustard flavour will be missing. To achieve this, you could stir in 2 teaspoons of English mustard paste 5–6 minutes before the end of cooking time.

2–3 tablespoons mustard oil

680g / 1½lb small new potatoes, boiled and peeled

½–1 teaspoon chilli powder

2 brown cardamom pods, bruised

4 green cardamom pods, bruised

½ teaspoon dry, ground ginger

2 teaspoons ground coriander (cilantro)

1 teaspoon salt or to taste

150g / 5oz low-fat set plain yogurt, whisked

Sprigs of fresh coriander (cilantro), to garnish

4–5 juliennes root ginger, to garnish

1   In a medium-sized saucepan, heat the oil to smoking point and fry the potatoes in two batches until well browned. Take the pan off the heat and drain the potatoes on absorbent paper. Using a toothpick, prick the potatoes all over to allow flavours to penetrate, then set them aside.

2   Place the pan back over a low heat and add the chilli powder followed by 2 tablespoons water. Cook for 1 minute and add the remaining spices. Cook for a further minute and sprinkle on 1 tablespoon water. Take care to keep the heat at minimum level as ground spices can burn easily, which will impart a bitter flavour. If this happens, you will need to throw it away and start again!

3   Add the browned potatoes, salt and the whisked yogurt (whisking the yogurt stops it curdling). Cover the pan tightly and reduce the heat to low. Cook until the sauce thickens and coats the potatoes (5–6 minutes). Remove from the heat and transfer to a serving dish. Garnish with the coriander (cilantro) and ginger juliennes and serve with chapattis.

Mashed Potatoes with Mustard, Chilli and Turmeric

Preparation time: 25–30 minutes
Cooking time: 5–6 minutes

Serves 4

When tossed in spiced olive oil, these lightly mashed potatoes have an exciting taste and appearance. They make a great accompaniment when served hot; sprinkled with garlic croutons, they are perfect as a salad or a just a moreish snack!

680g/1½lb boiled potatoes
1 tablespoon desiccated coconut
2 tablespoons light olive oil
½ teaspoon black mustard seeds
1 dried red chilli pepper, finely chopped or ¼ teaspoon crushed dried chilli pepper
½ teaspoon ground turmeric
½ teaspoon salt or to taste

1 Peel the potatoes and mash them roughly.

2 Soak the coconut in 60ml/2fl oz/¼ cup boiling water and set aside.

3 In a non-stick saucepan or a wok, heat the oil over a medium heat. When the oil is hot, but not smoking, throw in the mustard seeds. As soon as they start popping, switch off the heat source and add the chilli and turmeric. Let them cook for 25–30 seconds then add the potatoes and salt. Stir over a medium heat until the potatoes are heated through, as reheating them thoroughly in the seasoned oil will enhance the flavours. Just let them cool if you want to serve them cold.

Spiced Potato Sticks

Preparation time: 15 minutes
Cooking time: 15 minutes   Serves 4

These are cut like French fries, but are not deep-fried. Once tasted, it is quite easy to get addicted!

3 tablespoons sunflower or plain
   olive oil
1 teaspoon black mustard seeds
3 large cloves garlic, crushed
680g/1½lb/4½ cups potatoes, cut
   into 'French fries'
½ teaspoon chilli powder or to taste
1 teaspoon salt or to taste
2 tablespoons coriander (cilantro)
   leaves, chopped

1   Heat the oil over a medium heat in a non-stick frying pan
    (skillet). When the oil is hot, but not smoking, add the
    mustard seeds. Reduce the heat to low and add the garlic.
    Stir-fry until the garlic is lightly browned.

2   Add the potatoes, chilli powder and salt. Stir and cook for
    2–3 minutes, reduce the heat slightly and cover the pan.
    Cook for 5 minutes, increase the heat to medium again, stir
    and re-cover. Cook for a further 3–4 minutes and remove the
    lid. Continue to cook, stirring frequently, until the potatoes
    are lightly browned and tender. Stir in the chopped
    coriander (cilantro), remove from the heat and serve
    with Eastern Vegetarian Burgers *(page 78)* and Carrot Raita
    (page 16).

Spinach and Potatoes with Garlic and Fennel

Preparation time: 25 minutes
Cooking time: 25 minutes

Serves 4–6

One of my early childhood memories is spinach leaves collected straight from the garden, glistening with morning dew. If you do not have time to prepare fresh spinach, which needs thorough cleaning and washing, you can use frozen leaf spinach, but not the purée. You will need to thaw and drain it well. To freeze this recipe, do so before adding the potatoes; add them during reheating.

370g/13oz/2⅔ cups old potatoes, peeled, cut into 5cm/2-inch cubes

3 tablespoons sunflower or olive oil

½ teaspoon black mustard seeds

½ teaspoon fennel seeds

¼–½ teaspoon crushed dried chilli peppers

8 cloves garlic, peeled and crushed

1 onion, finely sliced

½ teaspoon ground fennel

1½ teaspoons ground cumin

½ teaspoon ground turmeric

275g/10oz/5 cups spinach, finely chopped

1 teaspoon salt or to taste

150g/5oz/⅔ cup canned chopped tomatoes, including juice

½ teaspoon garam masala

1 tablespoon tomato purée (paste)

1 Boil the potatoes until tender but still firm, then set aside.

2 Meanwhile, heat the oil in a sauté pan over a medium heat. When the oil is hot but not smoking, add the mustard seeds. As soon as they pop, add the fennel seeds, crushed chilli peppers and garlic. Stir-fry for 30 seconds.

3 Add the onion and stir-fry for 4–5 minutes or until soft and just beginning to colour.

4 Add the ground fennel, cumin and turmeric, and stir-fry for 1 minute. Add the spinach and salt, and stir-fry for 3 minutes until the spinach has shrunk to half the original amount.

5 Add the tomatoes, potatoes, garam masala and tomato purée (paste). Increase the heat to high and cook for 4 minutes, stirring frequently, then remove from the heat and serve with chappatis.

Mustard, Cumin and Fenugreek Potatoes

Preparation time: 15 minutes
Cooking time: 15–18 minutes

Serves 2–3

These potatoes, with their alluring taste and flavour, are the ones to use in filling the Rice and Lentil Pancakes on pages 87–89. They can also be served as a side dish or with any bread.

450g/1lb old potatoes, cut into 2.5cm/1-inch cubes
2 tablespoons sunflower or light olive oil
½ teaspoon black mustard seeds
½ teaspoon cumin seeds
5–6 fenugreek seeds
4–5 shallots, finely chopped
1 green chilli pepper, finely chopped (seeded if wished)
½ teaspoon ground turmeric
½ teaspoon hot chilli powder (optional)
½ teaspoon salt or to taste
2 tablespoons finely chopped coriander (cilantro) leaves

1   Boil the potatoes with a pinch of salt until *al dente*. Reserve 125ml/4fl oz/½ cup of the cooking liquid, drain well then refresh in cold water.

2   In a wok or non-stick pan, heat the oil over a medium heat. When the oil is hot, but not smoking, add the mustard seeds. As soon as they start popping, throw in the cumin seeds followed by the fenugreek seeds, shallots and chilli pepper. Stir and cook them for 4–5 minutes.

3   Add the turmeric, chilli powder (if using) and the potatoes. Stir for a couple of minutes, pour in the reserved cooking liquid and add the salt. Cook, uncovered, until the potatoes have absorbed all the liquid.

4   Stir in the coriander (cilantro) leaves and remove from the heat.

Roasted New Potatoes with Spicy Sesame Seed Crust

Preparation time: 10 minutes
Cooking time: 20–25 minutes

Serves 4

New potatoes are best left in their skins, not only because the young skin is full of flavour and interesting texture, but also for its nutritional value. Simply scrub and wash them under running water.

680g/1½lb small new potatoes
3 tablespoons light olive oil
Salt and pepper to taste
½ teaspoon hot chilli powder
1 teaspoon cumin seeds, lightly crushed
1 teaspoon coriander (cilantro) seeds, lightly crushed
2 tablespoons sesame seeds
1 tablespoon chickpea flour (besan), sieved

1   Preheat the oven to 190°C/375°F/Gas Mark 5.

2   Make several incisions on the potatoes without cutting them through. Put them in a roasting tin and drizzle the oil over them. Season with salt and pepper then roast in the upper part of the oven for 15–20 minutes until browned and almost tender.

3   Meanwhile, mix the remaining ingredients together in a small bowl and sprinkle the mixture evenly over the potatoes. Stir and mix until the spices coat the potatoes. Roast for a further 4–5 minutes, remove from the heat and serve.

New Potatoes with Mushrooms

Preparation time: 20 minutes
Cooking time: 30 minutes

Serves 4

New potatoes are best with a knob of butter and some mint, but cooked this way they taste really great! Use the smallest potatoes you can find for this recipe.

225g/8oz small new potatoes

2 tablespoons sunflower or plain olive oil

3–4 shallots, finely chopped

2–3 cloves garlic, crushed

1 teaspoon paprika

1 teaspoon ground coriander (cilantro)

½ teaspoon chilli powder

140ml/¼ pint/⅔ cup semi-skimmed milk

350g/12oz/4 cups whole button mushrooms

¾ teaspoon salt or to taste

140ml/¼ pint/⅔ cup half-fat single (half and half) cream

2 tablespoons ground almonds

1 Scrub and wash the potatoes and boil until tender.

2 Meanwhile, heat the oil gently and sauté the shallots for 3–4 minutes.

3 Add the garlic and fry for 1 minute.

4 With a little water, make a paste of the paprika, coriander (cilantro) and chilli powder. Add to the sautéed shallots and garlic and cook gently for about 2 minutes, sprinkling with a tablespoon of water to prevent the spices sticking to the bottom of the pan.

5 Add half the milk and increase the heat slightly. Stir and cook until the milk dries up. Repeat this process with the remaining milk.

6 Add the mushrooms, stir well and cover the pan. Reduce the heat to low and cook for 8–10 minutes.

7 Add the salt, cream, potatoes and ground almonds. Cover the pan and cook for 3–4 minutes. Remove from the heat and serve with any bread and a raita.

New Potatoes with Spinach and Almond Sauce

Preparation time: 20 minutes
Cooking time: 20 minutes

Serves 4

This superbly flavoured, nutritious dish can also be served cold. Traditionally, coconut is used, but I have opted for almonds instead, which are better for a low-fat diet. Although nuts are high in calories, they are an excellent source of protein in a vegetarian diet. They also contain useful amounts of B-vitamins. Team this with any Indian or Western bread to mop up all the sauce. It can also be used to moisten rice dishes.

450g/1lb small whole new potatoes

225g/8oz/4 cups fresh spinach, chopped

50g/2oz/½ cup blanched almonds, roughly chopped

2 green chilli peppers, seeded and chopped

2 teaspoons root ginger, peeled and chopped

1 teaspoon salt or to taste

125g/4oz/½ cup half-fat sour cream

1 tablespoon lime juice

1 tablespoon olive oil

½ teaspoon black mustard seeds

½ teaspoon cumin seeds

1 tomato, seeded and cut into julienne strips, to garnish

4–5 juliennes root ginger, to garnish

1 Scrub and wash the potatoes and boil until tender.

2 Meanwhile, put the spinach, almonds, chilli peppers and ginger in a saucepan and add 300ml/½ pint/1⅓ cups hot water. Bring to the boil, reduce the heat to low, cover and cook for 10 minutes. Remove from the heat and cool slightly.

3 Purée the spinach mixture until smooth and add the salt, sour cream and lime juice. Blend well.

4 In a small saucepan or steel ladle, heat the oil over a medium heat and add the mustard seeds. As soon as they pop, add the cumin seeds, allow to sizzle for 10–15 seconds, then pour this mixture over the puréed spinach. Reheat the spinach purée and transfer most of it to a serving dish. Pile the potatoes in the middle and drizzle the remaining sauce over them. Garnish with the tomato and ginger juliennes.

New Potatoes with Cinnamon

Preparation time: 25 minutes
Cooking time: 50–55 minutes

Serves 4

Packed with wonderful aromatic spices, this is a lovely way to serve new potatoes. A non-stick pan is essential for low-fat cooking, especially in this recipe where the potatoes are browned before adding spices.

450g/1lb/3 cups small new
    potatoes
3 tablespoons olive oil
1 teaspoon fennel seeds
3 × 2.5cm/1-inch pieces cinnamon
    stick
4 whole cloves
2 bay leaves, crumpled
5–6 shallots, finely chopped
4cm/1½-inch cube root ginger,
    peeled and finely grated
½ teaspoon ground fennel
½ teaspoon ground turmeric
1 teaspoon ground cumin
¼–½ teaspoon chilli powder
125g/4oz/½ cup canned chopped
    tomatoes, including juice
1 teaspoon salt or to taste
570ml/1 pint/2½ cups warm water
90g/3oz/⅓ cup low-fat natural
    yogurt
½ teaspoon sugar
½ teaspoon dried mint or 1
    tablespoon finely chopped fresh
    mint
½ teaspoon garam masala
2 tablespoons chopped coriander
    (cilantro) leaves

1 Scrub or scrape the potatoes, wash and dry thoroughly. Using a sharp knife, make several deep incisions in each potato without cutting right through.

2 In a non-stick pan, heat half the oil over a medium heat. When the oil is hot, fry the potatoes until well browned (8–10 minutes). Keep moving them around the pan to ensure even browning; they will brown very quickly towards the end. Turn off the heat, remove the potatoes with a slotted spoon and drain on absorbent paper. Do not worry if there is browned potato crust in the pan as this will add plenty of flavour to the dish.

3 Return the pan to medium heat and add the remaining oil. Add the fennel seeds, cinnamon, cloves and bay leaves, and stir-fry for 15 seconds.

4 Increase the heat to medium and add the shallots and ginger. Stir-fry for 4–5 minutes or until browned.

5 Add the ground fennel, turmeric, cumin and chilli powder. Stir-fry for 30 seconds and add the tomatoes. Stir-fry for 2–3 minutes or until the fat rises to the top.

6 Add the fried potatoes, salt and water. Bring to the boil and cook for 2 minutes. Stir once to reposition the potatoes, then reduce the heat to low. Beat the yogurt and sugar together and add to the potatoes. Cover the pan and simmer for 20 minutes. Stir occasionally and reposition the potatoes.

7 Add the mint and increase the heat to medium. Cook for 5 minutes. Stir in the garam masala and coriander (cilantro) leaves, remove from the heat and serve with any bread and Spicy Green Lentils *(page 69)*.

Mustard, Cumin and Chilli-flavoured Potatoes with Baby Spinach

Preparation time: 20–25 minutes
Cooking time: 45 minutes

Serves 4

This is a low-fat version of the ever-popular dish known as *saag-aloo*. Baby spinach leaves are used here, but the mature ones will also work well, if chopped finely.

3 tablespoons sunflower or plain olive oil
½ teaspoon black mustard seeds
½ teaspoon cumin seeds
1–2 dried red chilli peppers, chopped
1 medium onion, finely sliced
3 large cloves garlic, crushed
1 green chilli pepper, chopped, seeded if wished
680g/1½lb/4½ cups potatoes, peeled and cut into 2.5cm/1-inch cubes
1 teaspoon salt or to taste
1 teaspoon ground turmeric
1 tablespoon ground coriander (cilantro)
1 teaspoon ground cumin
225g/8oz/4 cups baby spinach leaves

1   Heat the oil in a large non-stick pan over a medium heat. When the oil is quite hot, but not smoking, add the mustard seeds. As soon as they pop, add the cumin seeds followed by the red chilli peppers. Let them sizzle for 5–10 seconds.

2   Add the onion, garlic and green chilli pepper. Stir-fry the ingredients for 5 minutes, reducing the heat slightly halfway through.

3   Add the potatoes and increase the heat to medium. Stir-fry for 5 minutes then reduce the heat slightly. Cover and cook for 3–4 minutes, stirring halfway through. The potatoes and onions should have browned well by now.

4   Stir in the salt and the spices. Reduce the heat to low, cover the pan and let the potatoes sweat for 8–10 minutes, stirring halfway through.

5   Add half the spinach and increase the heat to medium. Stir until the leaves wilt and add the remaining spinach. Again, stir until the leaves wilt, then reduce the heat to low. Cover the pan and cook for 3–4 minutes. Remove the lid and cook uncovered for a few minutes, letting the spinach juices evaporate, if necessary. Remove from the heat and serve with any bread or rice and a lentil or bean dish.

Cauliflower and Potato with Toasted Sesame Seeds and Coconut

Preparation time: 15–20 minutes
Cooking time: 25 minutes

Serves 4

Lightly coated with toasted sesame seeds and coconut, dotted with black mustard and cumin seeds, the potatoes and cauliflower have a heavenly appearance and a superb taste.

2 tablespoons sunflower or olive oil
½ teaspoon black mustard seeds
½ teaspoon cumin seeds
2–3 large garlic cloves, crushed
1–2 fresh green chilli peppers, chopped
½ teaspoon ground turmeric
350g/12oz/3 cups cauliflower florets (2.5cm/1 inch)
1 teaspoon salt or to taste
1½ tablespoons sesame seeds
1 tablespoon desiccated coconut
275g/10oz/2 cups potatoes, boiled, peeled and diced

1 In a non-stick wok, heat the oil over a medium heat. When hot, add the mustard seeds; as soon as they pop, reduce the heat to low and add the cumin seeds followed by the garlic and fresh chilli peppers. Stir-fry until the garlic browns slightly, then add the turmeric, cauliflower and salt. Stir and mix well, cover the pan and let the cauliflower sweat for 5–6 minutes.

2 Meanwhile, preheat a small, heavy-based pan over a medium heat for a minute or two. Reduce the heat to low and add the sesame seeds. Roast them, stirring constantly, for about 45 seconds and add the coconut. Continue to stir and roast until caramel brown (1–2 minutes). Remove from the pan and allow to cool.

3 Add the potatoes, increase the heat to medium and cook for 1–2 minutes, stirring constantly. Reduce the heat to low again and cover the pan. Cook the vegetables for 2–3 minutes.

4 Grind the roasted coconut and sesame seeds in a coffee grinder until smooth. The natural oils in the ingredients will cake the mixture to the sides of the bowl. When this happens, switch off the grinder, scrape off the mixture with a teaspoon and resume grinding. Stir this ground mixture into the potato and cauliflower, increase the heat slightly and cook for 1–2 minutes, stirring constantly. Remove from the heat and serve with Spicy Green Lentils *(page 69)* and boiled rice.

Sweet Potatoes with Fenugreek, Garlic and Chilli

Preparation time: 20 minutes
Cooking time: 20 minutes

Serves 4

Sweet potatoes grow in warm climates and India and Africa are the major growers. There are two varieties which look alike, but once you start peeling you will find either an orange or a creamy flesh underneath. Preparation and cooking methods are the same for both and they can be stored in the same way as standard potatoes. However, they cook more quickly than standard potatoes.

680g/1½lb/3 cups sweet potato, peeled and cut into bite-sized pieces

2 tablespoons sunflower or plain olive oil

½ teaspoon black mustard seeds

1 teaspoon cumin seeds

6–8 fenugreek seeds

6 large cloves garlic, crushed

½–1 teaspoon chilli powder

½ teaspoon ground turmeric

1 teaspoon salt or to taste

25g/1oz/¼ cup chickpea flour (besan)

1 Soak the sweet potatoes in cold water for about 10 minutes. Drain and rinse well.

2 Heat the oil over a medium heat in a large frying pan (skillet), preferably non-stick. When the oil is quite hot, but not smoking, throw in the mustard seeds and reduce the heat to low. Add the cumin seeds, fenugreek seeds and garlic. Stir-fry until the garlic is lightly browned.

3 Stir in the chilli powder and turmeric and add the potatoes and salt. Stir-fry for 2–3 minutes, then cover the pan and cook for 3–4 minutes. Remove the lid and increase the heat to high. Cook, stirring frequently, for a further 3–4 minutes or until the potatoes are tender and lightly browned.

4 Sprinkle the chickpea flour (besan) evenly on the potatoes, stir and cook for 1–2 minutes, remove from the heat and serve with Spicy Green Lentils *(page 69)* and Cumin Rice *(page 102).*

Broccoli and Cauliflower Coated with Spiced Chickpea Flour

Preparation time: 15–20 minutes
Cooking time: 12–15 minutes

Serves 4

Both cauliflower and broccoli are useful sources of vitamin C. Broccoli also contains betacarotene and iron. In order to retain maximum nutrients, the vegetables are cooked in their own juices with only a sprinkling of water.

⁂

2 tablespoons sunflower or plain olive oil
4 large cloves garlic, crushed
2 fresh red chilli peppers, cut into thick rings
275g/10oz/2½ cups bite-sized cauliflower florets
275g/10oz/2½ cups bite-sized broccoli florets
1 tablespoon chickpea flour (besan), sieved
1 teaspoon salt or to taste
½ teaspoon garam masala
½ teaspoon ground cumin
1 teaspoon ground coriander (cilantro)

1. Mix together the flour, salt, garam masala, cumin and coriander (cilantro). Set aside.
2. Heat the oil over a low heat in a wok or non-stick pan and fry the garlic and red chilli peppers gently until the garlic is lightly browned.
3. Add the vegetables and increase the heat slightly. Stir-fry for 3–4 minutes or until the vegetables begin to brown a little.
4. Reduce the heat to low and sprinkle the spice mix evenly on the vegetables. Cover the pan and cook for 5–6 minutes.
5. Sprinkle about a tablespoon of water on the vegetables and stir-fry until they are coated with the spiced flour. Cover the pan and cook until the vegetables are tender but firm, sprinkling a little more water if necessary. Remove from the heat and serve.

Mixed Vegetables Southern Style

Preparation time: 25 minutes
Cooking time: 30–35 minutes

Serves 4

This is a well-known, popular dish from southern India where a medley of vegetables is bathed in a pool of rich coconut milk with the distinctive flavour of fresh curry leaves. I have used reduced-fat canned coconut milk, which you can buy in supermarkets. It is difficult to find fresh curry leaves outside India, but the dried ones are easily available and can be used instead.

225g/8oz/1½ cups potatoes, peeled and cut into 5cm/2-inch cubes
125g/4oz/1 cup cut green beans
150g/5oz/1 cup carrots, scraped and cut into 5cm/2-inch cubes
225g/8oz aubergine (eggplant)
400ml/14fl oz/1¾ cups reduced-fat coconut milk
2 teaspoons chickpea flour (besan)
1 teaspoon salt or to taste
2 tablespoons sunflower or plain olive oil
6–7 shallots, finely chopped
6–8 fresh or 10–12 dried curry leaves
½ teaspoon dried chilli peppers, crushed
1 teaspoon ground coriander (cilantro)
½ teaspoon ground turmeric

1 Put all the vegetables, except the aubergine (eggplant), in a large pan and add 300ml/10fl oz/1⅓ cups hot water. Bring to the boil, reduce the heat to medium, cover the pan and cook for 5 minutes.

2 Meanwhile, peel and quarter the aubergine lengthways and cut into 5cm/2-inch pieces. Rinse and add to the vegetables in the pan.

3 Add two tablespoons of the coconut milk to the chickpea flour (besan), beat until smooth and blend with the remaining coconut milk. Pour into the pan and add the salt. Bring to a slow simmer (reduced-fat coconut milk will split if exposed to high heat), cover the pan and cook for 6–7 minutes.

4 Meanwhile, heat the oil in a small saucepan over a medium heat and cook the shallots for 4–5 minutes until softened. Add the curry leaves, crushed chilli peppers, coriander (cilantro) and turmeric. Stir for 15–20 seconds and pour the entire contents over the vegetables. Stir to distribute then remove from the heat and serve with Lemon Rice *(page 104)* and a raita.

Mushrooms and Garden Peas with Mint and Coriander

Preparation time: 15 minutes
Cooking time: 20 minutes

Serves 4

Mushrooms and peas make a good combination in terms of both nutrition and taste. Although mushrooms are relatively poor in nutritional value, the peas are rich in fibre, protein and vitamin C.

2 tablespoons sunflower or plain olive oil

5–6 shallots, finely chopped

½ cube root ginger, peeled and grated

2 green chilli peppers, seeded and chopped

½ teaspoon ground turmeric

½ teaspoon ground cumin

1 teaspoon ground coriander (cilantro)

½ teaspoon paprika

225g/8oz/2½ cups closed-cup mushrooms, quartered

150g/5oz/1 cup frozen garden peas

¾ teaspoon salt or to taste

1 tablespoon tomato purée (paste)

1 tablespoon chopped coriander (cilantro) leaves

10–12 fresh mint leaves, chopped

1   Heat the oil over a medium heat and fry the shallots, ginger and green chilli peppers until the shallots are soft but not brown (4–5 minutes).

2   Make a paste of the turmeric, cumin, coriander (cilantro) and paprika with a little water and add to the sautéed shallot mixture. Stir-fry for 30 seconds and add 2 tablespoons of water. Continue cooking, stirring constantly, for a further minute or so and add another 2 tablespoons of water. Stir and cook until the oil begins to rise to the surface of the spice paste.

3   Add the mushrooms, peas, salt and tomato purée (paste) blended with 3 tablespoons of water. Stir and mix well, reduce the heat to low, cover the pan and cook gently for 8–10 minutes. Stir halfway through.

4   Add the coriander (cilantro) and mint leaves, remove from the heat and serve with chapattis or boiled basmati rice accompanied by a protein-rich dish.

Mushroom Do-Piaza

Preparation time: 20–25 minutes
Cooking time: 20 minutes   Serves 4

Do-Piaza is a Mogul term meaning any meat cooked with vegetables and lashings of onions. I have created this vegetarian version with mushrooms as the main ingredient. For a variation, you could use cooked sliced beans instead of peas.

1 small onion, roughly chopped

1cm/½-inch cube root ginger, peeled and roughly chopped

4 cloves garlic, peeled and chopped

1 green chilli pepper, seeded and chopped

3–4 tablespoons water

2–3 tablespoons sunflower or corn oil

5–6 shallots, very finely chopped

1 teaspoon ground coriander (cilantro)

1 teaspoon ground cumin

¼ teaspoon crushed dried chilli peppers

1 teaspoon ground turmeric

125g/4oz/½ cup canned chopped tomatoes, including juice

1 tablespoon tomato purée (paste)

1 teaspoon salt or to taste

370g/13oz/4⅓ cups closed-cup mushrooms, thickly sliced

90g/3oz/⅔ cup frozen garden peas or cooked fresh peas

90ml/3fl oz/⅓ cup warm water

½ teaspoon garam masala

1   Purée the onion, ginger, garlic and fresh chilli with the water in a food processor or liquidizer.

2   In a wok or non-stick saucepan, heat the oil over a medium heat. When the oil is hot but not smoking, add the chopped shallots and stir-fry for 3–4 minutes or until beginning to colour.

3   Add the ground coriander (cilantro), cumin and crushed chilli peppers. Stir-fry for 30 seconds, then add the puréed ingredients and stir-fry over a low heat for 5–6 minutes.

4   Add the turmeric and half the tomatoes, increase the heat to medium and stir-fry for 2–3 minutes. Add the remaining tomatoes and stir-fry for 3–4 minutes or until the oil separates from the spice paste.

5   Add the tomato purée (paste), salt, mushrooms, peas and warm water, stir and mix well. Reduce the heat to low and simmer, uncovered, for 5–6 minutes. By this time, the natural juices from the mushrooms, combined with the little cooking liquid, will produce a thick, paste-like sauce.

6   Sprinkle with the garam masala and stir-fry for 1 minute. Remove from the heat and serve with chapattis or Chickpea Pilau *(see page 116)*.

Stir-fried Mushrooms with Mint and Coriander

Preparation time: 15–20 minutes plus time for boiling potatoes
Cooking time: 18–20 minutes

Serves 4–6

You can freeze this dish before adding the potatoes.

350g/12oz/9 cups large open-cup
    mushrooms
2 tablespoons sunflower or olive oil
6–8 shallots, finely chopped
4 cloves garlic, peeled and crushed
1 teaspoon ground cumin
1 teaspoon ground coriander
    (cilantro)
½–1 teaspoon chilli powder
½ teaspoon ground turmeric
1 teaspoon salt or to taste
225g/8oz old potatoes, boiled,
    peeled and cut into 2.5cm/1-
    inch cubes
½ teaspoon dried mint or 1
    tablespoon fresh mint, chopped
1 tablespoon tomato purée (paste)
¼ teaspoon garam masala
2 tablespoons finely chopped
    coriander (cilantro) leaves

1. Quarter the mushrooms and cut each quarter into two.
2. In a wok, heat the oil over a medium heat and add the shallots. Fry for 3–4 minutes and add the garlic; fry for a further minute.
3. Add the ground cumin, coriander (cilantro), chilli powder and turmeric. Stir-fry for 1 minute.
4. Add the mushrooms and salt, sprinkle with 3–4 tablespoons of water and reduce the heat to low. Cover the wok and simmer for 5 minutes.
5. Add the potatoes, mint and tomato purée (paste). Stir and mix well, cover again and simmer for 3–4 minutes.
6. Sprinkle with the garam masala and fresh coriander (cilantro). Stir, remove from the heat and serve with Cumin Rice *(page 102)* and a protein-rich dish.

Stir-fried Okra

Preparation time: 15 minutes
Cooking time: 15–18 minutes

Serves 4

Okra is widely available in supermarkets these days. In India, okra is also known as 'lady's finger' because of its shape. When buying okra, try and choose the small, tender ones and avoid those with blemished skins. Okra is a good source of vitamins A and C.

225g/8oz okra
2 tablespoons sunflower or olive oil
½ teaspoon cumin seeds
4 cloves garlic, peeled and crushed
1cm/½-inch cube root ginger, peeled and finely grated
1 teaspoon ground coriander (cilantro)
½ teaspoon ground cumin
½ teaspoon chilli powder
½ teaspoon ground turmeric
150g/5oz/¾ cup chopped canned tomatoes, including juice
1 teaspoon salt or to taste
½ teaspoon garam masala
2 teaspoons lime juice

1   Clean each okra by scrubbing gently and rinse several times. Trim off the hard heads.

2   Heat the oil over a medium heat. When the oil is hot, but not smoking, reduce the heat to low and add the cumin seeds. Let them sizzle for about 15 seconds.

3   Add the garlic and ginger and fry gently until lightly browned.

4   Add the coriander (cilantro), cumin, chilli powder and turmeric and stir-fry for 30 seconds.

5   Add the tomatoes and cook for 3–4 minutes, then add the okra and salt. Stir-fry for 3–4 minutes, reduce the heat to low and cook, covered, for 8–10 minutes when the okra will be tender but still firm.

6   Sprinkle with the garam masala and add the lime juice. Stir-fry for 1 minute then remove from the heat and serve with bread.

Okra in Sesame and Poppy Seeds with Peppers

Preparation time: 20–25 minutes
Cooking time: 15 minutes

Serves 4

A light and aromatic dish with an attractive appearance. The soft green colour of the okra contrasts beautifully with the bright-red sweet (bell) pepper and sliced onions, and the entire combination in a creamy sauce looks stunning.

225g/8oz/2¾ cups okra

1 sweet red (bell) pepper (about 150g/5oz/1¼ cups)

1 medium onion

1 tablespoon white poppy seeds

1 tablespoon sesame seeds

1 long slim dried red chilli pepper, chopped

2 tablespoons sunflower or corn oil

4–5 cloves garlic, peeled and crushed

½ teaspoon salt or to taste

90ml/3fl oz/⅓ cup warm water

1 Scrub each okra gently and rinse well in running water, then slice off the hard head.

2 Halve the pepper and remove seeds and white pith. Cut into 4cm/1½-inch strips.

3 Peel and halve the onion lengthways and cut into slices 5mm/¼-inch thick.

4 Grind the poppy seeds, sesame seeds and red chilli pepper in a coffee grinder until fine.

5 Heat the oil over a low heat and fry the garlic gently until it begins to brown.

6 Add the onion and stir-fry for 2–3 minutes, then add the ground ingredients. Stir-fry for 30 seconds.

7 Add the okra and salt, stir-fry for 30 seconds and add the water. Reduce the heat to low and cover the pan. Cook for 5 minutes.

8 Stir in the peppers, re-cover and cook for 4–5 minutes. Remove from the heat and serve.

Parsnips Seasoned with Hot Mustard Oil

Preparation time: 10–15 minutes

Cooking time: 10–12 minutes

Serves 4

Parsnips are easily available from autumn through to late spring. The sweet flesh of this root vegetable provides an exciting contrast in flavour when seasoned with pungent mustard oil. Make sure you heat the oil until it is well and truly smoking because it is at this point that mustard oil mellows and transforms into a deliciously nutty ingredient. If you can't get mustard oil, use an ordinary cooking oil, but add a dash of English mustard for that distinctive flavour.

680g/1½lb parsnips

2 tablespoons mustard oil

2 tablespoons red onion, finely chopped

1 green chilli pepper, seeded and finely chopped

2 tablespoons coriander (cilantro) leaves, finely chopped

Salt and freshly milled black pepper to taste

1 Peel and quarter the parsnips lengthways and cut the thicker ends to the same size as the rest. Chop evenly and boil in salted water for 7–8 minutes until tender but firm. Drain.

2 In a wok or non-stick pan, heat the oil over a high heat until smoking. Add the parsnips and the remaining ingredients. Stir, switch off the heat source and lightly mash a few pieces of parsnip with the back of a spoon. Blend everything well and serve.

Peppers with Chickpea Flour

Preparation time: 10 minutes
Cooking time: 8–9 minutes

Serves 4

This seriously delicious dish with a lovely, nutty taste takes less than 10 minutes to cook!

2 tablespoons sunflower or olive oil
½ teaspoon black mustard seeds
1 teaspoon cumin seeds
2 green (bell) peppers, seeded and
    cut into 2.5cm/1-inch cubes
2 sweet red (bell) peppers, seeded
    and cut into 2.5cm/1-inch cubes
½ teaspoon ground turmeric
½ teaspoon chilli powder
½ teaspoon garam masala
½ teaspoon salt or to taste
2 tablespoons chickpea flour
    (besan), sieved

1. In a non-stick wok, heat the oil over a medium heat. When the oil is quite hot, but not smoking, throw in the mustard seeds, followed by the cumin seeds.

2. Add the peppers and the remaining ingredients, except the chickpea flour (besan). Increase the heat slightly and stir-fry the peppers for 4–5 minutes.

3. Sprinkle the chickpea flour (besan) all over and stir-fry for a further minute. Remove from the heat and serve with a lentil dish and boiled basmati rice or Lemon Rice *(page 104)*.

Spiced Mustard Greens

Preparation time: 25 minutes
Cooking time: 50 minutes

Serves 4

This speciality from the state of Punjab is traditionally served with *makki ki roti,* a bread made of cornmeal. Both mustard and corn are grown extensively in the Punjab. Mustard greens are available in Indian stores, but you can use a mixture of chard and spinach and add a dash of prepared English mustard for the authentic Punjabi flavour. The traditional way to serve this dish is with small cubes of chilled butter placed on the spiced greens.

450g/1lb/10 cups fresh mustard greens, finely chopped
125g/4oz/2 cups fresh spinach leaves, finely chopped
3 tablespoons sunflower or plain olive oil
1 red onion, finely chopped
2.5cm/1-inch cube root ginger, finely grated
4–5 cloves garlic, crushed
1 green chilli pepper, seeded and chopped
225g/8oz/1 cup fresh tomatoes, skinned and chopped
1 teaspoon chilli powder
1 teaspoon salt or to taste
25g/1oz/¼ cup chilled half-fat butter, cut into small cubes (optional)

1. In a heavy saucepan, bring 300ml/½ pint/1⅓ cups water to the boil and add the greens and spinach. Cover and cook over a low heat for 25–30 minutes. Cool slightly and purée the leaves along with all the cooking liquid.

2. Heat two tablespoons of the oil in a saucepan or wok over a medium heat and fry the onion, ginger, garlic and chilli pepper for 7–8 minutes until the onions are browned.

3. Add the tomatoes and half the chilli powder and continue to cook for a further 3–4 minutes.

4. Add the puréed greens and salt. Cook for 10–12 minutes or until all the moisture evaporates and the greens have a solid appearance. Remove from the heat and transfer to a serving dish.

5. In a small pan or a ladle, heat the remaining oil over a medium heat and add the rest of the chilli powder. Let it sizzle for 15–20 seconds, then pour the chilli oil over the greens.

6. Top with the cubes of butter (if using) and serve.

Sweetcorn in Poppy, Sunflower and Coriander Seed Sauce

Preparation time: 15 minutes
Cooking time: 30 minutes

Serves 4–6

Corn is extremely popular in northern India. The swaying cornfields in the state of Punjab are a sight to behold. In India, the corn kernels are meticulously removed from the cob to produce delicious dishes. Of course, in the West we succumb to ready-to-use frozen or canned sweetcorn!

1 tablespoon white poppy seeds
1 tablespoon sunflower seeds
1 teaspoon coriander (cilantro) seeds
2 tablespoons sunflower or olive oil
½ teaspoon royal cumin (shahi zeera or kala zeera)
1 red onion, finely chopped
2.5cm/1-inch cube root ginger, finely grated
2 green chilli peppers, finely chopped
½ teaspoon turmeric
450g/1lb/2 cups frozen sweetcorn, thawed and drained or canned sweetcorn, drained and well-rinsed
225ml/8fl oz/1 cup semi-skimmed milk
1 teaspoon salt or to taste
125g/4oz fresh tomatoes, skinned and chopped
1 tablespoon coriander (cilantro) leaves, chopped

1   Grind the poppy seeds, sunflower seeds and coriander (cilantro) seeds in a coffee grinder until fine and set aside.

2   In a non-stick pan, heat the oil over a low heat and fry the royal cumin gently for 25–30 seconds, then increase the heat to medium and add the onion, ginger and chilli peppers. Fry until the onion is soft.

3   Add the turmeric and the ground ingredients. Cook for a further minute or so, then add the sweetcorn, milk and salt. Let it simmer gently, uncovered, for 8–10 minutes or until the sauce has thickened. Stir occasionally.

4   Add the tomatoes and coriander (cilantro) leaves and transfer to a serving dish. Serve with any bread.

Stir-fried Sweetcorn with Peppers and Spring Onions

Preparation time: 10–15 minutes
Cooking time: 10 minutes

Serves 4

Packed with vitamin C, both red and green sweet (bell) peppers are the central attractions. Quick and easy to make, this recipe has an appealing uncluttered taste.

2 tablespoons sunflower or plain olive oil

1 teaspoon cumin seeds

1 bunch spring onions (scallions), both green and white parts, chopped

125g/4oz/1 cup sweet (bell) red pepper, cut into 2.5cm/1-inch dice

125g/4oz/1 cup sweet (bell) green pepper, cut into 2.5cm/1-inch dice

½ teaspoon ground turmeric

½–1 teaspoon chilli powder

400g/14oz/2 cups frozen or canned sweetcorn

¾ teaspoon salt or to taste

1 tablespoon chapatti flour (atta)

2 teaspoons lemon juice

2 tablespoons coriander (cilantro) leaves, chopped

1 Heat the oil over a medium heat in a large frying pan (skillet) or wok. When hot, add the cumin seeds. As soon as they start crackling, add the spring onions (scallions) and stir-fry for a minute or two.

2 Add the peppers, increase the heat slightly and continue to stir-fry for a further minute or so.

3 Add the turmeric, chilli powder and sweetcorn. Stir-fry for 2–3 minutes and add the salt. Pour in 125ml/4fl oz/½ cup warm water. Stir.

4 Sprinkle the chapatti flour evenly on the vegetables, stir and cook for about a minute, then add the lemon juice and coriander (cilantro) leaves. Stir. Remove from the heat and serve with naan or chapatti accompanied by a raita.

Swede in Spice-perfumed Oil

Preparation time: 10–15 minutes
Cooking time: 10 minutes

Serves 4

Grated swede (rutabaga), tossed in spice-infused oil and cooked in its own juices, makes a delightful, quick and easy side-dish. Swedes contain chemical compounds believed to be helpful in fighting cancer. They are also low in calories and high in vitamin C.

3 tablespoons sunflower or plain olive oil
½ teaspoon black mustard seeds
¼ teaspoon fenugreek seeds
4 large cloves garlic, crushed
1–2 fresh green chilli peppers, sliced (seeded if wished)
450g/1lb/2½ cups grated swede (rutabaga)
1 teaspoon salt or to taste
2 tablespoons coriander (cilantro) leaves, chopped

1   Heat the oil over a medium heat in a shallow pan. When the oil is quite hot, but not smoking, add the mustard seeds.

2   As soon as the mustard seeds pop, reduce the heat to low and add the fenugreek seeds, followed by the garlic and chilli peppers. Let the garlic brown slightly.

3   Add the swede (rutabaga) and salt. Stir to mix well and cook for 2–3 minutes, stirring. Reduce the heat to low and cover the pan. Sweat the vegetables for 5–6 minutes. Stir in the coriander (cilantro) leaves, remove from the heat and serve with boiled basmati rice and a lentil dish.

Cauliflower Korma

Preparation time: 25 minutes
Cooking time: 20 minutes

Serves 4

Although kormas are traditionally meat-based, vegetarian versions are a popular alternative. Instead of cauliflower you could use a combination of vegetables such as green beans, carrots and potatoes.

50g/2oz/½ cup raw cashew nuts

565g/1¼lb/4½ cups bite-sized cauliflower florets

2 tablespoons sunflower or olive oil

4 green cardamom pods, bruised

2 × 5cm/2-inch pieces of cinnamon stick, halved

5–6 shallots, finely chopped

1–2 green chilli peppers, sliced diagonally

¾ teaspoon salt or to taste

150ml/5fl oz/⅔ cup half-fat single (half and half) cream

1 tablespoon lime juice

1 Soak the cashew nuts in 140ml/5fl oz/⅔ cup boiling water and set aside for 15 minutes.

2 Cook the cauliflower in boiling water for 2 minutes, drain and refresh with cold water. Set aside.

3 Heat the oil over a low heat and sauté the cardamom and cinnamon gently for 1 minute.

4 Add the shallots and chilli peppers and fry until the shallots have softened (4–5 minutes).

5 Add the cauliflower and salt and pour in 140ml/5fl oz/⅔ cup hot water. Mix well, cover the pan and cook for 2–3 minutes.

6 Meanwhile, purée the cashews with the water in which they were soaked and add to the cauliflower. Add the cream and lime juice, and stir gently until the cauliflower is well coated. Cook, uncovered, for 2–3 minutes, remove from the heat and serve with any bread and a raita.

Vegetable Korma

Preparation time: 20 minutes
Cooking time: 20 minutes

Serves 4

A combination of four vegetables has produced a korma with a fabulously rich flavour. To keep the fat content low, I have used semi-skimmed milk instead of cream, but you could use half-fat single (half and half) cream if you wish.

140ml/5fl oz/⅔ cup semi-skimmed milk

50g/2oz/½ cup raw cashew nuts

Small pinch of saffron threads, pounded

2 tablespoons rose water

2 tablespoons sunflower or plain olive oil

1 large onion, finely sliced

4 green cardamom pods, bruised

½ teaspoon royal cumin (shahi zeera or kala zeera)

2.5cm/1-inch cube root ginger, peeled and grated

4–5 cloves garlic, crushed

2 teaspoons ground coriander (cilantro)

½ teaspoon chilli powder

275g/10oz/2 cups potatoes, peeled and cut into 5cm/2-inch cubes

175g/6oz/1¼ cups carrots, sliced into 2.5cm/1-inch coins

225g/8oz/2 cups sliced green beans

175g/6oz/1¼ cups bite-sized cauliflower florets

1 teaspoon salt or to taste

1 tablespoon lemon juice

1   Heat the milk to almost boiling point and soak the cashews for 10–15 minutes.

2   In a small bowl, soak the pounded saffron in the rose water and set aside.

3   In a roasting pan, mix half the oil with the onion and place in the centre of an oven preheated to 190°C/375°F/Gas Mark 5. Cook for 12–15 minutes until the onion is a pale golden colour, stirring once or twice.

4   Heat the remaining oil over a low heat and add the cardamom, royal cumin, ginger and garlic. Fry gently for 2–3 minutes and stir in the coriander (cilantro) and chilli.

5   Add the potatoes, carrots, beans and 450ml/16fl oz/2 cups warm water. Bring to the boil, reduce the heat to medium and cover the pan. Cook for 5–6 minutes.

6   Meanwhile, blend the milk and cashews in a blender until smooth. Add the mixture to the vegetables, along with the cauliflower, salt, roasted onions and the saffron-infused rose water. Stir to mix thoroughly, re-cover the pan and cook for 5–6 minutes. Stir and reposition the vegetables once. Remove from the heat and serve with Tomato Pilau (*page 121*) and a raita.

Vegetables in Spiced Chickpea Flour Sauce

Preparation time: 15 minutes
Cooking time: 15–20 minutes

Serves 4

In this dish, fresh green chilli peppers and curry leaves provide a refreshing flavour and there is plenty of visual appeal in the rich golden colour of the sauce dotted with chopped tomatoes, mustard and cumin seeds.

---

2 tablespoons sunflower or plain olive oil

½ teaspoon black mustard seeds

1 teaspoon cumin seeds

6–8 fresh or 10–12 dried curry leaves

1–2 green chilli peppers, chopped (seeded if liked)

275g/10oz/2 cups potatoes, cut into 7.5cm/2-inch dice

275g/10oz/2½ cups bite-sized cauliflower florets

125g/4oz/½ cup chopped canned tomatoes, including the juice

1 teaspoon salt or to taste

¼–½ teaspoon chilli powder

½ teaspoon ground turmeric

50g/2oz/½ cup chickpea flour (besan), sieved

1 Heat the oil over a medium heat and add the mustard seeds. As soon as they pop, add the cumin seeds, curry leaves and green chilli peppers.

2 Add the potatoes and increase the heat to high. Stir-fry the potatoes until they begin to brown slightly. Reduce the heat to low and cover the pan. Cook for 2–3 minutes.

3 Add the cauliflower and increase the heat to high again. Sauté the vegetables for 2–3 minutes.

4 Reduce the heat to medium and add the remaining ingredients, except the chickpea flour (besan). Stir and cook for a minute or two.

5 Blend the chickpea flour with 140ml/¼ pint/⅔ cup cold water and add to the vegetables. Stir and cook for a minute and pour in 300ml/½ pint/1⅓ cups hot water. Cook for 2–3 minutes, stirring carefully. Remove from the heat and serve with hot naan.

Vegetables with Mustard, Garlic and Chilli

Preparation time: 25 minutes
Cooking time: 15 minutes

Serves 4

This is a quick and delicious dish with the nutty taste of mustard seeds and the unbeatable combination of garlic and chilli. The golden sauce produced by chickpea flour (besan) adds a spectacular visual appeal, showing off the coral-coloured carrots, the emerald-green beans and the cubes of white potato.

3 tablespoons sunflower or plain olive oil

½ teaspoon black mustard seeds

4–5 cloves garlic, crushed

1 fresh green chilli pepper, finely chopped

200g/7oz/1½ cups carrots, finely chopped

200g/7oz/2¼ cups green beans, finely chopped

275g/10oz/2 cups potatoes, finely chopped

1 teaspoon ground coriander (cilantro)

1 teaspoon ground cumin

½ teaspoon ground turmeric

½ teaspoon chilli powder

1 teaspoon salt

1 tablespoon chickpea flour (besan), sieved

4 spring onions (scallions), both green and white parts, chopped

1 Heat the oil over a low heat. When the oil is hot, but not smoking, add the mustard seeds. As soon as they pop, add the garlic and chilli and fry until the garlic is lightly browned.

2 Add all the vegetables except the spring onions (scallions) and increase the heat to high. Stir-fry for 5 minutes.

3 In a small bowl, mix together the coriander (cilantro), cumin, turmeric, chilli powder, salt and flour. Sprinkle the spice mixture evenly over the vegetables, reduce the heat to low, cover the pan and cook for 5 minutes.

4 Add the spring onions, stir and cook for 2–3 minutes, remove from the heat and serve with any bread and Spiced Chickpeas with Sun-dried Mango (*page 49*) or a lentil dish.

Nine-jewelled Vegetables

Preparation time: 30 minutes
Cooking time: 20 minutes   Serves 6

In the courts of the Mogul Emperor Akbar, there were nine members of outstanding ability. Akbar nicknamed them 'the nine jewels', and the palace chefs dedicated several dishes to them, such as this delectable recipe which consists of nine types of vegetable. As it can be time-consuming to prepare them all, don't worry about using nine different vegetables; just choose a colourful range of ingredients.

1 tablespoon unsalted cashew nuts

1 tablespoon sunflower seeds

2 tablespoons sunflower or light olive oil

4 green cardamom pods, bruised

1 × 5cm/2-inch piece cinnamon stick

5–6 shallots, finely chopped

2.5cm/1-inch cube root ginger, finely grated

1 green chilli pepper, chopped (seeded if wished)

1 teaspoon ground coriander (cilantro)

½ teaspoon chilli powder

⅓ teaspoon ground turmeric

175g/6oz/1 cup potatoes, peeled and cut into 5cm/2-inch cubes

125g/4oz/⅔ cup fresh green beans, cut into 5cm/2-inch pieces

90g/3oz carrots, cut into chunks

125g/4oz/1 cup aubergine (eggplant), cubed

150g/5oz/1 cup pumpkin or butternut squash, cut into 5cm/2-inch pieces

125g/4oz/1 cup turnip, cut into 2.5cm/1-inch cubes

1 teaspoon salt or to taste

½ teaspoon sugar

125g/4oz/1 cup cauliflower florets, divided into bite-sized pieces

90g/3oz/1 cup button mushrooms, halved

125g/4oz/2 cups fresh spinach leaves, chopped

140ml/5fl oz/⅔ cup half-fat single (half and half) cream

50g/2oz/¼ cup low-fat plain yogurt

1 tablespoon lemon juice

1 In a small heavy skillet, dry-roast the cashews and the sunflower seeds until lightly browned. Remove, cool and purée in a blender with 200ml/7fl oz/¾ cup warm water and set aside.

2 In a heavy saucepan, heat the oil gently and add the cardamom and cinnamon. Let them sizzle for 30–40 seconds.

3 Add the shallots, ginger and chilli pepper. Increase the heat to medium and fry until the shallots are soft and translucent (3–4 minutes).

4 Add the spices and stir, then add the potatoes, beans and carrots. Pour in 450ml/16fl oz/2 cups lukewarm water and bring to the boil. Reduce the heat to medium, cover and cook for 3–4 minutes.

5 Add the aubergine (eggplant), pumpkin, turnips, salt and sugar. Cover and cook for 5 minutes.

6 Add the cauliflower and mushrooms and stir. Pile the spinach leaves on top of the vegetables and cover the pan. Cook for 5 minutes.

7 Add the cashew and sunflower seed purée, cream and yogurt. Cook, uncovered, for 4–5 minutes.

8 Stir in the lemon juice and remove from the heat. Serve with any bread.

Winter Squash in Coconut Milk with Hot-oil Seasoning

Preparation time: 20 minutes
Cooking time: 18–20 minutes

Serves 4

This recipe produces a slightly sweet, hot and tangy flavour.

400ml/14fl oz/1¾ cups reduced-fat coconut milk

450g/1lb/2¼ cups pumpkin or butternut squash, peeled and cut into 5cm/2-inch dice

225g/8oz/1 cup potatoes, peeled and cut into 5cm/2-inch dice

1¼ teaspoons salt or to taste

8 fresh or 10–12 dried curry leaves

3–4 green chilli peppers, sliced lengthways (seeded if wished)

2 tablespoons sunflower or plain olive oil

4 large cloves garlic, crushed

1 teaspoon ground coriander (cilantro)

1 teaspoon ground cumin

½ teaspoon ground turmeric

1 tablespoon chickpea flour (besan), sieved

1½ tablespoons lime juice

1. Put the coconut milk into a saucepan with the ingredients up to and including the green chilli peppers. Bring to a slow simmer (the coconut milk will curdle if you cook it fast). Cover the pan and simmer gently for 5 minutes. Remove the lid and continue to cook gently for a further 5–6 minutes or until the vegetables are tender, stirring once or twice.

2. Heat the oil in a small saucepan over a low heat and fry the garlic until browned.

3. Add the spices and cook gently for 30–40 seconds, then stir into the cooked vegetables. Blend the chickpea flour (besan) with a little water and add to the vegetables along with the lime juice. Simmer gently for 2–3 minutes, remove from the heat and serve with any bread.

Spiced Turnips

Preparation time: 15 minutes
Cooking time: 50–55 minutes

Serves 4–6

Turnip is low in calories and contains plenty of fibre and vitamin C. In this superbly flavoured dish, a non-stick wok or pan is essential to keep the fat content low. For a variation, substitute half the turnips with potatoes or use yam *(suran)* instead of turnips. This recipe is suitable for freezing.

680g/1½lb/5 cups turnips

175g/6oz/1 cup low-fat natural yogurt

2 teaspoons chickpea flour (besan), sieved

3 tablespoons olive oil

1 red onion, finely sliced

1 teaspoon royal cumin (shahi jeera)

4 whole cloves

1cm/½-inch cube root ginger, peeled and cut into juliennes

2 teaspoons ground coriander (cilantro)

½ teaspoon ground turmeric

¼–½ teaspoon chilli powder

1 teaspoon salt or to taste

300ml/½ pint/1⅓ cups warm water

½ teaspoon garam masala

1–2 green chilli peppers, seeded and cut into juliennes

2 tablespoons chopped coriander (cilantro) leaves

1   Trim, peel and wash the turnips. Cut each one in half, then quarter each half so that you have chunks of approximately 4cm/1½ inches.

2   Put the yogurt in a bowl and beat with the chickpea flour (besan) until smooth. Set aside.

3   In a non-stick wok, heat half the oil over a medium-high heat. When the oil is hot, sauté the turnips until well browned (6–7 minutes). Drain on absorbent paper.

4   Reduce the heat slightly, add the remaining oil and the onion, royal cumin, cloves and ginger. Fry, stirring regularly, until lightly browned (about 8–9 minutes).

5   Add the coriander (cilantro), turmeric and chilli powder and stir-fry for 30 seconds. Make sure the pan is not too hot; if it is, remove from the heat and cool for a minute or so. Add half the yogurt and bring to a very slow simmer. Now add the remaining yogurt and let it bubble gently for about 2 minutes.

6   Add the turnips, salt and water. Stir and mix well. Cover the pan and simmer very gently for 25–30 minutes or until the turnips are tender.

7   Add the garam masala, chilli peppers and coriander (cilantro) leaves. Stir, remove from the heat and serve with any bread or boiled basmati rice and Spicy Green Lentils *(page 69)*.

Creamed Butternut Squash

Preparation time: 20–25 minutes
Cooking time: 40 minutes

Serves 4–6

Butternut squash is a nutritious and easily digestible vegetable. Its sweet, golden flesh, combined with the warm, assertive flavours of the winter spices (cinnamon, cardamom and cloves), creates fabulous taste sensations in this dish.

---

1 butternut squash or small pumpkin (about 550g/1¼lb/4 cups)

2 potatoes (about 200g/7oz/1⅓ cups)

3 tablespoons sunflower or olive oil

2 × 2.5cm/1-inch pieces cinnamon stick

4 green cardamom pods, split at the top of each pod

4 whole cloves

8 cloves garlic, peeled and crushed

1 small onion, finely chopped

1 tablespoon ground cumin

1 teaspoon ground turmeric

½–1 teaspoon crushed dried red chilli peppers

125g/4oz/½ cup canned chopped tomatoes, including juice

2.5cm/1-inch cube root ginger, peeled and grated

1 teaspoon salt or to taste

350ml/12fl oz/1½ cups warm water

½ teaspoon garam masala

3 tablespoons half-fat single (half and half) cream

2 tablespoons finely chopped coriander (cilantro) leaves

1. Halve or quarter the butternut squash or pumpkin and remove the seeds. Peel and cut into 2.5cm/1-inch cubes.

2. Peel the potatoes and cut into 1cm/½-inch cubes.

3. In a wok or medium saucepan, heat the oil over a low heat and add the cinnamon, cardamom and cloves. Let the spices sizzle for 30 seconds.

4. Add the garlic and onion. Fry for 6–8 minutes or until the onion begins to colour.

5. Add the cumin, turmeric and crushed chilli peppers, stir-fry for about a minute and add the tomatoes. Cook for 4–5 minutes or until the oil separates from the spice paste and begins to float.

6. Add the ginger, stir-fry for 1 minute then add the pumpkin, potatoes, salt and water. Increase the heat to high, bring to the boil and cook for 2–3 minutes. Now reduce the heat to low and cover the pan. Cook for 20–25 minutes, stirring occasionally.

7. Add the garam masala, cream and half the coriander (cilantro) leaves. Stir and cook for 1 minute, then remove from the heat. Garnish with the remaining coriander leaves and serve with any bread and a protein-rich dish.

Leeks in Chickpea Flour with Sweet Red Pepper

Preparation time: 20 minutes
Cooking time: 10 minutes

Serves 4–6

Chickpea flour (besan) is available in Asian stores, health-food shops and some good supermarkets. It can be stored like ordinary flour, in a cool dry place. Any leftovers from this recipe can be used as a filling for spicy toasted sandwiches (excellent made in an electric toasted sandwich maker). For a variation, add equal quantities of onion and cabbage instead of leeks. Stir-fry the onions for 2–3 minutes before adding the cabbage and pepper slices.

4 leeks (about 450g/1lb/4 cups)
1 red (bell) pepper (about 200g/7oz/1¼ cups)
2 tablespoons sunflower or olive oil
½ teaspoon black mustard seeds
½ teaspoon cumin seeds
8–10 fenugreek seeds
8 cloves garlic, peeled and crushed
¼ teaspoon crushed dried red chilli peppers
1 teaspoon salt or to taste
2 tablespoons chopped coriander (cilantro) leaves
125g/4oz/¾ cup chickpea flour (besan), sifted

1. Trim the leeks and halve them lengthways. Wash thoroughly, making sure you remove any grit between the leaves. Holding 3–4 halves of leeks together, slice them finely.

2. Remove the seeds and pith from the pepper and cut into 2.5cm/1-inch strips.

3. In a wok, heat the oil over a medium heat. When the oil is hot but not smoking, reduce the heat slightly and add the mustard seeds. As soon as they pop, reduce the heat to low and add the cumin and fenugreek seeds. Follow with the garlic. Stir-fry for 1 minute.

4. Add the crushed chilli peppers, stir-fry for 30 seconds and add the leeks, pepper slices and salt. Increase the heat to medium and stir-fry for 5 minutes.

5. Add the coriander (cilantro) leaves and 2 tablespoons of water, then sprinkle the chickpea flour (besan) evenly over the vegetables. Stir-fry for 1½ minutes and remove from the heat. Scrape off and mix in any flour that sticks to the bottom of the pan. This will add extra flavour. Serve with any bread or Toasted Sesame Rice (page 107) and a raita.

Chapter 8

Cooking Sauces, Marinades and Seasonings

Cooking sauces can quickly transform a simple ingredient into a gourmet meal. Although you can buy good-quality cooking sauces in the supermarket, nothing can match the taste and flavour of homemade versions. As most of the spices, especially turmeric, have natural preserving qualities, you can safely store your sauces in the fridge for up to 10 days, provided they are kept in airtight containers. They also freeze well.

Marinades and basting sauces are also included in this section so that you can rustle up a gourmet meal at lightning speed. Imagine getting home from work and being able to produce a first course of grilled (broiled) corn-on-the-cob basted with Minty Chilli and Lime Basting Sauce *(page 174),* followed by a main course of grilled smoked tofu with a sensational Apricot Sauce *(page 172),* accompanied by a bowl of steaming hot basmati rice simmered in Aromatic Stock *(page 173)!* With the recipes in this chapter, you cannot fail to produce gourmet meals in just under an hour. Here's wishing you a stress-free time in the kitchen!

Apricot Sauce

Preparation time: 20–25 minutes plus marinating
Cooking time: 35–40 minutes

Based on a recipe from the exquisite cuisine of Kashmir, this sauce has a sweet, savoury and tangy-hot flavour. It is ideal for pouring over smoked, grilled (broiled) tofu, boiled new potatoes, roasted mixed peppers, cooked chickpeas (garbanzos) etc. Once you have made your chosen dish, always taste it and adjust the seasoning accordingly.

14 dried ready-to-eat apricots, roughly chopped

2 tablespoons sunflower or light olive oil

6–7 shallots, roughly chopped

2.5cm/1-inch cube root ginger, chopped

3–4 cloves garlic, peeled and chopped

2 green chilli peppers, seeded and chopped

½ teaspoon ground cumin

1 teaspoon ground coriander (cilantro)

½ teaspoon salt or to taste

½ teaspoon sugar

2 tablespoons coriander (cilantro) leaves, chopped

90ml/3fl oz/⅓ cup half-fat single (half and half) cream

1   Roughly chop the apricots and soak them in 140ml/5fl oz/ ⅔ cup hot water for 15 minutes.

2   In a non-stick pan, heat the oil over a medium heat and sauté the shallots, ginger, garlic and chilli peppers until they begin to brown a little. Add the spices and sauté for about a minute then pour in 150ml/5fl oz/⅔ cup warm water. Add the salt and sugar and bring to the boil. Reduce the heat and simmer for 5–6 minutes. Remove from the heat and allow to cool slightly.

3   Place the apricots along with the water in which they were soaked in a blender and add the cooked spice mixture. Purée until smooth and return to the pan.

4   Add the coriander (cilantro) and cream. Simmer gently for 5–6 minutes, remove from the heat and use as desired. This sauce will keep well in the fridge for 3–4 days if cooled quickly and stored in an airtight container.

Aromatic Stock

Preparation time: 5–10 minutes
Cooking time: 35–40 minutes

Makes 1 litre/1¾ pints/4½ cups

This stock is great for livening up plain rice. Cook the rice in the stock instead of plain water. Use it to cook vegetables such as green beans, carrots, spinach, potatoes and broccoli. Cook the vegetables in just enough stock that they absorb all the liquid, resulting in a quick but flavoursome dish. The stock can be stored in the fridge in a covered container for up to two weeks.

1 teaspoon black peppercorns
2 tablespoons coriander (cilantro) seeds, crushed
2 tablespoons cumin seeds, crushed
2 × 5cm/2-inch pieces of cinnamon stick
4 green cardamom pods, bruised
2 brown cardamom pods, bruised
8 cloves
2 bay leaves
8 garlic cloves, lightly crushed
7.5cm/3-inch cube root ginger, sliced
1 teaspoon salt

1   Put all the ingredients in a large saucepan and pour in 1.2 litres/2 pints/5 cups water. Bring to the boil, then reduce the heat to low, cover the pan and simmer for 35–40 minutes.

2   Strain the stock and push the garlic and ginger through a sieve into the stock. Mix well, cool and store.

Minty Chilli and Lime Basting Sauce

Preparation time: a few minutes

Use this sauce to add zest to plain cooked or raw vegetables. Steam or boil the vegetables until *al dente* then brush with the sauce. Brown quickly under a hot grill (broiler). Try steamed corn on the cob (corncob), raw whole button mushrooms, courgettes (zucchini) quartered lengthways and steamed cauliflower florets. This quantity is enough for 450g/1lb vegetables.

Juice and zest of 1 lime
½ teaspoon ground cumin
½ teaspoon ground coriander
   (cilantro)
½–1 teaspoon hot chilli powder
½ teaspoon dried mint
1 tablespoon light olive oil
½ teaspoon salt
½ teaspoon sugar

1   Blend all the ingredients together thoroughly. The sauce is then ready to use or can be stored in the fridge in a screw-top jar for 4–5 days.

Spiced Corn on the Cob, page 9

Spiced Potato Canapés, page 2

Mung Bean Rolls, page 6

Pumpkin Soup, page 44

Spiced Oranges with Grenadine, page 190

Mango-flavoured Sweet Yogurt Drink (Lassi), and Pomegranate Crush, pages 256, 262

Spiced Fruit Salad, page 192

Minted Aubergine with Garlic and Fresh Coriander, page 127

Coconut, Coriander and Chilli Pesto

Preparation time: 5–10 minutes   **Makes about 225g/8oz**

This taste-bud reviver looks fresh and inviting. Use it as a dressing for boiled whole new potatoes, parsnips roasted with a drizzle of olive oil or steamed carrots.

25g/1oz/¼ cup desiccated coconut

3 tablespoons sunflower or
   vegetable oil

3–4 shallots, roughly chopped

2.5cm/1-inch cube root ginger,
   roughly chopped

2 garlic cloves, peeled and chopped

1–3 green chilli peppers

25g/1oz coriander (cilantro) leaves
   and stalks, roughly chopped

½ teaspoon salt

1½ tablespoons lemon juice

½ teaspoon salt or to taste

½ teaspoon sugar

90g/3oz/½ cup low-fat plain
   yogurt, beaten until smooth

1 Put the coconut in a bowl and pour over 140ml/5fl oz/⅔ cup boiling water. Set aside for 10 minutes.

2 Meanwhile, heat the oil in a non-stick sauté pan over a medium heat and fry the shallots, ginger, garlic and chilli peppers for 5–6 minutes. Remove from the heat.

3 Put the coconut and the water in which it was soaked in a blender and add the coriander (cilantro), sautéed ingredients, salt and lemon juice. Switch on the blender and leave it running on medium speed (it will take 5–7 minutes to get a smooth texture).

4 Add the beaten yogurt and use as required.

Lettuce and Peanut Sauce

Preparation time: 10 minutes
Cooking time: 10 minutes

Serves 4

Strange though it may sound, this unusual dish tastes great with boiled basmati rice and bread. A vegetarian diet can benefit from nuts as they provide protein and other nutrients that are generally derived from meat and poultry. Peanuts are an excellent source of essential fatty acids, which are beneficial to the heart.

50g/2oz/⅔ cup dry-roasted peanuts

175g/6oz/2 cups lettuce leaves

175g/6oz/1 cup fresh tomatoes, skinned, seeded and chopped

2 green chilli peppers, seeded and chopped

2 teaspoons root ginger, peeled and chopped

50g/2oz/¼ cup plain yogurt

1 tablespoon lime juice

½ teaspoon ground cumin

1 teaspoon salt or to taste

1 Grind the peanuts in a coffee grinder until fine and set aside.

2 Put the lettuce and tomatoes into a saucepan and add 300ml/½ pint/1⅓ cups water. Bring to the boil, reduce the heat to low and cook for 5 minutes. Remove from the heat and cool slightly, then purée in a blender.

3 Add the ground peanuts and the remaining ingredients. Blend well and serve at room temperature.

Spiced Salt

Preparation and cooking time: a few minutes

Spiced salt is wonderful for flavouring salads and steamed vegetables. Simply sprinkle on at the last minute and serve. On yogurt-based salads (raita), you can use it instead of plain salt, as long as you omit the other spices in the recipe. Add a pinch to plain boiled rice, pasta, potatoes etc. A coarse sea salt works better and the spices are best pre-roasted to activate their volatile oils and add maximum flavour. Try not to keep this salt for longer than 3–4 weeks because the flavours will begin to diminish after this time.

1 teaspoon peppercorns

2 teaspoons cumin seeds

2 teaspoons coriander (cilantro) seeds

1–2 dried red chilli peppers, chopped

3 tablespoons coarse sea salt

1 Preheat a small, heavy pan over a medium heat and add the spices. Stir them around for a minute or two until they release their aroma. Remove from the pan to stop them overheating. Let them cool then pound them together with the salt to a medium-coarse mixture. You could also use a coffee grinder, but take care not to grind them finely. Store in an airtight jar away from direct light.

Tomato and Fenugreek Sauce

Preparation time: 10 minutes
Cooking time: 45 minutes

Makes 850ml/1½ pints/3¾ cups

This sauce is ideal for a whole range of dishes, such as Vegetable Korma, cooked chickpeas (garbanzos), butterbeans and black-eye beans. Dried fenugreek leaves add that unmistakable taste and aroma typical of this sauce. The leaves will keep well for 5–6 months if stored in an airtight container.

3 tablespoons sunflower or light
    olive oil
1 large onion, roughly chopped
2.5cm/1-inch cube root ginger,
    chopped
4–5 cloves garlic, chopped
2 × 2.5cm/1-inch pieces of
    cinnamon stick
6 cardamom pods, bruised
5 cloves
2–3 green chilli peppers, seeded if
    wished
2 × 400g/14oz cans of chopped
    tomatoes, including juice
150g/5oz tomato purée (paste)
2 teaspoons sugar
2 teaspoons salt
1–2 teaspoons chilli powder
300ml/½ pint/1⅓ cups warm water
2 teaspoons dried fenugreek leaves
    (Kasoori methi)
140ml/5fl oz/⅔ cup half-fat single
    (half and half) cream

1 Heat the oil over a medium heat and sauté the onion, ginger, garlic, cinnamon, cardamom and cloves for 4–5 minutes.

2 Add the remaining ingredients except the fenugreek leaves and the cream. Bring to the boil, then reduce the heat to low and simmer, uncovered, for 30 minutes.

3 Remove the whole spices, purée the sauce and return to the saucepan. Add the fenugreek leaves and cream and simmer for 10 minutes. Cool and store.

Tomato and Onion Sauce

Preparation time: 10 minutes
Cooking time: 50–55 minutes

Makes 1.2 litres/2 pints/5 cups

This sauce is great for boiled or sautéed potatoes, garden peas, boiled chickpeas (garbanzos), tofu etc. Simply simmer your chosen ingredient in the required amount of sauce. Always taste and adjust the seasoning and finish the dish by adding fresh herbs such as mint, coriander (cilantro) or snipped chives. A dash of garam masala at the end of cooking will enhance the flavour. This sauce is suitable for freezing.

---

3 tablespoons sunflower or light olive oil

450g/1lb/2 cups onions, roughly chopped

50g/2oz garlic cloves, peeled and chopped

5cm/2-inch cube root ginger, peeled and roughly chopped

2 teaspoons ground coriander (cilantro)

1 teaspoon cumin

1 teaspoon ground turmeric

1½ teaspoons salt

425g/15oz/2 cups canned tomatoes, including the juice

1–2 teaspoons hot chilli powder

1   Heat the oil over a medium heat and sauté the onions, garlic and ginger until they begin to brown.

2   Add the coriander (cilantro), cumin and turmeric and cook for about a minute.

3   Add the salt, tomatoes, chilli powder and pour in 570ml/ 1 pint/2½ cups hot water. Bring to the boil, reduce the heat to low, cover the pan and simmer for 25–30 minutes. Remove from the heat and allow to cool, then purée in a blender or food processor or press through a sieve. Store in the fridge for 8–10 days. Alternatively, divide into smaller quantities and freeze.

Tomato, Black Pepper and Coriander Sauce

Ready in 45 minutes   **Makes about 425ml/¾ pint/2 cups**

Coarsely crushed black pepper is the distinctive flavour in this sauce. Combined with lemon juice and tomatoes, the peppery taste is perfect for boiled basmati rice. Alternatively, simply toss some cooked green beans or a combination of frozen garden peas and boiled and diced potatoes in the required amount of sauce. It is also good with grilled tofu and sautéed Quorn pieces. Try sautéed chestnut mushrooms in just enough sauce to coat them.

3 tablespoons sunflower or light olive oil

5cm/2-inch piece of cinnamon stick, halved

4 green cardamom pods, bruised

4 cloves

2.5cm/1-inch cube root ginger, roughly chopped

4–5 large garlic cloves, chopped

2 medium onions, roughly chopped

1 teaspoon paprika or mild chilli powder

½ teaspoon ground turmeric

1 tablespoon roasted and ground coriander (cilantro) seeds

1 tablespoon black peppercorns, coarsely crushed

255g/9oz/1⅓ cups chopped canned tomatoes, including the juice

230ml/8fl oz/1 cup warm water

Juice of ½ lemon

1¼ teaspoons salt or to taste

2 tablespoons finely chopped coriander (cilantro) leaves

1   In a wok or non-stick pan, heat the oil over a medium heat and add the cinnamon, cardamom and cloves. Let them sizzle gently until the cardamom pods have plumped up then add the ginger, garlic and onions. Fry for 4–5 minutes until the onions begin to brown.

2   Add the paprika or chilli powder, turmeric, coriander (cilantro) seeds and black pepper. Cook for about a minute and add the tomatoes and warm water. Bring to the boil, reduce the heat to low and simmer for 15–20 minutes. Remove the whole spices, purée the sauce and return it to the pan.

3   Add the lemon juice, salt and coriander (cilantro) leaves. Simmer for 1–2 minutes and remove from the heat.

4   Cool and store in the fridge. It will freeze well.

Saffron and Yogurt Marinade

Preparation time: 10 minutes

This marinade will keep in the fridge for 4–5 days. Use to marinate vegetables and tofu. You can use a single vegetable or a combination of two or more. Alternatively, combine tofu, mushrooms, green and red (bell) peppers and marinate for 2–3 hours, then grill (broil) under a hot grill (broiler) or roast in a hot oven until the vegetables are tender but still firm and have brown patches. It also works well with small boiled (not too soft) whole potatoes. Prick the potatoes all over with a fork and marinate for at least an hour. Grill until browned. This quantity is enough for 1kg/2lb of vegetables.

Pinch of saffron threads, pounded
1 tablespoon hot milk
125g/4oz/⅔ cup fat-free Greek
    yogurt, whisked
125ml/4fl oz/½ cup half-fat single
    (half and half) cream
3–4 cloves garlic, crushed to a fine
    pulp
2.5cm/1-inch cube root ginger,
    finely grated
½ teaspoon ground turmeric
½ teaspoon garam masala
½–1 teaspoon chilli powder
½ teaspoon ground coriander
    (cilantro)
½ teaspoon ground cumin
Salt to taste
1 teaspoon sugar
2 teaspoons sieved chickpea flour
    (besan)
1 tablespoon coriander (cilantro)
    leaves, finely chopped

1 Soak the saffron in the hot milk and set aside for 20 minutes.
2 Mix the remaining ingredients together and add the saffron infused milk. Stir until well blended and use as required.

Chapter 9

Desserts

Indian desserts are generally dairy-based and quite heavy so are not traditionally served at the end of meals. Nevertheless, desserts are very important to every Indian household. Sweets are believed to be the food of the gods and they are offered at the altar on religious occasions and to welcome guests into the house. They are served at celebration meals, such as weddings, Diwali (the festival of light) and other religious festivals.

As a meal seems incomplete without a dessert, however, I always serve one so that the meal ends with a sweet note. Choosing the right kind of dessert needs a little care and skill. This is true of any cuisine as the dessert has to complement the starter and main course. If you have chosen a rich main course such as Lentils in the Royal Style *(page 70)* or Smoked Tofu in Saffron-cream Sauce *(page 77)*, go for a light, fruit-based dessert such as Papaya with Lime Dressing *(page 188)* or Pomegranate Sorbet *(page 189)*. Similarly, a light main course can be followed by a rich dessert. You could choose from Indian Bread Pudding *(page 241)*, Soft Carrot Fudge *(page 246)* or similar. The recipes in this chapter are suitable for a low-fat diet. For a selection of rich desserts, see Chapter 10.

Spiced Pineapple Compote

Preparation time: 20 minutes
Cooking time: 40–45 minutes

Serves 4

Mogul cooking is renowned for fruit compotes, some simple and some quite exotic. This pineapple compote is easy to make and keeps very well for several days in the fridge. Serve as a dessert for a refreshing end to a spicy meal.

---

1 large ripe pineapple
Pinch of saffron strands
175g/6oz/¾ cup granulated sugar
2 star anise
1 × 5cm/2-inch piece cinnamon stick
50g/2oz seedless raisins
2 tablespoons brandy (optional)
Greek yogurt or low-fat fromage frais, to serve
Silver leaf (varak) or silver dust (optional)

1   Slice off the ends of the pineapple, then cut it lengthways into 8 boat-shaped pieces. Remove the central hard core from each piece. Using a sharp knife and a sawing action, peel the skin from one end to the other. Remove the 'eyes' and cut the pieces into 5cm/2-inch pieces.

2   Pound the saffron strands lightly and soak in 1 tablespoon of hot water. Set aside.

3   Put 570ml/1 pint/2½ cups of water into a saucepan and add the sugar. Bring to a rolling boil and add the star anise and cinnamon. Reduce the heat slightly and continue to boil for 10–12 minutes.

4   Add the pineapple, bring back to the boil and cook over a medium heat for 8–10 minutes until the syrup thickens.

5   Add the steeped saffron with the water and the raisins. Continue to cook for 5–6 minutes until the pineapple is tender, but still firm.

6   Stir in the brandy (if using) and remove from the heat.

7   Serve hot or cold with yogurt or fromage frais, garnished with the silver leaf or silver dust (if using).

Saffron-flavoured Pineapple

Preparation time: 10–15 minutes   Serves 6

Pineapples came to India from South America. Today, pineapple is very popular all over India. I have flavoured this lovely fruit with saffron and cinnamon. It makes a wonderfully refreshing way to finish a spicy meal.

1 medium pineapple or
    2 × 350g/12oz cans pineapple in
    syrup
570ml/1 pint/2½ cups water
125g/4oz/⅔ cup caster
    (confectioner's) sugar
3 × 2.5 cm/1-inch pieces cinnamon
    stick
½ teaspoon saffron strands,
    pounded
2 teaspoons ground arrowroot
275g/10oz/1⅓ cups low-fat,
    unflavoured fromage frais
370g/13oz can guava halves,
    drained

1   Skin the pineapple and remove the 'eyes' with a small, sharp knife. Cut across into 12 slices and remove the hard core with an apple corer. If using canned pineapple, drain and reserve the syrup, then go to Step 4.

2   If using fresh pineapple, put the water, sugar and cinnamon in a large saucepan and place over a high heat. Bring to the boil, then add the pineapple rings. Cook for 8–10 minutes, and transfer the pineapple to a large plate with a slotted spoon.

3   Return the saucepan to the heat and add the saffron. Bring to the boil, reduce the heat to medium and cook for 6–7 minutes or until the syrup has reduced to nearly half its original volume.

4   If using canned pineapple, measure 425ml/14fl oz/2 cups of the syrup and place over a high heat. Add the cinnamon and bring to the boil. Reduce the heat to low and simmer for 5–6 minutes. Add the saffron and simmer for 6–8 minutes.

5   Strain the syrup, return to the saucepan and place over a medium heat. When the syrup begins to bubble, blend the arrowroot with a little water and add, stirring. Cook for 2–3 minutes when the syrup will thicken slightly. Remove from the heat and allow to cool.

6   Stack 2 pineapple rings together and place in an individual serving dish. Fill the hollow with fromage frais, spreading about 1 tablespoon on the top but leaving a thin border of pineapple showing.

7   Carefully remove the seeds from the guava halves with a teaspoon, then place the guavas on the fromage frais, hollow-side down.

8   Pour on enough saffron-flavoured syrup to cover the pineapple, but not the fromage frais, and chill until required.

Mangoes with Curd Cheese and Rose Water

Preparation time: 15–20 minutes plus chilling

Serves 4

This dessert works best with Alphonso mangoes, which are imported from India. They are available fresh in Indian stores during the mango season (May to August), but are also sold in cans, sliced or puréed. Canned mangoes from supermarkets work well too.

2 × 425g cans of mangoes
225g/8oz/1 cup low-fat curd cheese
1½ tablespoons caster (confectioner's) sugar or to taste
2 tablespoons rose water
¼ teaspoon ground cardamom or nutmeg
4 kiwi fruits, cut into cubes
Seeds of ½ a pomegranate

1 Purée the mangoes along with the syrup and add the curd cheese, sugar, rose water and most of the cardamom or nutmeg. Mix until well blended.

2 Arrange alternate layers of kiwi and pomegranate seeds in individual serving dishes and top with the mango mixture. Sprinkle with the reserved cardamom or nutmeg. Chill for at least 30 minutes.

Seasoned Mango with Coconut

Preparation time: 15 minutes
Cooking time: 5 minutes

Serves 4

Ripe mangoes, coated with coconut and seasoned with mustard and coriander (cilantro), make a superb dessert. You can also serve this as a side dish with summer meals instead of a salad.

4–5 ripe, firm mangoes
2 teaspoons soft brown sugar
¾ teaspoon salt or to taste
1 tablespoon lime juice
25g/1oz/⅓ cup desiccated coconut
2 dried red chilli peppers, chopped
1 tablespoon sunflower oil
½ teaspoon black mustard seeds
½ teaspoon ground coriander
   (cilantro)

1   Peel the mangoes, slice off the flesh and chop into bite-sized pieces.
2   Put the mangoes into a mixing bowl and add the sugar, salt and lime juice. Mix well.
3   Grind the coconut and red chilli peppers in a coffee grinder until fine and add to the mango. Mix thoroughly.
4   Heat the oil in a small saucepan over a medium heat. When the oil is hot, but not smoking, add the mustard seeds. As soon as they pop, stir in the ground coriander (cilantro), allow to cook for 5–10 seconds and remove from the heat. Pour the seasoned oil over the mango mixture and mix well. Serve at room temperature or chilled.

Mango Sauce

Preparation time: 10 minutes

Makes about 450ml/16fl oz/2 cups

Use this sauce to transform fresh fruit salads or pour over canned and drained fruits to make an instant dessert. It also tastes delicious and looks fabulous served with mixed summer berries or watermelon balls.

2 × 425g/15oz cans sliced mango
Finely grated rind of 1 lime
1 tablespoon lime juice
2 tablespoons caster
    (confectioner's) sugar or to
    taste
½ teaspoon dry ground ginger
½ teaspoon ground nutmeg
½ teaspoon ground cardamom
    seeds

1   Drain and purée the mangoes. Mix with the remaining ingredients and chill for a couple of hours.

Papaya with Lime Dressing

Preparation time: 20 minutes plus chilling

Serves 4–6

Papaya (pawpaw) is a nutritious tropical fruit with an exotic, juicy, sweet-tart flavour. As with other orange-fleshed fruits, it is a rich source of betacarotene, one of the antioxidants that fight heart disease.

2 ripe papaya (pawpaw) (total weight approx. 685g/1½lb)
125g/4oz/½ cup strawberries
2–3 kiwi fruits
225g/8oz/1 cup half-fat crème fraîche
Finely grated zest and juice of 1 lime
50g/2oz/¼ cup sieved icing (powdered) sugar

1   Trim both ends of the papaya (pawpaw) and cut in half lengthways. Carefully ease away the seeds with a teaspoon and scrape off the white membrane.

2   Halve the strawberries and peel and quarter the kiwis, then cut each quarter in half. Combine all the fruits in a large mixing bowl, cover and chill for at least an hour.

3   Beat the crème fraîche, lime zest and juice and the icing (powdered) sugar together. Taste the mixture and add a little more sugar if liked.

4   Arrange layers of fruits and lime-flavoured crème fraîche in stemmed glasses and serve.

Pomegranate Sorbet

Preparation time: 30 minutes plus freezing

Serves 4–6

This fat-free sorbet, with its attractive colour and clean, light taste, makes a fabulous dessert. It is also ideal as a palate cleanser between courses. Pomegranates are available during autumn through to late spring. Look for the ones with a reddish tinge on the skin as they are likely to have sweet, rich, red seeds.

8 large pomegranates
175g/6oz/1 cup caster
   (confectioner's) sugar
140ml/5fl oz/⅔ cup water
2 × 2.5cm/1-inch pieces of
   cinnamon stick
Juice of 1 lime
3 tablespoons grenadine
¼ teaspoon ground nutmeg
Few sprigs of fresh mint

1 Halve each pomegranate across its width. Hold each half seed side down and tap gently all the way round the skin with the handle of a large knife. This loosens the seeds inside. Now peel the pomegranates like an orange, removing the white pith and skin next to the seeds. Collect all the seeds in a large bowl. Reserve a few seeds for decoration and purée the remainder in a blender. Strain the seed purée into a large bowl, pushing through with a spoon in order to extract as much juice as possible. You should have 1.2 litres/2 pints/5 cups.

2 Put the sugar, water and cinnamon into a saucepan and bring to the boil, then simmer gently for 6–8 minutes. When cool, mix the syrup, lime juice, grenadine, nutmeg and pomegranate juice together.

3 Remove the cinnamon sticks and pour the mixture into an ice cream box or other suitable freezer container. Chill for 3–4 hours or overnight then place in the coldest part of the freezer for about 2 hours. Remove, whisk with an electric hand whisk or balloon whisk and return to the freezer for a further 2 hours and whisk again. Place the container back in the freezer for 3–4 hours or overnight before serving. Serve decorated with the reserved seeds and sprigs of fresh mint.

Spiced Oranges with Grenadine

Preparation time: 20–25 minutes   **Serves 4**

Fresh oranges with grenadine look fabulous and taste special. You can use canned mandarin oranges to save time, but they will need to be drained. Save a little of the syrup to use as suggested for the fresh oranges here.

8–10 large oranges, such as navel
1 teaspoon ground cinnamon
4 dessertspoons grenadine
Sliced kiwi fruits, to garnish

1   Peel the oranges. Using a small, sharp knife, remove the white pith. Separate the segments, taking care to remove and discard the membrane.

2   Put the orange segments into a bowl and sprinkle with the ground cinnamon. Mix well.

3   Spoon the grenadine into 4 glass serving bowls or stemmed glasses. Lift the orange segments with a slotted spoon and pile on top of the grenadine, then carefully spoon over the juice left behind.

4   Top with kiwi fruit and serve.

Exotic Fruit Salad

Preparation time: 15 minutes

Serves 4–6

This fruit salad is served with Cointreau-laced crème fraîche, but it is also good with Greek yogurt mixed with icing (powdered) sugar to taste.

1 large ripe fresh mango

1 small ripe papaya (pawpaw)

1 × 425g/15oz can of lychees, drained

1 × 425g/15oz can of pineapple cubes in natural juices, drained

300ml/½ pint/1⅓ cups half-fat crème fraîche

Finely grated rind of 1 orange

2 tablespoons icing (powdered) sugar

2 tablespoons Cointreau

1 tablespoon orange juice

1 Peel the mango, slice off the flesh and chop into bite-sized pieces.

2 Cut the papaya (pawpaw) in half lengthways and remove the black seeds. Scrape off the white membrane under the seeds. Peel and chop the papaya into bite-sized pieces.

3 Arrange the fruits in layers in 4 individual glass serving dishes or stemmed glasses.

4 In a mixing bowl, mix together the crème fraîche with the remaining ingredients and top each serving dish with the mixture. Serve chilled if liked.

Spiced Fruit Salad

Preparation time: 25–30 minutes   **Serves 4**

This is a stunning combination of delicately spiced fruits. For a variation, use a fresh, ripe mango instead of papaya (pawpaw) and fresh lychees instead of grapes.

2 ripe pomegranates
1 large ripe papaya (pawpaw)
1 small or ½ medium pineapple
175g/6oz/1 cup seedless green
    grapes
175g/6oz/1 cup seedless black
    grapes
½ teaspoon ground dry ginger
¼ teaspoon freshly milled black
    pepper
½ teaspoon ground cumin
Pinch of chilli powder
¼ teaspoon dried mint or 6–8 fresh
    mint leaves, finely chopped
½ teaspoon salt

1   Cut the pomegranates into halves and remove the seeds by peeling off the outer skin as you would peel an orange. If you find this difficult, gently ease away the seeds with a fork and discard the outer skin. Remove the white membrane and skin next to the seeds and reserve the seeds.

2   Cut the papaya (pawpaw) in half lengthways and remove the black seeds, scraping off the white membrane you will find under the seeds. Cut the papaya into 2.5cm/1-inch cubes.

3   Peel the pineapple and remove the 'eyes' with a small, sharp knife. Remove the central hard core and cut the pineapple into bite-sized pieces.

4   Halve the grapes and combine all the prepared fruits in a large mixing bowl. Add the remaining ingredients, except the salt, and mix thoroughly. Chill for 1–2 hours. Stir in the salt and serve.

Summer Fruits with Rose Cream

Preparation time: 15–20 minutes   **Serves 4**

You can use any combination of summer fruits here. A delicious rose-flavoured syrup, *Rooh Afza,* is used to flavour the crème fraîche and colour the cream a soft pink. It is also great for flavouring ice cream, yogurt and fromage frais. Diluted with water, the syrup makes a delicious summer drink served in tall glasses with crushed ice, known as the summer drink of the East. All Indian stores sell Rooh Afza, but other rose-flavoured drinks are also sold in supermarkets.

200g/7oz/1 cup peaches, stoned and sliced
150g/5oz/1 cup blackberries
150g/5oz/1 cup strawberries
170g/6oz/1 cup redcurrants
300ml/½ pint/1⅓ cups low-fat crème fraîche
5 tablespoons rose syrup (Rooh Afza)

1   Layer the fruits in four individual stemmed glasses.
2   Beat the crème fraîche and rose syrup together until well blended.
3   Pile the crème fraîche on top of the fruits and serve.

Summer Fruit Platter with Yogurt Dip

Preparation time: 15–20 minutes   **Serves 4**

These yogurt dips taste sensational with summer fruits. If you prefer, use plain fromage frais instead of yogurt.

350g/12oz/1½ cups low-fat Greek yogurt

2 tablespoons rose syrup (Rooh Afza)

50g/2oz/¼ cup ready-to-use chocolate sauce

680g/1½lb/3 cups mixed summer fruits such as strawberries, raspberries, peaches, mangoes

1 Divide the yogurt equally into two mixing bowls.

2 Add the rose syrup to one and the chocolate sauce to the other. Beat each mixture with a fork until smooth and well blended. Transfer to small serving bowls and chill.

3 Arrange the fruits on a large platter, place the bowls of yogurt dip in the centre and serve.

Rose-flavoured Yogurt Dessert with Summer Fruits

Preparation time: 5–6 minutes plus time for straining the yogurt   **Serves 6**

The much-loved southern Indian dessert, known as *shrikand,* is traditionally flavoured with saffron. Transform this into a spectacular summer dessert by replacing the saffron with rose syrup and mixing crushed blueberries into the yogurt. Serve garnished with bunches of fresh redcurrants and it is as pretty as a picture. The rose syrup gives the dessert a baby-pink background which shows off the blueberries and redcurrants exceptionally well.

3 × 425g/15oz cartons of
    wholemilk set yogurt
90g/3oz/⅓ cup caster
    (confectioner's) sugar
4 tablespoons Rooh Afza or other
    rose-flavoured syrup
225g/8oz/1¾ cups trimmed
    blueberries
125g/4oz/⅔ cup redcurrants,
    divided into small bunches

1   Line a colander or large sieve with a very fine, clean muslin cloth and pour the yogurt over it. Cover it loosely and place over a large bowl to collect the whey, which will separate from the yogurt. Leave in the fridge for 5–6 hours or overnight.

2   Next, remove the strained yogurt from the cloth and put into a food processor with the remaining ingredients, except the blueberries and redcurrants. Blend until smooth. Add the blueberries and pulse the ingredients in order to crush the fruits. Transfer to a serving bowl and arrange the bunches of redcurrants on top. Serve chilled.

Chapter 10

High Days and Holidays

The recipes in this section are for those occasions when you feel in the mood to indulge yourself a little! While it is important to make sure that everyday meals are nutritionally balanced and healthy, everyone deserves a treat now and again.

I have divided this chapter into three sections: first courses, savoury dishes and desserts. In the first category you will find such classics as Spiced Onion Fritters *(bhajiyas) (page 199)* and Cauliflower Fritters *(pakoras) (page 197)*. The Savoury Dishes section has Bombay Potato served with soft baps *(page 211)* and do-piaza with hard-boiled (hard-cooked) eggs *(page 214)*. Desserts include Goan Coconut Pancakes *(page 244)*, Sweet Samosas *(page 252)* and an irresistible White Chocolate Kulfi with Passion Fruit Sauce *(page 251)*!

Recipes from this chapter should be regarded as occasional treats by anyone following a low-fat diet. On the other hand, you may like to cook some of these recipes for family and friends.

Cauliflower Fritters

Preparation time: 15 minutes
Cooking time: 15–20 minutes

Serves 8–10

Fritters using raw vegetables are known as *pakoras* and are very popular all over India. Chickpea flour (besan) is the key ingredient in making fritters. Its nutty taste gives them an earthy character. They are generally spiced in different ways, according to regional variations.

1 cauliflower (about 370g/13oz
    when outer leaves removed)
1 medium onion, roughly chopped
1cm/½-inch cube root ginger,
    peeled and roughly chopped
4 cloves garlic, peeled and roughly
    chopped
2 green chilli peppers, seeded
15g/½oz/¼ cup coriander (cilantro)
    leaves including the tender
    stalks, roughly chopped
140ml/5fl oz/⅔ cup water
200g/7oz/1½ cups chickpea flour
    (besan), sieved
90g/3oz/½ cup ground rice
1¼ teaspoons salt or to taste
½ teaspoon chilli powder (optional)
½ teaspoon ground turmeric
90ml/3fl oz/⅓ cup water
Oil for deep frying

1. Divide the cauliflower into 2.5cm/1-inch florets.
2. Put the onion, ginger, garlic, fresh chilli peppers and coriander (cilantro) leaves in a blender, add the first measure of water and blend until smooth.
3. In a large mixing bowl, combine the sieved chickpea flour, ground rice, salt, chilli powder (if used) and turmeric. Add the blended ingredients and the remaining water and mix until you have a thick batter.
4. Heat the oil in a wok or other pan suitable for deep frying over a medium heat. The temperature of the oil should be about 170°C. Drop a tiny amount of the batter, about the size of a lemon pip, into the oil. If it surfaces immediately without browning, then the oil is at the right temperature.
5. Increase the heat slightly and dip each cauliflower floret in the batter, making sure it is fully coated. Fry as many fritters as you can in a single layer without overcrowding the pan. Each batch will take 6–7 minutes to brown. Turn them over once or twice. Drain on absorbent paper.

Aubergine Fritters

Preparation time: 25 minutes
Cooking time: 20–25 minutes

Serves 4

I do not find it necessary to soak the aubergine (eggplant) in salted water before cooking. This is traditionally done to remove any bitterness from the skin, but modern cultivation methods have eliminated this problem. However, you do need to soak it in order to prevent discolouring, and this can be done for just as long as it takes you to get the other ingredients ready.

2 aubergines (eggplants) (approx. 450g/1lb)
1 teaspoon salt or to taste
1 teaspoon cumin seeds
1 teaspoon onion seeds
½ teaspoon aniseeds
1–2 green chilli peppers, finely chopped
175g/5oz/1½ cups chickpea flour (besan)
90g/3oz/½ cup fine cornmeal (polenta)
Oil for deep frying
2 tablespoons chopped coriander (cilantro) leaves
1 tablespoon chopped mint leaves
1½ tablespoons bought chilli sauce

1   Slice the aubergines (eggplants) into 5mm/¼-inch rounds, soak in salted water and set aside until you are ready, then drain, rinse and pat dry.

2   Combine all the spices in a mixing bowl and sieve the chickpea flour over them. Add the cornmeal and mix well. Gradually add 250ml/9fl oz/1¼ cups cold water and mix until you have a batter of coating consistency.

3   Start heating the oil in a deep frying pan or wok over a medium-high heat. Meanwhile, mix the coriander (cilantro) and mint leaves with the chilli sauce and ¼ teaspoon salt. Spread about ¼ teaspoon of this mixture on a slice of aubergine and cover with another slice to make a sandwich. Dip the sandwich in the spiced batter, making sure it is fully coated and held firmly together. Put as many sandwiches as you can accommodate in the oil without overcrowding the pan. Fry until crisp and golden brown (4–5 minutes). Drain on absorbent paper and serve immediately, garnished with mixed salad leaves and accompanied by a chutney.

Spiced Onion Fritters

Preparation time: 15–20 minutes
Cooking time: 25–30 minutes

Makes 18

Spiced Onion Fritters *(bhajiyas)* are an ever-popular snack. You will find that the home-made version is quite different from those you may have eaten elsewhere.

150g/5oz/1¼ cups chickpea flour
  (besan), sieved
50g/2oz/⅓ cup ground rice
¼ teaspoon bicarbonate of soda
  (baking soda)
1 teaspoon onion seeds (kalonji)
1 teaspoon cumin seeds
2 teaspoons ground coriander
  (cilantro)
1 teaspoon ground turmeric
½ teaspoon crushed dried chilli
  peppers
2 green chilli peppers, chopped
1 teaspoon salt or to taste
15g/½oz fresh coriander (cilantro),
  chopped
350g/12oz/3 cups onions,
  shredded
Oil for deep frying

1 In a large mixing bowl, combine the chickpea flour, ground rice and soda. Add the remaining ingredients except the fresh coriander (cilantro), onions and oil. Mix thoroughly.

2 Add the coriander and onions and gradually pour in 170ml/6fl oz/¾ cup cold water. Mix until the flour and spices coat the onions. The batter should lightly bind the onions so that you can pick up small portions with your fingers.

3 Heat the oil in a deep-fat fryer or wok over a medium heat. Check that the temperature is correct by dropping a tiny portion of the batter, the size of a lemon pip, into the hot oil. If it floats immediately to the surface without browning, then the oil is just right.

4 Pick up small portions of the onion mixture, roughly the size of a golf ball, and flatten them slightly so they are not too compact. You will find using your fingers will work better, but using two spoons, one to pick up the mixture and the other to push it into the pan, is also an easy way. Fry in the hot oil in a single layer until well browned all over (8–9 minutes). Do make sure that the temperature of the oil is constant throughout. Drain on absorbent paper and serve.

Spicy Potato Fritters

Preparation time: 25–30 minutes
Cooking time: 20 minutes

Serves 4

Use floury potatoes for these fritters. They are delicious served as a side dish or as delightful morsels to accompany drinks.

450g/1lb potatoes
2 tablespoons sunflower or
    vegetable oil
½ teaspoon cumin seeds
1 medium onion, finely chopped
1 green chilli pepper, seeded and
    chopped
2 teaspoons fresh ginger, grated
¼ teaspoon ground turmeric
2 tablespoons fresh coriander
    (cilantro), finely chopped
1 teaspoon salt or to taste
2 tablespoons cornflour
    (cornstarch)
1 large (extra large) egg
Oil for deep frying

1 Peel and cut the potatoes into small pieces and boil with plenty of salted water until tender, but not mushy. Leave to drain and dry in a colander, then mash lightly.

2 In a small saucepan, heat the oil over a medium heat and add the cumin seeds. As soon as they splutter, add the onion, green chilli pepper and ginger. Fry for 3–4 minutes until the onion is soft.

3 Stir in the turmeric, coriander (cilantro) leaves and salt, remove from the heat and add the mashed potatoes, cornflour (cornstarch) and egg. Stir until all the ingredients are well blended.

4 In a wok or other suitable pan, heat the oil for deep frying over a medium-high heat. The temperature of the oil should be about 170°C. Drop a tiny amount of the potato mixture (the size of a lemon pip) into the oil to test the temperature. If the potato mixture starts sizzling and floats to the top immediately, then the oil is at the right temperature.

5 Pick up 1 tablespoon of the potato mixture and, with another spoon, make a rough croquette shape, then gently push it into the hot oil. Fry as many as the pan will hold in a single layer without overcrowding the pan. Too many fritters in the pan will lower the temperature of the oil, causing them to break up, so watch it! Fry until well browned (5–6 minutes) and drain on absorbent paper.

Sweet Potato Fritters

Preparation time: 20 minutes
Cooking time: 20–25 minutes

Serves 4–6

Sweet potatoes are available in most Asian stores as well as good supermarkets. They can be peeled just like ordinary potatoes. Cooked in a spicy batter, they produce a wonderful contrast of flavours and textures.

450g/1lb/3 cups sweet potatoes
175g/6oz/1 cup chickpea flour (besan), sieved
90g/3oz/⅓ cup ground rice or cornmeal
1 teaspoon salt or to taste
1 teaspoon carum seeds (ajowan)
½–1 teaspoon crushed dried chilli peppers
1 teaspoon ground turmeric
1 tablespoon ground cumin
15g/½oz/¼ cup fresh coriander (cilantro) leaves, including tender stalks, finely chopped
300ml/½ pint/1⅓ cups water
Oil for deep frying

1 Peel the sweet potatoes. Working from both ends, cut as many 5mm/¼-inch slices as possible. When the diameter of the slices gets bigger, cut the potato in half lengthways, and slice each half as before. Cut exceptionally large slices into quarters. You will have a few uneven slices because of the varied sizes of sweet potatoes. Soak the sliced potatoes in salted water for 15 minutes, then drain and rinse.

2 Sift the flour into a medium-sized mixing bowl. Add the remaining ingredients except the coriander (cilantro), water and oil. Mix thoroughly with a wooden spoon, then add the coriander. Gradually add the water while you continue to mix. Make sure the batter is smooth. When all the water is added, you should have a smooth, thick batter.

3 Heat the oil in a wok or other deep frying pan over a medium heat. If you have a cooking thermometer, check that the temperature of the oil is 160°C–170°C. Alternatively, drop a small portion of the batter (about the size of a pea) into the oil. If it floats to the surface straight away without browning, then the temperature is right.

4 Dip each slice of potato in the batter, making sure it is fully coated, and shake any excess batter back into the bowl. Fry as many slices as you can manage in a single layer without overcrowding the pan. Cook until evenly browned on both sides, turning over at least twice. Each batch will take 5–6 minutes. Drain on absorbent paper. Serve with a relish as a starter or with drinks.

Bread Fritters

Preparation time: 10–15 minutes
Cooking time: 25–30 minutes

Serves 4

Here is an idea to liven up stale bread. Pakoras must be eaten hot to enjoy them at their best.

3 tablespoons chilli sauce

1 teaspoon mint sauce

1 tablespoon mango chutney,
    mashed to a pulp

6 large slices slightly stale white
    bread, crusts removed

125g/4oz/1 cup chickpea flour
    (besan)

2 green chilli peppers, chopped

2 tablespoons chopped coriander
    (cilantro) leaves

1 teaspoon aniseed

1½ teaspoons garam masala

½ teaspoon ground turmeric

¾ teaspoon salt or to taste

½ teaspoon chilli powder (optional)

Oil for deep frying

1   Mix the chilli sauce, mint sauce and mango chutney together and use as a spread to make 3 sandwiches with the bread. Cut each sandwich into 4 squares.

2   Mix the remaining ingredients, except the oil, in a bowl and gradually add 175ml/6fl oz/¾ cup cold water. Stir until you have a thick batter of coating consistency.

3   Heat the oil in a deep pan or wok over a medium heat. The temperature of the oil should be about 170°C. Test the temperature by dropping a tiny amount of the batter, about the size of a lemon pip, into the oil. If it floats quickly to the surface without browning, then the temperature is just right.

4   Dip each sandwich square into the batter. Make sure they are well coated all over, including the edges. Fry in the hot oil until crisp and well browned. Drain on absorbent paper and serve.

Cumin and Nutmeg-flavoured Vegetable Soup

Preparation time: 10 minutes
Cooking time: 40 minutes

Serves 4

This wonderfully satisfying soup is also quick to make. Serve it with any snack in this section.

⌘⌘⌘⌘⌘⌘⌘⌘⌘⌘⌘⌘

50g/2oz/¼ cup butter

4–5 shallots, finely chopped

2 large cloves garlic

½–1 teaspoon salt or to taste

125g/4oz/1 cup potatoes, finely chopped

125g/4oz/1 cup carrots, finely chopped

125g/4oz/1 cup green beans, finely chopped

450ml/16fl oz/2 cups hot water

2 vegetable stock cubes

125g/4oz/1 cup frozen or canned (drained) sweetcorn kernels

300ml/10fl oz/1⅓ cups milk

1 teaspoon ground cumin

½ teaspoon ground nutmeg

½ teaspoon freshly milled black pepper

1 tablespoon cornflower (cornstarch), blended with a little water

125ml/4fl oz/½ cup double (heavy) cream

1   Reserve 1 tablespoon of the butter. Melt the remainder gently over a medium-low heat and fry the shallots for 2–3 minutes.

2   Meanwhile, crush the garlic cloves with a pestle or the back of a wooden spoon. Discard the skin and crush the cloves with the salt to a fine pulp. Add this to the shallots and fry for 2–3 minutes.

3   Add the potatoes, carrots and beans. Fry for 2–3 minutes and add the water and crumbled stock cubes. Bring to the boil, cover and reduce the heat to low. Cook for 15 minutes.

4   Add the sweetcorn and milk. Bring back to the boil, reduce the heat, re-cover and simmer for 5 minutes.

5   Melt the reserved butter in a small saucepan over a low heat. When it stops sizzling, stir in the cumin, nutmeg and pepper. Let them sizzle gently for 15–20 seconds then stir into the soup.

6   Add the blended cornflour (cornstarch) and cream. Simmer for 1–2 minutes, remove from the heat and serve sprinkled with more freshly milled black pepper, if liked.

Vermicelli and Vegetable Soup

Preparation time: 20–25 minutes
Cooking time: 35 minutes

Serves 4

This is a filling soup with delicate spicing. Serve with any snack in this section or just a hot roll and butter if you prefer.

40g/1½oz/1 cup plain vermicelli
50g/2oz/¼ cup butter
2 cloves garlic, peeled and chopped
½ teaspoon salt or to taste
1 medium onion, finely chopped
90g/3oz/½ cup carrots, cut into
 bite-sized cubes
150g/5oz/1 cup potatoes, cut into
 bite-sized cubes
50g/2oz/½ cup frozen garden peas
50g/2oz/½ cup frozen or canned,
 drained sweetcorn
300ml/10fl oz/1⅓ cups milk
140ml/5fl oz/⅔ cup single (half
 and half) cream
1½ tablespoons cornflour
 (cornstarch), blended with a
 little water
1½ teaspoons ground cumin
½ teaspoon ground coriander
 (cilantro)
½ teaspoon crushed black pepper
1 tablespoon fresh coriander
 (cilantro), finely chopped

1 Break up the clusters of vermicelli and put them in a pan of boiling water. Boil for 1 minute and drain. Rinse thoroughly in cold water and leave to drain.

2 Reserve 2 tablespoons butter and melt the remainder gently. Crush the garlic to a smooth pulp with the salt and fry with the onion for 4–5 minutes or until the onion is soft.

3 Add the carrots and potatoes and fry for 3–4 minutes. Pour in 570ml/1 pint/2½ cups hot water. Bring to the boil, reduce the heat to low, cover and simmer for 10 minutes.

4 Add the peas, sweetcorn and milk. Bring back to the boil, reduce the heat to medium and cook, uncovered, for 5 minutes.

5 Add the cream, vermicelli and blended cornflour (cornstarch). Cook for a further 3–4 minutes.

6 Meanwhile, melt the remaining butter over a medium heat. When the foam subsides, take the pan off the heat and add the spices. Let them sizzle gently for 15–20 seconds then pour the spiced butter over the soup. Stir and cook for 1–2 minutes, add the coriander (cilantro) leaves, remove from the heat and serve.

Pomegranate Soup

Preparation time: 20–25 minutes
Cooking time: 10–12 minutes

Serves 4

This soup has a rich but delicate flavour. The emerald-green colour comes from fresh spinach leaves and the jewel-like, ruby-red pomegranate seeds look quite stunning.

2 pomegranates
1 tablespoon butter
1 small onion, finely chopped
2 teaspoons fresh ginger, finely
    chopped
20 spinach leaves
½ teaspoon ground cumin
Salt and pepper to taste
4 tablespoons double (heavy) cream
2 tablespoons lightly whipped
    cream, to garnish

1   Cut each pomegranate in half. Hold one half cut-side down and tap it all the way round with the handle of a knife or other similar object. This will loosen the seeds and make it easier to remove them. Once you have removed all the seeds, discard any white membrane clinging to the seeds.

2   Melt the butter gently over a low heat and fry the onion and ginger until the onion is soft, but not brown.

3   Reserve one tablespoon of pomegranate seeds and add the rest to the onions, followed by the spinach and cumin. Pour in 450ml/16fl oz/2 cups warm water. Bring to the boil, reduce the heat to low, cover and cook for 5–6 minutes. Remove from the heat, cool slightly then purée the ingredients in a blender. Season with salt and plenty of freshly milled black pepper.

4   Put the soup into individual serving bowls, float a little whipped cream into each bowl and top with the reserved pomegranate seeds.

Indian Cheese Kebab

Preparation time: 20 minutes plus marinating
Cooking time: 8–10 minutes   Serves 4

The only Indian semi-hard cheese, known as *paneer,* is packed with protein and essential nutrients. On its own it has no flavour, but it does absorb spices extremely well. In this vegetarian version of the famous kebab, the cubes of paneer have a light and delicate aroma with a complex but well-balanced taste. Paneer is available in larger supermarkets and Indian stores. Cyprus halloumi cheese is a good substitute.

225g/8oz paneer, cut into 2.5cm
   (1-inch) cubes
1 tablespoon lemon juice
½ teaspoon salt or to taste
90g/3oz set wholemilk plain
   yogurt
4 large cloves garlic, chopped
2.5cm/½-inch cube root ginger,
   chopped
½ teaspoon carum seeds (ajowan)
½–1 teaspoon chilli powder
½ teaspoon ground turmeric
1 tablespoon chickpea flour (besan)
3 tablespoons sunflower or plain oil

1 Put the paneer in a saucepan and add plenty of hot water. Place the pan over a high heat and bring to the boil. As soon as the paneer begins to float, drain into a colander and leave to dry. This exercise prepares the paneer to absorb all the flavours of the spices.

2 Mix the remaining ingredients well in a large mixing bowl and add the cubed paneer *(tikkas)*. Stir until the tikkas are fully coated, cover and refrigerate for 3–4 hours or overnight, but bring to room temperature before cooking.

3 Preheat the grill (broiler) to high and line a grill pan with foil (remove the grid). Brush the foil and 4 skewers with some oil. Thread the marinated tikkas onto the skewers, shaking any excess marinade back into the bowl. Grill (broil) the prepared tikkas 7.5cm/3 inches away from the heat source for 4–5 minutes. Turn the skewers over, baste with the extra marinade and grill for 2–3 minutes or until slightly charred. Serve as a starter with a salad or as a snack with Minted Yogurt and Coriander Sauce *(page 40)* or Mint and Onion Chutney *(page 37)*.

Batter-fried Spiced Yam Slices

Preparation time: 15 minutes plus 30 minutes to soak the yam
Cooking time: 12–15 minutes

Serves 6–8

Suran or yam is also known as elephant yam and its use in Indian cooking dates back to Aryan times. If you have not cooked or eaten yam before, try this delicious, spicy recipe. You can buy yam in good supermarkets and Asian stores.

900g/2lb yam
1 teaspoon salt or to taste
1 teaspoon ground turmeric
1–1¼ teaspoons chilli powder
1 teaspoon carum seeds (ajowan)
25g/1oz chickpea flour (besan), sifted
1 heaped tablespoon ground rice
Oil for deep frying

1   Peel the yam and cut into 5mm/¼-inch slices. As yam has rather thin ends and is quite thick in the middle, cut the bigger slices in half. Soak the slices in cold water for 30 minutes, then drain but do not dry them.

2   Put the salt, turmeric, chilli powder, carum seeds, flour and ground rice in a large bowl and mix well. Add the yam slices and mix until fully coated with the spiced flour.

3   Heat the oil for deep frying in a wok or other suitable pan over a medium-high heat. Fry the yam slices in batches in a single layer for 3–4 minutes or until crisp and golden brown. Drain on absorbent paper. Serve with drinks or as a starter with a chutney.

Batter-fried Spiced Spinach Leaves

Preparation time: 15 minutes
Cooking time: 6–8 minutes

Serves 4

These large, crunchy spinach leaves have the distinctive nutty flavour of chickpea flour and are spiced with cumin seeds, onion seeds and chilli peppers. They go down a treat with a drink or any soup.

12 large spinach leaves
90g/3oz/¾ cup chickpea flour (besan)
40g/1½oz/¼ cup fine cornmeal (polenta)
½ teaspoon ground turmeric
½ teaspoon chilli powder
1 teaspoon cumin seeds
1 teaspoon onion seeds (kalonji)
½ teaspoon salt or to taste
170ml/6fl oz/⅔ cup water
Oil for deep frying

1   Wash spinach leaves carefully without damaging them, leaving the stalks intact. Dry thoroughly on absorbent paper.

2   Sieve the chickpea flour (besan) into a large mixing bowl and add the rest of the ingredients, except the water and oil. Mix the dry ingredients well and gradually add the water; continue to mix until you have a thick batter of coating consistency.

3   Heat the oil in a wok or other suitable pan over a medium-high heat. It is important that the oil is at the right temperature. If you have a cooking thermometer, make sure that the oil is at least 180°C. Otherwise, drop a tiny amount of batter in the hot oil. If it floats immediately without browning, then the oil is at the right temperature.

4   Hold each spinach leaf by its stem and dip it in the batter, making sure it is fully coated. The stem should also be coated lightly. Depending on the size of the pan, fry 2–3 leaves at a time until golden brown and crisp (approx. 1½ minutes). Drain on absorbent paper and serve immediately with a dip, if liked.

Deep-fried Spinach Balls

Preparation time: 15–20 minutes
Cooking time: 20–25 minutes

Makes 24

I am always surprised when people dismiss spinach as uninteresting and tasteless. For me, spinach is a wonderful vegetable, offering complete flexibility in the way it can be cooked. Even if you are generally not interested in spinach, just try this recipe once and you'll love it! For a variation, use fenugreek instead of spinach.

This recipe is suitable for freezing. Thaw and reheat under a preheated medium grill (broiler) for 5–6 minutes, turning over halfway through. Place the grill 15–25cm/6–10 inches away from heat.

150g/5oz/1 cup chickpea flour (besan), sieved
50g/2oz/⅓ cup ground rice
1 teaspoon salt or to taste
¼–½ teaspoon chilli powder (optional)
1 teaspoon ground cumin
2 teaspoons ground coriander (cilantro)
1 teaspoon ground turmeric
1 teaspoon fennel seeds
1–2 green chilli peppers, seeded and finely chopped
150g/5oz/2½ cups spinach leaves, finely chopped
150g/5oz/1¼ cups onions, chopped
140ml/¼ pint/⅔ cup water
Oil for deep frying

1 Sift the flour into a large mixing bowl and add the remaining ingredients, except the water and oil.

2 Mix the ingredients together, then gradually add the water until you have a thick, paste-like consistency. Divide the mixture into 4 equal parts and make 6 walnut-sized balls from each part.

3 Heat the oil in a wok or pan over a medium heat. Check the temperature with a cooking thermometer, if you have one, and ensure it is 160°C–170°C. If you do not have a thermometer, take a tiny amount of the paste (about the size of a pea) without the vegetables, and drop it in the oil. If it surfaces immediately without browning, then the temperature is just right.

4 Fry the spinach balls in a single layer in batches for 8–10 minutes, turning over occasionally. Drain on absorbent paper. Serve as a starter with a chutney or with drinks.

Nutty Potato Nuggets

Preparation time: 30 minutes
Cooking time: 15 minutes

Makes 20

These lightly spiced morsels are delicious hot or cold. You can serve them for a buffet party or as a starter with a small salad and a chutney. Floury potatoes work best for this recipe.

1 tablespoon sunflower or olive oil
½ teaspoon black mustard seeds
1 red onion, finely chopped
2 cloves garlic, crushed
1–2 fresh green chilli peppers, seeded and finely chopped
3 tablespoons finely chopped coriander (cilantro) leaves
1 teaspoon salt or to taste
½ teaspoon chilli powder or to taste
2 tablespoons mixed nuts such as cashews, almonds and pistachios, chopped
2 tablespoons sunflower seeds, lightly crushed
1 tablespoon lemon juice
450g/1lb potatoes, boiled in their jackets, peeled and roughly mashed
1 tablespoon plain (all-purpose) flour
1 tablespoon milk
1 medium egg
125g/4oz/½ cup fresh white breadcrumbs
Olive oil for deep frying

1   Heat the first measure of oil in a small non-stick pan or wok over a medium heat and add the mustard seeds. As soon as they pop, add the onion, garlic and chilli. Fry until the onion is just soft, then stir in the coriander (cilantro) leaves, salt, chilli powder, nuts and sunflower seeds. Stir-fry the ingredients for about 30 seconds, mix in the lemon juice and remove from the heat.

2   Put the potatoes in a large mixing bowl and add the onion mixture. Mix thoroughly and divide into two equal portions. Make 10 equal-sized nuggets out of each portion and dust each nugget lightly in the flour.

3   Beat the milk and egg together. Dip the nuggets in this mixture then roll them in the breadcrumbs.

4   Heat the oil in a wok over a medium-high heat and fry the nuggets in batches until crisp and golden brown. Drain on absorbent paper.

Savoury Dishes

Bombay Potato

Preparation time: 20–25 minutes
Cooking time: 30 minutes

Serves 4

Bombay Potato, as a dish, does not exist in India! Since it is such a popular dish in Britain, I have teamed it with soft rolls, fried in butter, to create a dish similar to the famous Bombay street snack known as *pao-bhaji*. The Bombay version also has vegetables added to the potatoes. Pao (bread) bhaji (dry-spiced vegetables) is a delicious snack for which a special spice mix *(pao-bhaji masala)* is available in Indian stores. You can, however, cook this delicious potato dish using the following ingredients.

4 tablespoons sunflower or plain olive oil
½ teaspoon black mustard seeds
1 teaspoon cumin seeds
1 large onion, finely chopped
2.5cm/1-inch cube root ginger, peeled and grated
4 large cloves garlic, crushed
150g/5oz/¾ cup chopped canned tomatoes, including juice
1–1½ teaspoons chilli powder
680g/1½lb/4½ cups potatoes, cut into 2.5cm/1-inch dice
1 teaspoon salt or to taste
2 tablespoons coriander (cilantro) leaves, chopped
1 teaspoon garam masala

1 Heat the oil over a medium heat. When the oil is quite hot, but not smoking, add the mustard seeds, followed by the cumin.

2 Add the onion and fry for 3–4 minutes, stirring frequently.

3 Add the ginger and garlic; continue to fry for a further 3–4 minutes.

4 Add the tomatoes and chilli powder; cook for 2–3 minutes.

5 Add the potatoes, salt and 450ml/15fl oz/2¼ cups hot water. Bring to the boil, reduce the heat to low, cover and cook for 12–15 minutes or until the potatoes are tender. The mixture should have quite a mushy consistency.

6 Stir in the coriander (cilantro) leaves and garam masala, remove from the heat and serve with soft rolls, split and lightly fried in butter. The amount of butter you use depends on how you feel about your waistline. From what I have seen, they don't worry about it in Bombay! This dish also tastes wonderful with naan or chapattis accompanied by a lentil or chickpea (garbanzo) dish.

Broccoli with Eggs

Preparation time: 15 minutes

Cooking time: 10–12 minutes

Serves 4

Broccoli is a good source of iron, betacarotene and vitamin C. This simple, nutritious and visually appealing dish takes only about 10 minutes to cook.

3 tablespoons sunflower or plain olive oil

1 large red onion, finely sliced

2 fresh red chilli peppers, sliced (seeded if wished)

½ teaspoon ground turmeric

1 teaspoon ground cumin

400g/14oz/3½ cups broccoli florets (approx. 5cm/2 inches)

1 teaspoon salt or to taste

4 large (extra large) eggs, beaten

1   Heat the oil over a medium heat and fry the onion and chilli peppers for 3–4 minutes, stirring frequently.

2   Add the turmeric and cumin and fry for 30 seconds.

3   Add the broccoli and salt, increase the heat to high and stir-fry for 2–3 minutes or until the broccoli has brown patches. Reduce the heat to low, cover the pan and cook for 5 minutes.

4   Pour the beaten eggs all over the pan and the broccoli. Stir until the eggs coat the broccoli, remove from the heat and serve with chapattis or parathas, or with boiled basmati rice and a lentil dish.

Egg Cutlets

Preparation time: 25 minutes
Cooking time: 25 minutes

Makes 12

You will need pre-boiled potatoes for this recipe. While you are boiling the eggs, you can cut the potatoes into small pieces and pop them in the microwave or cook them on the stove top. Leave the cooked potatoes in a colander to drain.

6 hard-boiled (hard-cooked) eggs
350g/12oz/2½ cups potatoes, diced, boiled and mashed
3 tablespoons sunflower or plain olive oil
1 medium onion, finely chopped
2.5cm/1-inch cube root ginger, peeled and grated
2 green chilli peppers, finely chopped (seeded if liked)
½ teaspoon ground turmeric
½ teaspoon chilli powder or to taste
½ teaspoon garam masala
15g/½oz coriander (cilantro) leaves, chopped
1 teaspoon salt or to taste
2 tablespoons plain (all purpose) flour
1 large (extra large) egg, beaten
90g/3oz/1½ cups fresh soft breadcrumbs
Oil for deep frying

1 Shell the eggs and halve them. Scoop out the yolks and mash them. Chop the whites finely and mix the egg yolks and whites with the mashed potatoes.

2 Heat the oil over a medium heat and fry the onion, ginger and chilli peppers until the onion is soft, but not brown.

3 Add the spices, fresh coriander (cilantro) and salt. Stir and cook for a minute or two, remove from the heat and add to the potato and egg mixture. Mix until the ingredients are well incorporated.

4 Divide the mixture into 12 equal-sized portions and form into oval-shaped flat cutlets approximately 2.5cm/½-inch thick. Dust in flour and dip in beaten egg, then roll in breadcrumbs. Fry in hot oil until crisp and golden brown. Drain on absorbent paper. Serve with Coriander and Coconut Chutney *(page 36)* and any bread.

Egg Do-Piaza

Preparation time: 30 minutes
Cooking time: 50–55 minutes

Serves 4

A favourite recipe from north and north-east India, Egg Do-Piaza is delicious with boiled basmati rice or naan. If you don't mind missing the distinctive flavour of chickpea flour (besan), use plain flour to coat the eggs.

4 hard-boiled (hard-cooked) eggs
Sunflower oil for shallow frying
1 large onion, finely sliced
2 tablespoons chickpea flour
    (besan), sieved
1 large (extra large) egg, beaten
1 teaspoon salt or to taste
½ teaspoon chilli powder
½ teaspoon ground turmeric
1 teaspoon ground cumin
1 teaspoon ground coriander
    (cilantro)
1 tablespoon ghee or unsalted
    butter
2.5cm/1-inch piece cinnamon stick,
    halved
4 green cardamom pods, bruised
225g/8oz/1 cup chopped canned
    tomatoes, including the juice
125g/4oz frozen garden peas
½ teaspoon garam masala
2–3 tablespoons coriander
    (cilantro) leaves, chopped

1   Shell the eggs and halve them lengthways.

2   Heat the oil for shallow frying to cover the base of the pan to a depth of about 2.5cm/1 inch. Fry the onion over a medium heat until well browned (10–12 minutes) and drain on absorbent paper.

3   Meanwhile, put the chickpea flour into a bowl and add a little water to make a smooth, thick paste. Add the beaten egg, a little at a time, while you beat the mixture with a fork. Beat in ¼ teaspoon each of the salt, turmeric, chilli powder, cumin and coriander (cilantro).

4   When the onion has been removed from the pan, dip each egg half in the spiced batter and fry over a medium heat until browned all over. Drain on absorbent paper.

5   In a separate pan, melt the butter over a low heat and add the cinnamon and cardamom. Let them sizzle for 15–20 seconds and add the remaining turmeric, chilli, cumin and coriander. Fry gently for 1 minute and add half the tomatoes. Cook for a further 2–3 minutes and pour in 140ml/5fl oz/⅔ cup warm water. Add the reserved salt, the fried eggs and the peas. Stir gently, reduce the heat to low, cover the pan and cook for 5–6 minutes. Stir in the garam masala and coriander (cilantro) leaves and remove from the heat. Serve garnished with the fried onions, accompanied by any bread.

Indian Fried Eggs

Preparation time: 10–15 minutes
Cooking time: 6–8 minutes

Serves 4

Hard-boiled (hard-cooked) eggs, when sautéed and sprinkled with a touch of spices, make a wonderful snack or a satisfying light meal if served with hot crusty bread spread with a little butter, and a salad.

4 hard-boiled (hard-cooked) eggs
1 tablespoon sunflower or plain
    olive oil
½ teaspoon cumin seeds, crushed
½ teaspoon freshly milled black
    pepper
¼ teaspoon ground turmeric
Salt to taste
1 tablespoon coriander (cilantro)
    leaves, chopped

1   Shell the eggs and make 4–6 deep gashes lengthways on each. Set aside.

2   Heat the oil over a medium heat in a small non-stick frying pan (skillet) and add the crushed cumin seeds. Let them sizzle for 15–20 seconds and add the pepper, turmeric and salt. Reduce the heat to low and add the eggs; cook gently, turning the eggs around the pan until they form a light crust.

3   Stir in the coriander (cilantro) leaves, remove from the heat and serve.

South Indian Fried Eggs

Preparation time: 20–25 minutes
Cooking time: 25–30 minutes

Serves 4

This seriously delicious dish is based on a recipe known as 'Egg Roast', which I first came across in Kerala, southern India. The roast was, in fact, hard-boiled (hard-cooked) eggs, fried with spices until browned. I have added potatoes to my version here to make a more substantial dish.

⤜᧞᧞᧞᧞᧞᧞᧞᧞᧞᧞᧞᧞᧞᧞᧞᧞᧞᧞᧞⤛

4 hard-boiled (hard-cooked) eggs

5 tablespoons sunflower or soya oil

1 teaspoon cumin seeds

450g/1lb/3¼ cups potatoes, cut into slices 2.5cm/1-inch thick

½ teaspoon chilli powder

½ teaspoon ground turmeric

½ teaspoon salt or to taste

½ teaspoon freshly milled black pepper

1cm/½-inch cube root ginger, grated

2 cloves garlic, crushed

1 large onion, finely sliced

1 tablespoon extra oil

175g/6oz/1 cup fresh tomatoes, chopped

1–2 green chilli peppers, seeded and chopped

2 tablespoons fresh coriander (cilantro), chopped

1　Shell the eggs and make at least 6 deep gashes lengthways on each. Set aside.

2　Heat the oil over a medium heat in a large non-stick frying pan (skillet) and add the cumin seeds. Let them sizzle for 15–20 seconds and add the potatoes, half the chilli powder, half the turmeric and salt. Stir, cover and cook for 4–5 minutes, stirring halfway through. Re-cover and cook for a further 2–3 minutes or until the potatoes are tender and brown. Add the pepper, transfer to a heatproof dish and keep warm in a low oven.

3　In the remaining oil, fry the ginger and garlic for 1 minute and add the onion. Stir-fry for 8–9 minutes or until caramel brown. Reduce the heat slightly towards the end if necessary. Add salt to taste and spread the onions on top of the potatoes. Keep hot.

4　Add 1 tablespoon of oil to the pan and place over a medium heat. When the oil is hot, remove the pan from the heat and add the remaining chilli powder, turmeric and eggs. Return the pan to the heat and fry the eggs, stirring constantly, until evenly browned.

5　Add the tomatoes, chilli peppers and coriander (cilantro) leaves. Stir and cook gently for 2–3 minutes.

6　Season to taste and arrange on the potato and onion mixture. Serve with warmed chapattis or any dhal and boiled basmati rice.

Spicy Mushroom Omelette

Preparation time: 10–15 minutes
Cooking time: 10–15 minutes

Makes 2

Besides being rich in protein, eggs are also a good source of vitamins and minerals. This omelette is wonderful served with diced new potatoes sautéed in a little butter with a couple of whole garlic cloves.

2 large (extra large) eggs
50g/2oz/¼ cup butter
1 medium onion, finely chopped
2 green chilli peppers, seeded and
    chopped
½ teaspoon ground turmeric
2 tablespoons coriander (cilantro)
    leaves, chopped
175g/6oz/2 cups closed-cup
    mushrooms, chopped
½ teaspoon salt or to taste

1   Preheat the grill (broiler) to medium.

2   Beat the eggs with 2 tablespoons of cold water and set aside.

3   Reserve about 2 teaspoons of butter and melt the remainder over a medium heat in an omelette pan. Fry the onion and chilli peppers until the onion is just beginning to brown.

4   Add the turmeric, stir and add the fresh coriander (cilantro), mushrooms and salt. Stir-fry for 3–4 minutes. Remove half the mushrooms and set aside.

5   Pour half the eggs all around the pan to cover the mushrooms completely. Reduce the heat to low and cook until the omelette is set (2–3 minutes), then place the pan under the preheated grill. Cook until the top is set and lightly browned. Fold and serve.

6   Return the reserved butter and mushrooms to the pan and make the second omelette the same way.

Mushroom-topped Crumpets

Preparation time: 15 minutes

Cooking time: 15 minutes

Serves 4

With their deliciously spiced topping, these crumpets make a quick and filling snack. Serve them with a bowl of soup for a quick meal.

⋙⋘ ⋙⋘ ⋙⋘ ⋙⋘ ⋙⋘ ⋙⋘ ⋙⋘ ⋙⋘ ⋙⋘

50g/2oz/¼ cup butter

1 small red onion, finely chopped

1–2 green chilli peppers, chopped

1 teaspoon ground cumin

175g/6oz/1 cup fresh tomatoes, chopped

2 tablespoons coriander (cilantro) leaves, chopped

175g/6oz/2 cups closed-cup mushrooms, chopped

Salt to taste

8 crumpets

90g/3oz/¾ cup Cheddar cheese, grated

1   Melt the butter over a medium heat and fry the onion and green chilli peppers until the onion is soft.

2   Add the cumin, tomatoes and fresh coriander (cilantro). Stir, then add the mushrooms and seasoning. Mix thoroughly and remove from the heat.

3   Place the crumpets upside down on a grill (broiler) pan and grill (broil) for a minute or two. Remove the pan from the grill and turn the crumpets over. Divide the mushroom mixture equally between the crumpets and top with the grated cheese. Grill until bubbling and golden brown.

Lentil and Spinach Cutlets

Preparation time: 10 minutes plus soaking time for the lentils
Cooking time: 20–25 minutes

Makes 12

This is a wonderful way to treat yourself when you have been generally following a low-fat diet. In fact, apart from the oil used for shallow frying, the remaining ingredients are low in fat and high in nutritional value.

125g/4oz/⅔ cup red split lentils
   (masoor dhal)
125g/4oz/⅔ cup yellow split lentils
   (channa dhal) or yellow split
   peas
1 green chilli pepper, chopped
2.5cm/1-inch cube root ginger,
   peeled and chopped
2 small garlic cloves, peeled and
   chopped
12–15 fresh mint leaves
1 red onion, finely chopped
1 teaspoon salt or to taste
225g/8oz/4 cups fresh spinach,
   finely chopped
Sunflower or olive oil for shallow
   frying

1 Wash both types of lentils and soak for 3–4 hours or overnight. Drain well.

2 Put the lentils, chilli pepper, ginger, garlic and mint in a food processor and blend until smooth. Turn the mixture into a large bowl, add the remaining ingredients except the oil and mix thoroughly.

3 Halve the mixture and make 6 cutlets out of each half.

4 Pour enough oil into a frying pan (skillet) to cover the base to a thickness of about 1cm/½ inch and heat over a medium heat. Fry the cutlets gently for 10–12 minutes, turning them over as they brown. Drain on absorbent paper. Serve with Pumpkin Raita *(page 20)* and Roasted New Potatoes with Spicy Sesame Seed Crust *(page 140)*.

Butterbeans in Creamed Butter Sauce

Preparation time: 20 minutes
Cooking time: 20 minutes   **Serves 4**

The buttery texture of the beans complements the sauce in which they are cooked, giving it an opulent taste and appearance. Traditionally, dried butterbeans are soaked and boiled until tender before cooking with any spices. Canned butterbeans, if drained and rinsed well, are a quick and easy alternative.

2–3 tablespoons sunflower or plain
    olive oil
1 red onion, finely chopped
4–5 cloves garlic, peeled and
    crushed to a fine pulp
1cm/½-inch cube root ginger,
    peeled and finely grated
2 green chilli peppers, chopped
    (seeded if liked)
2 teaspoons ground coriander
    (cilantro)
½ teaspoon ground cumin
½ teaspoon ground turmeric
½–1 teaspoon chilli powder or to
    taste
1 teaspoon salt or to taste
1 teaspoon sugar
125g/4oz/½ cup chopped canned
    tomatoes, including juice
1 tablespoon tomato purée (paste)
140ml/5fl oz/⅔ cup warm water
2 teaspoons dried fenugreek leaves
400g/14oz can butterbeans,
    drained and well rinsed
225g/8oz boiled potatoes, peeled
    and cut into 2.5cm/1-inch cubes
50g/2oz/¼ cup half-fat butter
140ml/5fl oz/⅔ cup half-fat single
    (half and half) cream
¼ teaspoon garam masala
1 tablespoon coriander (cilantro)
    leaves, finely chopped

1   Heat the oil over a medium heat and add the onion. Fry,
    stirring regularly, for 5–6 minutes or until the onion is soft,
    but not brown.

2   Add the garlic, ginger and chilli peppers and cook for 1
    minute then add the ground coriander (cilantro), cumin,
    turmeric, chilli powder, salt, sugar, tomatoes and tomato
    purée (paste). Stir and cook for 2–3 minutes.

3   Add the water and bring to the boil. Reduce the heat to low,
    cover the pan and simmer for 10–12 minutes. Remove from
    the heat and allow to cool slightly, then purée the
    ingredients until smooth.

4   Return the sauce to the heat and add the fenugreek leaves,
    butterbeans, potatoes, butter and cream. Cook gently over a
    low heat for 6–8 minutes.

5   Sprinkle over the garam masala and add the coriander
    (cilantro) leaves, stir and cook for 1–2 minutes and remove
    from the heat. Serve with boiled basmati rice and a salad.

Creamed Lentil Kebabs

Preparation time: 35–40 minutes plus time for soaking the lentils

Cooking time: 35 minutes   **Serves 4**

Yellow split peas can be used if you cannot get split lentils, although they do not have the wonderful nutty taste.

For the Kebabs:

125g/4oz/½ cup yellow split lentils (channa dhal)

125g/4oz/½ cup red split lentils (masoor dhal)

3 tablespoons coriander (cilantro) leaves and stalks, roughly chopped

1 fresh green chilli pepper, seeded and chopped

2.5cm/1-inch cube root ginger, peeled and roughly chopped

½ teaspoon salt or to taste

1 small onion, finely chopped

Oil for deep frying

1 tablespoon plain (all purpose) flour

For the sauce:

3–4 tablespoons sunflower or plain olive oil

1 large onion, roughly chopped

4 cloves garlic, peeled and chopped

1cm/½-inch cube root ginger, peeled and chopped

2 teaspoons ground coriander (cilantro)

½ teaspoon ground cumin

½ teaspoon chilli powder

½ teaspoon paprika

1 tablespoon tomato purée (paste)

90g/3oz/½ cup passata (Italian sieved tomatoes)

1 teaspoon salt or to taste

230ml/8fl oz/1 cup warm water

90ml/3fl oz/⅓ cup single (half and half) cream

¼ teaspoon garam masala

2 tablespoons coriander (cilantro) leaves, chopped

1 Wash the lentils in several changes of water. Soak for 2–3 hours and drain thoroughly.

2 Grind the lentils, coriander (cilantro) leaves, chilli pepper, ginger and salt in a food processor until you have a granular mix. Transfer the lentil mixture to a medium mixing bowl and add the onion. Mix well, cover and chill for 30 minutes.

3 Divide the mixture into 4 portions and make 5 equal sized flat cakes out of each (20 kebabs).

4 Heat the oil over a medium heat in a wok or other suitable pan. Roll each kebab in flour, making sure it is fully coated, and fry in batches until well browned. Each batch will take 10–12 minutes. Drain on absorbent paper.

5 To make the sauce, heat half the oil over a medium heat and add the onion, garlic and ginger. Fry for 4–5 minutes, remove from the pan and allow to cool slightly, then purée in a food processor or blender with 3–4 tablespoons water.

6 Add the remaining oil to the same pan and place over a low heat. Add the ground coriander (cilantro), cumin, chilli powder and paprika and let them bubble very gently for 1 minute.

7 Add the puréed ingredients and increase the heat to medium; stir-fry for 2 minutes and add the tomato purée (paste). Stir and cook for a further 2 minutes or until the oil floats on the surface, reducing the heat if necessary.

8 Add the passata, salt and water; cook for 3–4 minutes, stirring constantly.

9 Add the fried kebabs and cream; simmer, uncovered, for 2–3 minutes. Add the garam masala and coriander (cilantro) leaves; stir gently, taking care not to damage the kebabs. Cook for 1 minute, remove from the heat and serve with naan or boiled basmati rice.

Spicy Mushy Peas with Fried Rolls

Preparation time: 10 minutes
Cooking time: 10–15 minutes

Serves 4

Mushy peas are gorgeous when spiced up. The sweetness of the peas provides a perfectly balanced background for the spices used here. When served on lightly sautéed soft rolls, they make a delicious and filling snack.

2 tablespoons sunflower or plain olive oil

1 teaspoon cumin seeds

1cm/½-inch cube root ginger, peeled and grated

2 cloves garlic, crushed

1 green chilli pepper, chopped

½ teaspoon ground turmeric

¼ teaspoon chilli powder

2 tablespoons chopped coriander (cilantro) leaves

½ teaspoon salt or to taste

400g/14oz can mushy peas

200g/7oz can baked beans

8 soft rolls and butter, to serve

Lightly crushed fried or grilled pappadums, to serve

1 Heat the oil over a medium heat and throw in the cumin seeds. As soon as they start popping, add the ginger, garlic and green chilli pepper. Stir-fry until they brown a little.

2 Add the turmeric and chilli powder. Stir, then add the fresh coriander (cilantro), salt, peas and beans. Reduce the heat to low and cook gently until the peas and beans are heated through. Remove from the heat.

3 Split the rolls and butter them to your liking. Now fry them gently, buttered side down first, turning them over once or twice. Fry until the buttered side is browned and slightly crispy.

4 Top the browned side of the rolls with the mushy-pea mixture and sprinkle with the crushed pappadums. Eat immediately.

Pan-fried Carrot Cakes

Preparation time: 15–20 minutes
Cooking time: 30 minutes

Makes 10

As well as being rich in fibre and vitamin A, carrots are a good source of betacarotene, which is beneficial in fighting certain types of cancer.

175g/6oz/1 cup carrots, grated
1 small onion, finely chopped
2 green chilli peppers, chopped
15g/½oz coriander (cilantro) leaves, chopped
3 tablespoons plain (all purpose) flour
2 tablespoons semolina (cream of wheat)
2 large (extra large) eggs
90ml/3fl oz/⅓ cup milk
¾ teaspoon salt or to taste
¼–½ teaspoon chilli powder (optional)
Oil for shallow frying

1 In a mixing bowl, combine all the ingredients, up to and including the semolina.

2 Beat the eggs and milk together and add the salt and chilli powder (if using). Beat until well blended and gradually add to the carrot mixture. Mix until all the ingredients are incorporated.

3 Heat 2 teaspoons of oil in a non-stick omelette pan and add 1 heaped tablespoon of the carrot mixture. Let it spread gently into a cake 7.5cm/3 inches in diameter. If the pan is big enough, carry out this process for another cake simultaneously.

4 Cook the cakes until the undersides are well browned and turn them over. Cook for 2–3 minutes or until browned, reducing the heat if necessary. Keep the cooked cakes hot in a low oven in an open tray until you finish cooking all of them. Serve immediately.

Paneer Tikki

Preparation time: 10–15 minutes
Cooking time: 10 minutes

Makes 8

Paneer is a cheese widely used in Indian cooking for savoury as well as sweet dishes. An unripened cheese, its bland background absorbs any flavour that is added. Hard tofu or Cyprus halloumi cheese can be used as a substitute.

2 large slices white bread, a day or two old
225g/8oz/1 cup paneer, roughly chopped
15–20 fresh mint leaves, chopped or ½ teaspoon dried mint
2 tablespoons coriander (cilantro) leaves, chopped
1cm/½-inch cube root ginger, peeled and grated
25g/1oz/¼ cup flaked almonds, lightly crushed
1–2 green chilli peppers, chopped
1 teaspoon garam masala
½ teaspoon chilli powder (optional)
1 teaspoon salt or to taste
1 tablespoon lemon juice
1 large (extra large) egg, beaten
Oil for shallow frying

1 Soak the bread in water for a minute or two then squeeze out the liquid by crumbling the slices between your palms. Place in a large mixing bowl and add the remaining ingredients except the oil. Mix well to form a binding consistency.

2 Halve the mixture and make 4 equal-sized flat cakes of 5mm/¼-inch thickness out of each half.

3 Pour enough oil into a frying pan (skillet) to cover the base to a thickness of about 2.5cm/1 inch, and heat over a medium heat. Fry the tikkis until well browned on both sides. Drain on absorbent paper.

Indian Cheese with Roasted Peppers

Preparation time: 20–25 minutes
Cooking time: 15–20 minutes

Serves 4

Olive oil, roasted (bell) peppers and garlic, together with roasted cumin, add sensational taste and flavour to this quick and simple dish.

⁓⁓⁓⁓⁓⁓⁓⁓⁓⁓

1 large green (bell) pepper
1 large sweet red (bell) pepper
1½ teaspoons cumin seeds
2 tablespoons sunflower or plain olive oil
3–4 large cloves garlic, crushed
½ teaspoon chilli powder
¼ teaspoon salt or to taste
225g/8oz/1 cup paneer or Cyprus halloumi cheese, cut into 2.5cm/1-inch slices
2–3 tablespoons snipped chives

1   Roast the peppers either under a preheated hot grill (broiler) or over a naked flame on the hob until the skin is charred, turning them around frequently. Put them in a plastic bag and tie it up. Set aside for 20–25 minutes then scrape off the skin, de-seed them and remove the pith. Cut into 2.5cm/1-inch strips and reserve any accumulated juices.

2   Meanwhile, preheat a small, heavy pan over a medium heat. Add the cumin seeds and reduce the heat to low. Roast them gently, stirring, until they are just a shade darker. Transfer to a plate to prevent over-cooking and crush them when cool.

3   Heat the oil over a low heat in a frying pan (skillet) and fry the garlic gently until just beginning to brown.

4   Add the chilli powder, salt (remember to reduce the quantity of salt if you are using halloumi) and paneer or halloumi. Stir gently and cook for 2–3 minutes.

5   Add the crushed cumin and the prepared peppers. Stir until the peppers are heated through then stir in the chives. Serve with any bread or Tomato Pilau *(page 121)*.

Minted Indian Cheese in Chilli and Tomato Sauce

Preparation time: 20 minutes
Cooking time: 30–35 minutes

Serves 4

Indian cheese *(paneer)* is quite bland on its own, but it readily absorbs other flavours. In this recipe it has been given a fresh taste.

4 tablespoons sunflower or plain olive oil

1 large onion, finely chopped

2.5cm/1-inch cube root ginger, peeled and grated

4 large cloves garlic, crushed

2 teaspoons ground coriander (cilantro)

1 teaspoon ground cumin

½ teaspoon ground turmeric

225g/8oz/1 cup fresh tomatoes or canned, drained tomatoes, skinned and chopped

275g/10oz/2 cups potatoes, cut into 5cm/2-inch cubes

½–1 teaspoon salt

450g/1lb/2 cups paneer or Cyprus halloumi cheese, cut into 5cm/2-inch cubes

2 green chilli peppers, whole

1 green chilli pepper, seeded and sliced lengthways

1 teaspoon garam masala

1 tablespoon fresh mint leaves, chopped

1　Heat the oil over a medium heat and fry the onion, ginger and garlic until the onion is caramel brown (6–7 minutes). Stir frequently.

2　Add the coriander (cilantro), cumin and turmeric. Stir and cook for 1 minute.

3　Add the tomatoes, stir-fry for 3–4 minutes, reduce the heat slightly and continue to fry for a further 2–3 minutes.

4　Add the potatoes, salt (1 teaspoon with paneer, ½ teaspoon with halloumi) and 600ml/1 pint/2½ cups hot water. Bring to the boil, cover, reduce the heat to low and cook for 10 minutes.

5　Add the paneer or halloumi and all the green chilli peppers. Re-cover and cook for 10–15 minutes or until the potatoes are tender.

6　Add the garam masala and fresh mint, cook for a minute or two and remove from the heat. Serve with boiled basmati rice or warmed pitta or naan and a raita.

Stir-fried Indian Cheese

Preparation time: 10–15 minutes
Cooking time: 15 minutes

Serves 4

This quick and easy recipe provides plenty of protein for the vegetarian. For a sustaining meal, place the cheese mixture on one side of a hot chapatti and add chopped or sliced tomatoes, cucumber and crisp lettuce. Roll it up and serve with a soup. Alternatively, serve the cheese with a vegetable curry or a lentil dish and rice.

1 teaspoon cumin seeds

3 tablespoons sunflower or plain
    olive oil

1 large onion, finely chopped

1–2 green chilli peppers, chopped
    (seeded if wished)

¼ teaspoon ground turmeric

225g/8oz/1 cup grated paneer or
    Cyprus halloumi cheese

1 tablespoon natural yogurt,
    preferably thick

Salt, to taste

¼–½ teaspoon chilli powder

1 tablespoon fresh coriander
    (cilantro), chopped

Sliced tomatoes and sprigs of fresh
    coriander (cilantro), to serve

1 Preheat a small, heavy-based pan over a medium heat. Dry-roast the cumin seeds until they are a shade darker. Remove from the pan, cool and crush with a pestle or the back of a wooden spoon. Set aside.

2 Heat the oil over a medium-high heat in a non-stick frying pan (skillet) and fry the onion for 2 3 minutes. Reduce the heat to medium and continue to fry, stirring frequently, for a further 4–5 minutes or until the onion is lightly browned.

3 Add the chilli peppers and turmeric. Stir for 30 seconds and add the paneer or halloumi. Stir-fry for a minute or two and add the yogurt. Season with salt to taste (you may not need any salt with halloumi as it is already salted). Continue to stir-fry for 3–4 minutes.

4 Add the chilli powder and roasted cumin and stir. Add the coriander (cilantro) leaves, stir and remove from the heat. Arrange the sliced tomatoes in a serving dish to form a border and place the cheese in the middle. Garnish with sprigs of fresh coriander.

Spinach with Fried Indian Cheese

Preparation time: 25–30 minutes
Cooking time: 20 minutes

Serves 4

This is one of those all-in-one dishes that provide you with protein, carbohydrate, vitamins and minerals. For a variation, use frozen garden peas instead of spinach, thawing them first. Fresh peas are lovely and should be cooked before adding to the sauce. You can also use tofu instead of the paneer. This recipe is suitable for freezing (the texture of the cooked potatoes will change when thawed).

3 tablespoons sunflower or corn oil
225g/8oz/1 cup paneer, cubed
6 cloves garlic, peeled and crushed
1 small onion, very finely chopped
2.5cm/1-inch cube root ginger, peeled and finely grated
2 teaspoons ground coriander (cilantro)
½ teaspoon ground cumin
125g/4oz/½ cup canned chopped tomatoes, including juice
½ teaspoon ground turmeric
½ teaspoon paprika
¼–½ teaspoon chilli powder
150g/5oz/2½ cups spinach, finely chopped, or frozen leaf spinach, thawed and drained
300ml/½ pint/1⅓ cups warm water
175g/6oz/1¼ cups boiled potatoes, cut into 2.5cm/1-inch cubes
1 teaspoon salt or to taste
½ teaspoon garam masala
4 tablespoons single (half and half) cream

1   Heat the oil in a wok or non-stick frying pan (skillet). When the oil is hot but not smoking, fry the cubes of paneer until lightly browned, tossing and turning them constantly. This will take only 1½–2 minutes. Drain on absorbent paper.

2   Add the remaining oil to the wok and heat for a minute or so over low heat. Add the garlic and stir-fry for 30 seconds, then add the onion and stir-fry for 3–4 minutes.

3   Add the ginger, ground coriander (cilantro) and cumin, stir-fry for 30 seconds and add the tomatoes. Stir-fry for 2 minutes or until the oil floats on top.

4   Add the turmeric, paprika and chilli powder and stir-fry for 30 seconds. Add the spinach, increase the heat to high and stir-fry for 2–3 minutes, then add half the water. Cook for 3 minutes or until the water dries up, tossing and turning the ingredients constantly.

5   Add the fried paneer, potatoes, salt and remaining water. Cook for 1 minute, then reduce the heat to low and simmer for 5 minutes, uncovered. Add a little more water if necessary.

6   Sprinkle on the garam masala, stir in the cream, remove from the heat and serve with Peshawari Naan *(page 238)* and a raita.

Indian Cheese and Potato Cakes

Preparation time: 25 minutes
Cooking time: 10–12 minutes

Makes 12

If using halloumi cheese instead of paneer, remember to reduce the amount of salt. Do make sure that you peel the potatoes after boiling, rather than before, to avoid any stickiness.

2 large slices white bread (about 125g/4oz)

370g/13oz/2¼ cups potatoes, boiled, peeled and mashed

200g/7oz/1 cup paneer or halloumi cheese, grated or mashed

1–2 green chilli peppers, seeded and finely chopped

2–3 cloves garlic, peeled and crushed

½ teaspoon chilli powder (optional)

1 teaspoon salt or to taste

1½ teaspoons bottled mint sauce or 1 tablespoon finely chopped mint mixed with 1 tablespoon lime juice

15g/½oz/¼ cup coriander (cilantro) leaves, finely chopped

1 small onion, finely chopped or minced

25g/1oz/⅕ cup plain (all purpose) flour, seasoned

1 large (extra large) egg, beaten

Oil for shallow frying

1. Lay the slices of bread side by side on a large plate and pour over enough cold water to soak them for a few seconds. Hold the bread, one slice at a time, crumpled between your palms and squeeze out all the water. Put in a large mixing bowl.

2. Add the remaining ingredients except the flour, egg and oil. Using a potato masher, mash the ingredients until thoroughly blended together. Alternatively, put all the ingredients (except the onion, flour, egg and oil) in a food processor and blend until smooth. Add the onions and mix.

3. Halve the mixture and make 6 equal-sized balls from each. Flatten the balls into smooth, round cakes.

4. Put oil in a frying pan (skillet) to a depth of 5mm/¼ inch and heat over a medium heat. Dust each cake in the seasoned flour, making sure it is fully coated. Dip the cakes in the beaten egg and fry until well browned on both sides. Drain on absorbent paper. Serve with a raita or chutney.

Peas with Indian Cheese and Sweetcorn

Preparation time: 15–20 minutes
Cooking time: 30 minutes

Serves 4–6

Mattar-paneer is a very popular dish in northern India, especially in the state of Punjab. I have added sweetcorn *(makki)* to the traditional combination.

4 tablespoons sunflower or corn oil

225g/8oz/1 cup paneer, cut into
    2.5cm/1-inch cubes

1 teaspoon royal cumin (shahi
    jeera)

1 large onion, finely chopped

5–6 cloves garlic, peeled and
    crushed

2.5cm/1-inch cube root ginger,
    peeled and finely grated

2 tablespoons ground coriander
    (cilantro)

½ teaspoon ground cumin

½ teaspoon ground turmeric

½ teaspoon chilli powder

1 tablespoon tomato purée (paste)

225g/8oz/1⅔ cups frozen
    sweetcorn, thawed, or canned
    sweetcorn, drained and rinsed

150g/5oz/¾ cup frozen garden
    peas, thawed, or cooked fresh
    peas

300ml/½ pint/⅔ cup warm water

90g/3oz/½ cup canned chopped
    tomatoes

½ teaspoon dried mint

1 teaspoon salt or to taste

140ml/¼ pint/⅔ cup single (half
    and half) cream

3–4 green chilli peppers

2 tablespoons chopped coriander
    (cilantro) leaves

1 Heat the oil over a medium heat. When the oil is hot but not smoking, stir-fry the paneer cubes until golden brown. Take care while frying paneer, as the oil tends to splutter quite a bit. Drain on absorbent paper.

2 Allow the oil to cool slightly, removing the pan from the heat if necessary. Add the royal cumin (shahi jeera) and stir-fry for 15 seconds. Add the onion, increase the heat slightly, and stir-fry for 4–5 minutes.

3 Add the garlic, ginger, coriander (cilantro) and cumin. Reduce the heat slightly and stir-fry for 1 minute. Add 2 tablespoons of water and stir-fry until the water evaporates.

4 Add the turmeric and chilli powder and stir-fry for 30 seconds. Add 2 tablespoons of water and stir-fry again until the water evaporates.

5 Add the tomato purée (paste), stir-fry for 30 seconds, then add the sweetcorn, peas and water. Bring to the boil, reduce the heat to low and simmer for 5 minutes.

6 Add the fried paneer, tomatoes, mint, salt, cream and chilli peppers. Increase the heat slightly and cook for 5 minutes. Stir in the coriander (cilantro) leaves and remove from the heat. Serve with Saffron Rice (page 100) or Peshawari Naan (page 238), accompanied by a raita.

Indian Cheese Pilau

Preparation time: 20–25 minutes plus soaking time for the rice
Cooking time: 25 minutes

Serves 4

If you cannot find paneer (Indian cheese), use Cyprus halloumi cheese or hard tofu.

225g/8oz/1½ cups basmati rice

50g/2oz/¼ cup ghee or unsalted butter

6 green cardamom pods

2 × 5cm/2-inch pieces cinnamon stick, halved

6 whole cloves

1 large onion, finely sliced

2.5cm/1-inch cube root ginger, peeled and grated

2–3 large cloves garlic, crushed

½ teaspoon ground turmeric

1 teaspoon salt or to taste

225g/8oz/1 cup paneer, cut into 2.5cm/1-inch cubes

2 tablespoons coriander (cilantro) leaves, chopped

125g/4oz/½ cup fresh tomatoes, skinned and chopped

1 Wash the rice in cold water at least twice and soak for 15–20 minutes. Drain thoroughly.

2 Heat the ghee or butter gently over a medium-low heat.

3 Split the top of each cardamom pod and add to the fat along with the cinnamon and cloves. Let them sizzle for 15–20 seconds.

4 Add the onion, increase the heat slightly and fry, stirring regularly, for 6–7 minutes or until lightly browned.

5 Add the ginger and garlic, stir-fry for 1 minute and add the rice, turmeric and salt. Stir and cook for 2–3 minutes.

6 Add the cheese, stir gently and fry for 2–3 minutes.

7 Add 450ml/16fl oz/2 cups hot water and the coriander (cilantro) leaves. Bring to the boil, reduce the heat to low, cover the pan and cook for 10 minutes. Remove from the heat and scatter the tomatoes on top. Cover and leave undisturbed for 6–7 minutes, then fork through and serve with a raita.

Lentil Pilau

Preparation time: 20 minutes plus soaking time for the lentils
Cooking time: 25 minutes   **Serves 4**

This recipe is adapted from the Anglo-Indian dish, kedgeree. I have used moong dhal as they are the fastest-cooking lentils.

225g/8oz/1½ cups basmati rice

125g/4oz/½ cup yellow split lentils (moong dhal)

3 tablespoons ghee or unsalted butter

1 red onion, finely sliced

2 × 5cm/2-inch pieces of cinnamon stick, halved

6 cloves

1–2 green chilli peppers, seeded and chopped

1cm/½-inch cube root ginger, peeled and grated

2 bay leaves, crumpled

2 teaspoons ground coriander (cilantro)

1¼ teaspoons salt or to taste

2–3 hard-boiled (hard-cooked) eggs, quartered lengthways, to garnish

1 Wash the rice and the lentils together then soak in cold water for 20 minutes. Leave to drain in a colander.

2 Heat the ghee or butter over a medium heat and fry the onion, stirring frequently, until well browned (8–9 minutes). Lift the onion with a slotted spoon and press down with another spoon to remove excess fat. Drain on absorbent paper.

3 In the same fat, fry the remaining ingredients, except the ground coriander (cilantro) and salt, for 15–20 seconds.

4 Stir in the coriander followed by the rice, lentils, salt and half the fried onion. Stir-fry for 2–3 minutes and pour in 570ml/ 1 pint/2½ cups hot water. Bring to the boil, reduce the heat to low, cover the pan and cook for 10 minutes. Remove from the heat and leave undisturbed for 6–7 minutes. Fork through the pilau and serve garnished with the hard-boiled (hard-cooked) eggs and the remaining fried onions, accompanied by a raita.

Indian-style French Toast

Preparation time: 15 minutes
Cooking time: 15 minutes   **Serves 4**

These lightly spiced toasts are ideal for a weekend breakfast. Make sure that the plain side of the toast is well browned and crispy.

4 large (extra large) eggs
½ teaspoon salt or to taste
1 small onion, finely chopped
1–2 fresh green chilli peppers,
  seeded and chopped
2 tablespoon coriander (cilantro)
  leaves, chopped
Oil and butter for frying
8 slices brown or white bread

1   Beat the eggs and add the salt, onion, chilli peppers and coriander (cilantro). Mix well.

2   Preheat an omelette pan over a low heat and add 1 teaspoon oil and ½ teaspoon butter. When the mixture begins to bubble, fry one side of a slice of bread until it browns, increasing the heat slightly if necessary.

3   Spread 2 tablespoons of the egg mixture on the uncooked side and allow the egg to soak in, then turn it over. Let the mixture set for a minute, then press it down with a spoon so that the bread sits evenly on the pan. Cook for a minute or two or until well browned. Turn it over again and cook the plain side until crisp.

Plain Naan

Preparation time: 15–20 minutes plus time for proving the dough (batter)
Cooking time: 18–20 minutes

Makes 6

Naan is a Persian word simply meaning 'bread'. I have used soda water in the dough (batter) to make the naan wonderfully soft and fluffy.

450g/1lb/3¼ cups self-raising flour
1 teaspoon salt
1 teaspoon sugar
1 dessertspoon easy-blend yeast
90g/3oz/½ cup ghee or unsalted butter, melted
300–350ml/10–12fl oz/1⅓–1½ cups soda water

1   Put the flour, salt, sugar and yeast into a warmed steel bowl and mix thoroughly. If you store your flour in a fairly cool place, leave it in a warm room for at least 30 minutes.

2   Make sure the ghee or butter is lukewarm; reserve one tablespoon and work the remainder into the flour with your fingertips.

3   Gradually add the soda water and mix until you have a fairly sticky dough (batter). You can make the dough in a food processor with a dough hook if you wish. When the dough is formed, add the reserved fat and knead until the dough does not stick to the bowl or the hook.

4   For the hand-mixed method, transfer the dough to a pastry board and knead with your hands for 2–3 minutes. Add the reserved ghee or butter and knead until the dough stops sticking to your fingers and the board.

5   Cover the bowl with plastic wrap and leave in a warm place for 45–50 minutes.

6   Knock back the dough and divide into 6 equal portions; cover and leave to rise again for 15–20 minutes.

7   Preheat the oven to 220°C/425°F/Gas Mark 7. Line a baking sheet with greased greaseproof (wax) paper.

8   Use a large pastry board or flat surface to roll out the naan. Lightly grease your palms with a little oil then grease a portion of dough by patting and tossing from one palm to another. Roll out to a disc of approximately 15cm/6 inches and gently pull the lower end to form a teardrop shape. However, the shape of the naan is not important. You can make them round or square if you like!

9   Bake in the top shelf of the oven for 8–9 minutes.

Peshawari Naan

Preparation time: 15–20 minutes plus time for proving the dough (batter)

Cooking time: 18–20 minutes
                                                                    Makes 6

Peshawari Naan needs no introduction! It must be the most popular bread on the menu of most Indian restaurants. Here is my version, which is suitable for freezing.

450g/1lb/3¼ cups plain (all
purpose) flour

1 teaspoon baking powder

1 teaspoon salt

1 tablespoon sugar

1 dessertspoon easy-blend yeast

160g/5½oz/⅔ cup ghee or unsalted
butter, melted

250ml/9fl oz/1¼ cups warm milk

15g/½oz seedless raisins, coarsely
chopped

25g/1oz/⅓ cup flaked almonds,
lightly crushed

Little extra flour for dusting

1 tablespoon natural yogurt

1 tablespoon white poppy seeds or
sesame seeds

1 Put the flour, baking powder, salt, sugar and yeast in a large,
warmed mixing bowl and mix thoroughly. Add half the
melted ghee or butter and mix well. Gradually add the
warm milk and mix into a stiff dough (batter). Alternatively,
use a food processor with a dough hook.

2 For both methods, now add the remaining melted ghee or
butter and knead for 2–3 minutes for the hand method, and
50–60 seconds in the food processor. The dough will be very
sticky at this stage – do not panic!

3 For the hand method, transfer the dough to a pastry board,
add the raisins and almonds, and knead until it stops sticking
to the board and your fingers. Make sure the raisins and
almonds are well distributed. If using a food processor, add
the raisins and nuts and run it until the bowl and the dough
hook are clean.

4 Put the dough in a large plastic bag and tie securely, leaving
room for expansion. Put the bag in a warmed bowl,
preferably a steel one as it will retain the heat better. If you
do not have one, use a saucepan. Leave in a warm place (the
airing cupboard is ideal) for 1–1½ hours to prove.

5 Halve the dough and make 3 equal portions from each.
Rotate each portion between your palms, and press gently to
flatten into a round cake. Cover the flattened cakes and set
aside for 10 minutes. Preheat the oven to 220°C/425°F/Gas
Mark 7.

6 Lightly dust each cake in flour and roll out to a 15cm/6-inch
circle. Place one hand on the top end of the circle and gently
pull the lower end to form a teardrop shape. This shape is
not absolutely necessary. You can make your naan round or
even square if you like!

7 Preheat a baking sheet and place greased greaseproof (wax)
paper or baking parchment on top. Put 2–3 naans on the
baking sheet (depending on size), and brush the tops with a
little yogurt. Sprinkle with poppy or sesame seeds and bake
on the top shelf of the oven for 8–9 minutes or until puffed
and lightly browned. Serve with any vegetable curry or lentil
dish.

Cheese, Chilli and Coriander Baguettes

Preparation time: 10 minutes
Cooking time: 5–6 minutes

Serves 4

This is a perfect accompaniment to any soup. The quantities given here are not meant for full-length baguettes (French sticks). I used two batons, which are a little less than half the length of a full baguette.

125g/4oz/1 cup Cheddar or red Leicester cheese, grated
2 green chilli peppers, seeded and chopped
2 tablespoons coriander (cilantro) leaves, chopped
1 large (extra large) egg, beaten
2 batons or 1 medium-sized baguette

1 Preheat the grill (broiler) to medium.
2 Mix together the cheese, chilli peppers, coriander (cilantro) and egg.
3 Halve the baguettes lengthways and place on a grill pan, cut-side down. Grill (broil) for about a minute. Turn them over and spread the mixture equally on each half. Grill until the top is well browned.

Desserts

Indian Bread Pudding

Preparation time: 15 minutes plus chilling
Cooking time: 20–25 minutes

Serves 4

You can cut the bread in any shape you like for this yummy bread pudding. In this recipe, the bread is cut into half-moon or triangle shapes. This is a quick version of the traditional method, but is equally delicious. Silver leaf *(varak)* is traditionally used to decorate the pudding, but you can use silver dust, which is used for decorating cakes.

125g/4oz/½ cup dried milk powder

4–5 tablespoons single (half and half) cream

4 large slices white bread

Oil for deep frying

300ml/10fl oz/1⅓ cups full-cream milk

125g/4oz/½ cup caster (confectioner's) sugar

Pinch saffron threads, pounded

25g/1oz/¼ cup unsalted pistachio nuts, chopped

Silver leaf or silver dust (optional)

1   Mix the milk powder and cream together until you have a binding consistency. Cover and chill for 1–2 hours.

2   Trim the crusts from the bread and cut the bread slices into half-moon shapes or triangles.

3   Heat the oil in a wok or other suitable pan over a medium heat. Fry the slices of bread until well browned. Drain on absorbent paper.

4   In a separate pan, combine the milk, sugar and saffron and bring to simmering point. Add the fried bread and cook until the bread has absorbed all the milk.

5   Transfer the bread to a serving plate and spread the dried milk mixture over the top. If the mixture is hard, use a fork to break up the lumps. Garnish with the pistachio nuts and silver leaf or silver dust (if using). Serve at room temperature.

Bibinca
(Goan Christmas Cake)

Preparation time: 20 minutes
Cooking time: 55–60 minutes

Christmas is a major festival in Goa, where Christianity is one of the three main religions. Bibinca is a delicious coconut cake made at Christmas by Goan housewives. It needs no advance preparation – you can even make it on Christmas Eve! Alcohol, nuts and raisins are not traditionally used, but I like to include them to give the cake a more festive look and taste.

~~~

1   Soak the raisins in the rum for 30 minutes, stirring several times.
2   Mix the flour, nutmeg, cinnamon and salt in a large mixing bowl and set aside.
3   Put the sugar, cinnamon stick and cardamom pods in a saucepan and add 500ml/18fl oz/2¼ cups water. Place over a high heat and bring to the boil. Reduce the heat to medium and cook for 10 minutes. Remove from the heat and allow to cool.
4   Blend the coconut milk powder with 140ml/¼ pint/⅔ cup hot water to make a thick paste. Stir in the Malibu, then strain over the syrup. Beat with an electric beater or a wire whisk. Do not panic if the coconut milk looks curdled when you add the syrup; once you start beating, it will turn into a lovely, smooth mixture. Cool the mixture and beat in the egg yolks. Divide the mixture into 3 equal portions (use a measuring jug).
5   Preheat the grill (broiler) to medium and cook the nuts until lightly browned (1½–2 minutes). Remove and allow to cool. Now turn the temperature up to medium-high. Preheat the oven to 200°C/400°F/Gas Mark 6. Line a 23cm/9-inch round cake tin with non-stick baking parchment.

90g/3oz/½ cup seedless raisins

1 tablespoon dark rum

255g/9oz/1¼ cups plain (all purpose) flour

½ teaspoon freshly grated nutmeg

½ teaspoon ground cinnamon

Pinch of salt

255g/9oz/1¼ cups caster (confectioner's) sugar

5cm/2-inch piece cinnamon stick

8 green cardamom pods, bruised

255g/9oz/1¼ cups coconut milk powder

2 tablespoons Malibu

12 medium egg yolks

25g/1oz/¼ cup whole raw cashew nuts

25g/1oz/¼ cup blanched almonds

125g/4oz/½ cup ghee or unsalted butter

2 tablespoons apricot jam

6   Heat 1½ tablespoons ghee or butter in a 20cm/8-inch non-stick frying pan (skillet) over a medium heat and spread 4 tablespoons (approximately 90ml/3fl oz) of the batter over the base of the pan. Allow to set then place the pancake under the grill and cook until browned. Remove the pan from the grill and spread 1 tablespoon melted fat on the cooked side. Spread 4 tablespoons batter over this and sprinkle 1 teaspoon melted fat on the surface. Return the pan to the grill. Allow to brown and repeat until you have used up the first quantity of batter.

7   Spread half the raisins on the pancake. Cover with 5 tablespoons of the batter and sprinkle a teaspoon of melted fat on the surface. Return to the grill and cook until browned. Repeat until you have used up the second quantity of batter and spread the remaining raisins on top. Continue layering and grilling until the third quantity of batter is used up. Remove the pan from the grill when the last layer is just set, but not brown.

8   When the pancakes are ready, loosen the edges with a thin spatula and shake the pan to loosen the cake. Lift it out carefully (use two wide spatulas) and place in the prepared cake tin. Bake in the centre of the oven for 15 minutes or until well browned. Leave to cool in the tin, then turn the cake out onto a cake board.

9   Heat the apricot jam and brush generously all over the surface of the cake. Arrange the nuts on top and glaze them with any remaining jam.

Goan Coconut Pancakes with Malibu and Lime Sauce

Preparation time: 10 minutes plus time for resting the batter
Cooking time: 15 minutes

Makes 10

Coconut plays a prominent part in all Goan sweets. Malibu is not traditional, but adds a special zest. Take care not to boil the sauce once you have added the coconut as coconut milk will curdle at high temperatures.

For the pancakes:
125g/4oz self-raising flour
½ teaspoon ground nutmeg
Pinch of salt
2 medium eggs
300ml/½ pint/1⅓ cups coconut
   milk
2 tablespoons melted butter
Sunflower or soya oil for frying

For the sauce:
300ml/½ pint/1⅓ cups water
90g/3oz/⅓ cup caster
   (confectioner's) sugar
Juice and rind of 1 lime
25g/1oz/2 tablespoons seedless
   raisins
25g/1oz/¼ cup raw, unsalted
   cashews, chopped
90g/3oz creamed coconut, grated
4 tablespoons Malibu

1 Mix the flour, nutmeg and salt and set aside.
2 Beat the eggs and gradually add the coconut milk, followed by the melted butter.
3 Add the flour, one tablespoon at a time, and continue to mix until you have a smooth batter. Alternatively, blend all the ingredients together in an electric blender or food processor. Let the batter stand for 15–20 minutes.
4 Heat 1 teaspoon oil over a medium heat in a non-stick frying pan (skillet) with a diameter of 15–18cm/6–7 inches. Using a ladle large enough to hold 4 tablespoons of batter, pour and spread it quickly. Allow to cook for 30 seconds then flip it over. Cook for a further 30 seconds and fold it into a triangle. Transfer to an oven-proof plate and continue to cook and fold the remaining pancakes in the same way. Put the pancakes in a warm oven while you make the sauce. Alternatively, you could reheat individual portions in a microwave.
5 Put the water and sugar into a saucepan and bring to the boil. Reduce the heat to medium and add the remaining ingredients, except the coconut and Malibu. Cook for 6–7 minutes.
6 Add the grated coconut, reduce the heat to low and simmer for 4–5 minutes. Stir in the Malibu and remove from the heat.
7 Place 2 pancakes per person on individual serving plates and divide the sauce, raisins and nuts equally among them.

Cinnamon and Star Anise Sago Dessert with Malibu-Raspberry Coulis

Preparation time: 10 minutes
Cooking time: 15 minutes

Serves 4–5

A traditional recipe from Goa with a Portuguese influence, this dessert is known as *sabu dane che alone*. Here it is served with a modern twist by adding raspberry coulis laced with Malibu. You can, however, omit the Malibu if you wish. If you cannot get star anise, use cloves. The flavour will be different, but just as tasty.

125g/4oz/⅔ cup sago or tapioca

25g/1oz ghee or unsalted butter

2 star anise

2.5cm/1-inch piece cinnamon stick

25g/1oz/¼ cup raw cashew nuts, split

25g/1oz/¼ cup seedless raisins

300ml/½ pint/1⅓ cups full-fat milk

140ml/¼ pint/⅔ cup hot water

90g/3oz/½ cup creamed coconut, cut into small pieces

90–125g/3–4oz/½–⅔ cup caster (confectioner's) sugar

For the sauce:

450g/1lb/2 cups raspberries, fresh or frozen

125g/4oz/⅔ cup caster (confectioner's) sugar

2 tablespoons Malibu

1 Rinse the sago or tapioca and soak in cold water for 10–15 minutes.

2 In a non-stick saucepan, melt the ghee or butter over a low heat and add the star anise, cinnamon, cashews and raisins. Fry gently until the cashews begin to brown and the raisins are puffed.

3 Add the milk, water, coconut and sugar. Stir over a medium heat until the coconut is dissolved, then drain and add the sago or tapioca. Cook until the mixture thickens. Stir constantly towards the end to ensure the thickened mixture does not stick to the bottom of the pan. When the mixture comes away from the bottom and sides of the pan, the dessert is ready. This will take 10–12 minutes.

4 Put into individual ramekins or a decorative mould. Leave at room temperature for at least an hour, then serve surrounded by the sauce.

5 To make the sauce, put the raspberries and sugar in a saucepan and place over a high heat. Add 140ml/¼ pint/⅔ cup water and stir until the sugar has dissolved. Purée in a blender, then push the mixture through a sieve. Discard the seeds. Mix the sauce with the Malibu. The sauce can be made 2–3 days in advance and stored in the fridge. It will freeze well too.

Soft Carrot Fudge

Preparation time: 15–20 minutes
Cooking time: 50 minutes

Serves 6

Soft fudges (*halva*) were introduced to India by the Moguls. They generally have a high fat content, though I have tried to keep this within a reasonable limit. The fudge is decorated with edible silver leaf (*varak*), reminiscent of the Mogul era. Alternatively, you can sprinkle the fudge with silver dust.

400g/14oz/3 cups carrots, scraped
    and finely grated
570ml/1 pint/2½ cups full-cream
    milk
6 cardamom pods
1 × 5cm/2-inch piece cinnamon
    stick
Pinch saffron strands, pounded
1 tablespoon hot milk
125g/4oz/½ cup granulated sugar
140ml/5fl oz/⅔ cup double (heavy)
    cream
½ teaspoon freshly grated nutmeg
50g/2oz/½ cup ghee or unsalted
    butter
25g/1oz/¼ cup seedless raisins
25g/1oz/¼ cup raw shelled
    pistachio nuts
25g/1oz/¼ cup blanched slivered
    almonds
1 tablespoon rose water
Silver leaf or silver dust (optional)

1 Put the carrots, milk, cardamom and cinnamon into a heavy saucepan and bring to the boil. Reduce the heat to medium and cook for 5 minutes, then simmer gently until the milk has evaporated (15–20 minutes). Stir frequently to ensure it does not stick to the pan.

2 Meanwhile, soak the pounded saffron in the hot milk for 10–15 minutes.

3 Add the sugar to the carrot mixture and continue to cook, stirring constantly, until the mixture is dry again (5–6 minutes).

4 Stir in the cream, saffron and milk and the nutmeg. Cook, stirring constantly, for 2–3 minutes and remove from the heat.

5 In a small saucepan, melt the butter or ghee gently and fry the raisins and nuts until the raisins are puffed and the nuts are lightly browned. Stir them into the carrot mixture.

6 Transfer the fudge to a serving dish and sprinkle the rose water over the top. Garnish with the silver leaf or sprinkle with some silver dust (if using).

Dried Milk Balls in Syrup

Preparation time: 20 minutes
Cooking time: 20 minutes

Makes 16

This recipe, known as *gulab jamoon,* is traditionally made with *khoya* and *chenna.* Both of these are dairy products and rather time-consuming to make. Full-cream dried milk powder is an easy alternative, which you can buy from Asian shops. If you cannot get it, use dried skimmed milk powder and single (half and half) cream.

〜〜〜〜〜〜〜〜〜〜〜〜〜〜

175g/6oz full-cream milk powder or dried skimmed milk powder with 150ml/¼ pint/⅔ cup single (half and half) cream

90g/3oz semolina (cream of wheat)

2 teaspoons plain (all purpose) flour

1 teaspoon ground cardamom

1 teaspoon baking powder

40g/1½oz ghee or unsalted butter, melted

140ml/¼ pint/⅔ cup milk

1 teaspoon saffron strands soaked in 2 tablespoons hot milk

350g/12oz/1¾ cups granulated sugar

680ml/1½ pints/4 cups water

Oil for deep frying

2 tablespoons rose water

Whipped double (heavy) cream mixed with 2 tablespoons rose water, to serve

1   In a large mixing bowl, combine the milk powder, semolina (cream of wheat), flour, ground cardamom and baking powder. Add the ghee or butter and rub in until blended.

2   Add the milk (if you are using skimmed milk powder, you need to add the cream instead of the milk) and the saffron strands along with the milk in which they were soaked. Mix until a soft dough (batter) is formed and knead it on a pastry board until smooth. Divide the dough in half and make 8 equal-sized balls out of each portion. Rotate the balls between your palms to make them as smooth as possible, without any surface cracks.

3   Put the sugar and water in a saucepan and bring to the boil. Stir until the sugar has dissolved. Turn the heat down and simmer the syrup for 6–8 minutes. Remove from the heat and stir in the rose water.

4   Meanwhile, heat the oil in a wok over a low heat and deep-fry the milk balls gently until a rich dark-brown. When you first put them in the hot oil, they will sink. After a couple of minutes they will start floating in the oil; if they do not, gently ease them away from the base of the pan using a thin spatula. Turn them over once or twice until they brown.

5   Lift the milk balls with a slotted spoon and put them into the prepared syrup. Allow them to soak in the syrup while you fry the next batch. Leave them all soaking in the syrup for a couple of hours before serving.

Sweet Rice Flakes

Preparation time: 5 minutes
Cooking time: 15 minutes

Serves 4–5

If you thought rice flakes were meant only for soggy milk puddings, I am sure this recipe will change your mind. This is ideal for picnics and barbecues or if you fancy some comfort food, any time! Ideally, use Indian rice flakes as they have long, slender flakes and a creamy colour, and give the recipe more bite than the thinner and lighter Western counterpart. However, family and friends have devoured this recipe irrespective of which type of rice flakes I have used!

You need a large sieve for frying batches of rice flakes by lowering the sieve into the hot oil. A deep-fat fryer is not suitable, neither is the frying basket as it has large holes. Use a wok or a deep pan.

For a savoury version, omit the sugar and sprinkle with ground roasted cumin and coriander (cilantro) plus a little chilli powder while the rice flakes are hot. Add more nuts and freshly milled black pepper.

Sunflower oil for deep frying
25g/1oz/¼ cup natural cashew
 pieces
25g/1oz/¼ cup almonds, slivered
25g/1oz/¼ cup raw pistachio nuts
255g/9oz rice flakes
1½ tablespoons caster
 (confectioner's) sugar
½ teaspoon salt

1 Heat the oil over a medium heat. Using a sieve, fry the nuts, one variety at a time, as they will need different cooking times. Cashews are ready when they are a medium-brown colour. Almonds will brown and crackle gently when they are ready. Pistachios are ready when they are light brown. Drain them on absorbent paper.

2 Increase the heat to high and allow the oil to heat until smoking point. Half-fill a sieve with rice flakes and lower into the hot oil. They will puff up immediately and fill the sieve. As soon as the sieve is full, drain the rice flakes on absorbent paper. When you have finished frying them all, and while the rice flakes are still hot, sprinkle with the sugar and salt and mix thoroughly.

3 Stir in the fried nuts. I crush the pistachios very lightly to reveal the green insides for a striking effect.

Rose and Saffron-scented Rice Dessert with Mango

Preparation time: 10 minutes
Cooking time: 10 minutes

Serves 4

Indian rice pudding is highly aromatic with a thinner consistency than its Western counterpart. You will love this recipe for its incredible speed and fabulous flavours. It is equally delicious chilled or at room temperature.

Good pinch saffron strands, pounded

125ml/4fl oz/½ cup hot full-cream milk

2 tablespoons ghee or unsalted butter

6 green cardamom pods, bruised

2.5cm/1-inch piece cinnamon stick

565g/20oz (approx.) can of creamed rice

2–3 tablespoons double (heavy) cream

1–2 tablespoons caster (confectioner's) sugar

1 large, ripe mango

1 tablespoon rose water

1 tablespoon shelled, unsalted pistachio nuts

Few fresh rose petals, washed, to garnish

1 Soak the pounded saffron in the milk and set aside.

2 Melt the ghee or butter gently over a low heat and add the cardamom and cinnamon. Let them sizzle until the cardamom pods are puffed.

3 Add the creamed rice and saffron milk. Bring to a slow simmer and add the cream and sugar. Let it bubble gently for 5 minutes, then remove from the heat and set aside to cool. To speed this up, stand the pan in a bowl of iced water.

4 Meanwhile, peel the mango and slice off the two large pieces on either side of the stone, then the two thinner sides. Chop all the slices into bite-sized pieces. Scrape off all the flesh next to the stone and add to the rice pudding, along with the chopped mango. Stir in the rose water.

5 Toast the pistachio nuts quickly under the grill (broiler) or in the microwave. Cool, crush and sprinkle over the dessert. Serve garnished with the rose petals.

Iced Mango Dessert

Preparation time: 5 minutes plus freezing
Cooking time: 10 minutes

Serves 8

This popular Indian iced dessert is known as *kulfi,* a term derived from the conical metal moulds in which it is frozen. Opinions vary as to the origins of this dessert. Some believe it was brought to India from Kabul by the mighty Moguls. Others claim it originated in India after the arrival of the Moguls.

Traditional kulfi moulds are available in some Asian shops, but you can use small plastic containers or decorative individual jelly moulds instead. To give you an idea of the size, traditional moulds hold about two tablespoons of kulfi mix. I often set them in ice lolly moulds too.

370g/13oz can evaporated milk
300ml/½ pint/1⅓ cups single (half and half) cream
1½ tablespoons ground almonds
175g/6oz/1 cup granulated sugar
1 teaspoon ground cardamom
450g/1lb mango purée
25g/1oz shelled unsalted pistachio nuts, roasted and lightly crushed

1 Mix the evaporated milk and cream together in a heavy-based saucepan and place over a medium heat.
2 Mix together the ground almonds and sugar, then sprinkle onto the milk mixture, stirring.
3 Continue to stir and cook until the mixture has thickened slightly (6–8 minutes).
4 Add the ground cardamom, stir and mix thoroughly, and remove from the heat. Allow to cool completely, keeping an eye on the mixture and stirring now and again to prevent a skin forming. When completely cold, stir in the mango purée.
5 Fill small containers of your choice with the mixture and put in the freezer for 4–5 hours. Leave at room temperature for 5–6 minutes before removing from the moulds. The texture of kulfi is much harder than that of conventional ice cream.
6 Served sprinkled with roasted pistachio nuts.

White Chocolate Kulfi with Passion Fruit Sauce

Ready in 15 minutes, excluding freezing time   **Serves 4–6**

This is a quicker version of the traditional *kulfi* (iced dessert) with a modern twist. Instead of freezing the dessert in several small, conical containers as is traditionally done, freeze it in one decorative mould to save time. Unmould and leave the dessert in the fridge for 20–25 minutes to soften, then cut into slices and serve. You can serve it with or without the sauce, but the sauce does add texture and taste.

For the kulfi:
400g/14oz can of evaporated milk
**300ml/½ pint/1⅓ cups double
    (heavy) cream**
**50g/2oz/¼ cup caster
    (confectioner's) sugar**
150g/5oz white chocolate

For the sauce:
5 large passion fruit
125ml/4fl oz/½ cup water
**90g/3oz/¼ cup caster
    (confectioner's) sugar**
2 teaspoons arrowroot
**1–2 tablespoons crème de menthe
    (optional)**

1   Put the evaporated milk, double (heavy) cream and caster (confectioner's) sugar into a saucepan and place over a low heat. Stir until the mixture is lukewarm and the sugar has dissolved. Remove and set aside.

2   Break up the chocolate into small pieces and put in a heat-proof bowl. Place the bowl over a pan of simmering water on a low heat and leave to melt fully. There is no need to stir the chocolate until it has melted. Stir and pour it into the milk/cream mixture. Mix well then put into your chosen container and place in the freezer for at least 5 hours.

3   To make the sauce, remove the pulp from the passion fruit and put into a saucepan. Add the water, sugar and arrowroot blended with a little water. Stir over a low-medium heat until the sauce has thickened. Add the crème de menthe (if using), remove and cool. Can be stored in the fridge for 7–8 days.

Sweet Samosas

Preparation time: 20 minutes
Cooking time: 30–35 minutes

Makes 12

These delicious morsels, known as *neuris,* are traditionally cooked during the Hindu festival of light, Diwali. The use of filo pastry is not traditional but intentional on my part to reduce both labour and the fat content of the dish. They are perfect with a cup of tea or coffee after a meal or at afternoon tea.

90g/3oz/½ cup desiccated coconut

50g/2oz/¼ cup light soft brown sugar

25g/1oz/¼ cup raw cashews, lightly crushed

25g/1oz/¼ cup seedless raisins

225ml/8fl oz/1 cup evaporated milk

½ teaspoon freshly ground nutmeg

½ teaspoon ground cinnamon

12 sheets filo pastry (approximately 28 × 18cm/11 × 7 inches)

Sunflower or light olive oil to brush over the pastry

1   Put the coconut, sugar, cashews, raisins and evaporated milk into a small, heavy-based saucepan and place over a medium heat.

2   Stir until the milk starts bubbling, reduce the heat to low and cook, uncovered, until the coconut has absorbed all the milk (about 8–10 minutes). Remove the pan from the heat and stir in the nutmeg and cinnamon. Allow to cool completely and divide the mixture into 12 equal portions.

3   Preheat the oven to 180°C/350°F/Gas Mark 4 and line a baking sheet with greased greaseproof (wax) paper or non-stick baking parchment.

4   Place a sheet of filo pastry on a pastry board and brush well with oil. Fold the pastry in half lengthways, brush with oil again and fold it across.

5   Place a portion of filling on one half of the pastry and fold the other half over it. Seal the edges with cold water, press with a fork and trim with scissors.

6   Place the samosas on the prepared baking sheet and brush liberally with oil. Bake in the centre of the oven for 20–25 minutes until golden brown.

Dried Fruit and Nut Dessert

Preparation time: 10 minutes
Cooking time: 30–35 minutes

Serves 4

This delicious dessert with dried fruit and nuts is flavoured with saffron and rose water and a hint of spices. Traditionally, it is chilled and served in earthenware bowls. The addition of evaporated milk is not traditional, but I use it to speed up the cooking process.

½ teaspoon saffron strands, pounded

2 tablespoons very hot milk

1 tablespoon ghee or unsalted butter

40g/1½oz/¼ cup ground rice

25g/1oz/¼ cup raw cashews, split

25g/1oz/¼ cup seedless raisins

570ml/1 pint/2½ cups milk

300ml/½ pint/1⅓ cups evaporated milk

50g/2oz/⅓ cup caster (confectioner's) sugar

½ teaspoon ground cardamom

½ teaspoon ground nutmeg

1 tablespoon rose water

50g/2oz/⅓ cup ready-to-eat apricots, sliced

25g/1oz/¼ cup walnut pieces, lightly browned in a little ghee or butter

1 tablespoon unsalted shelled pistachio nuts, lightly crushed and browned as for walnuts

1 Soak the saffron strands in the hot milk and set aside.

2 Melt the ghee over a low heat in a wok or heavy-based saucepan and add the ground rice, cashews and raisins. Stir-fry for 1 minute and add the milk. Increase the heat to high and stir until smoke rises, then reduce the heat and cook for 10–12 minutes or until the mixture thickens slightly, stirring constantly.

3 Add the evaporated milk and sugar; continue to stir and cook until the mixture resembles the consistency of pouring custard.

4 Add the saffron-infused milk, ground cardamom and nutmeg; stir and cook for 1 minute.

5 Add the rose water, stir and remove from the heat. Stir in half the apricots and allow to cool thoroughly; stir frequently to prevent a skin forming.

6 Transfer to a serving dish and chill for 3–4 hours. Top with the remaining apricots and fried nuts.

Chapter 11

Drinks

Consuming alcoholic drinks is not the norm in India, though this trend is changing fast. Being a land rich in fresh fruits and vegetables, India has a great repertoire of drinks made from these ingredients, which are drunk by themselves or at meal-times. The most popular non-alcoholic drink is *lassi,* which is made from yogurt blended with water. Lassi is drunk in copious amounts during the summer months. It can be either sweet or savoury, and in the following pages you will find recipes for exotic rose-flavoured lassi and the ever-popular mango lassi. To make a savoury lassi, simply add salt, freshly milled black pepper and a few crushed cumin seeds to the yogurt and water *(see page 258).*

There is the divine Pomegranate Crush *(page 262)* made with the juice extracted from its jewel-like, ruby red seeds. Cardamom Coffee *(page 260)* will help you keep warm during the winter, and a glass of Tamarind Drink *(page 264)* provides a quick remedy for indigestion or stomach upsets. All the drinks in this chapter are not only delicious, but healthy too.

Spiced Tea

Preparation time: 5 minutes **Serves 4**

Spiced tea *(masala chai)* is very popular in the cold, hilly terrain of Indian, especially during the winter months. It is brewed in an infusion of winter spices, such as cardamom, cinnamon and cloves, which are known to create body heat. Serve Spiced Tea after dinner or at any other time as a warming drink.

700ml/1¼ pints/2¾ cups water

1 × 5cm/2-inch piece cinnamon
   stick

6 green cardamom pods, split at the
   top of each pod

4 whole cloves

½ teaspoon fennel seeds

4 teaspoons Assam or Darjeeling
   leaf tea

Milk and sugar to taste

1   Put the water, cinnamon, cardamom, cloves and fennel in a saucepan and bring to the boil. Reduce the heat to low, cover and simmer for 5 minutes.

2   Rinse out a teapot with boiling water and add the tea leaves. Strain the spiced liquid into the teapot and brew for 4–5 minutes.

3   Put milk and sugar to taste in individual cups and strain the tea over.

Mango-flavoured Sweet Yogurt Drink (Lassi)

Preparation time: 10 minutes   **Serves 4**

Fresh, ripe mango is best for this recipe. If they are not ripe when you buy them, leave them for several days at room temperature. They will be soft to the touch when fully ripened.

2 large, ripe mangoes, peeled and chopped
90g/3oz/½ cup caster (confectioner's) sugar, or to taste
450g/1lb/2 cups low-fat plain yogurt
3 tablespoons rose water or 1 teaspoon rose essence
Crushed ice, to serve

1 Put all the ingredients in a blender and add 570ml/1 pint/2½ cups water. Blend until smooth. Taste and add more sugar if necessary.
2 Pour into a jug and chill for several hours. Serve in tall glasses lined with crushed ice.

Variations

As well as mango, the following flavours are great too.

Pineapple Lassi: Add 225g/8oz/1 cup chopped fresh pineapple or canned pineapple in natural juice, drained.

Berry Lassi: In the summer, make use of the fabulous fresh berries. Blueberries make a very pretty and delicious glass of lassi. Strawberries and blackberries are also great. You will need to strain these before placing in the fridge to chill. Approximately 225g/8oz/1 cup of berries will be enough for four. Always taste it and adjust the sugar level.

Rose-flavoured Yogurt Drink (Lassi)

Preparation time: 5 minutes   **Serves 4**

This is a healthy and nourishing breakfast drink. Yogurt provides calcium and B-vitamins. It is known to aid digestion and help prevent constipation and diarrhoea. Lassi, both sweet and savoury, is drunk at breakfast time in the state of Punjab, where the drink originated. I have used *Rooh Afza* (a rose-scented syrup), which gives the drink a pink tinge. You can buy it from Indian stores, but there are other rose-flavoured drinks available in supermarkets. As an alternative, you can use rose water and sugar to taste.

255g/9oz/1¼ cups low-fat plain yogurt
570ml/1 pint/2½ cups water
4–5 tablespoons Rooh Afza or other rose-flavoured syrup
Crushed ice, to serve
Sprigs of fresh mint, to garnish

1   Blend everything together in a blender and pour into tall glasses lined with plenty of crushed ice.
2   Serve garnished with the mint.

Savoury Yogurt Drink

Ready in 5 minutes   **Makes 1.2 litres/2 pints/5 cups**

This lightly-spiced lassi is indeed a welcome sight during the oppressive Indian summer months served in tall glasses lined with crushed ice. Serve any time as a refreshing drink or with meals.

½ teaspoon cumin seeds
½ teaspoon black peppercorns
450g/1lb/2 cups set low-fat natural
    yogurt
12–14 mint leaves
1½ teaspoons salt or to taste
2 teaspoons sugar
570ml/1 pint/2½ cups water
Crushed ice, to serve

1   Preheat a wok or other small, heavy-based pan over a medium heat. Add the cumin and peppercorns; stir and roast for a minute or two until they release their aroma. Remove from the pan and allow to cool, then crush with a pestle and mortar.

2   Put the crushed spices in a blender and add the yogurt, mint, salt, sugar and half the water. Blend until the mint and spices are thoroughly incorporated. Mix in the remaining water, then pour into tall glasses lined with crushed ice.

Melon Drink

Preparation time: 10 minutes   **Serves 4**

You can use either watermelon or honeydew for this recipe. With a delicate touch of spice, it is a very refreshing and low-calorie drink, especially if you use watermelon. Melon is believed to stimulate efficient function of the kidneys.

½ **large honeydew or medium-sized watermelon**
Juice of 1½ limes
1 teaspoon salt
1 teaspoon sugar
¼ **teaspoon chilli powder**
½ **teaspoon roasted ground cumin seeds**
450ml/16fl oz/2 cups water
Crushed ice, to serve

1   Peel the melon and remove the seeds, then roughly chop. Place in a blender with the remaining ingredients and blend until smooth.

2   Line four tall glasses with plenty of crushed ice. Pour the drink over the crushed ice and serve.

Cardamom Coffee

Ready in 5 minutes   **Serves 4**

Indian cuisine is well known for its enticing aromas and captivating flavours. Tea and coffee flavoured with aromatic spices are popular all over the country. Try this cardamom-flavoured coffee, which is delicious served hot during the winter months. It is equally enjoyable cold in the summer. In India, it is often served in tall glasses with a scoop of vanilla ice cream.

6 green cardamom pods, bruised
300ml / ½ pint / 1⅓ cups semi-skimmed milk
Instant coffee and sugar to taste

1   Put the cardamom pods in a saucepan and add 570ml/ 1 pint/2½ cups water. Bring to the boil and reduce the heat to low. Cover and simmer for 5–6 minutes.
2   Add the milk and bring to the boil again. Remove and discard the cardamom pods.
3   Put coffee and sugar to taste in individual cups and pour over the milky mixture. Stir and serve.

Lemon and Lime Drink

Preparation time: 10 minutes   **Serves 4**

This is a popular and refreshing drink during the summer months. It is known as 'fresh lime-soda' and is the Indian equivalent of home-made lemonade. It is very cooling and can be served before, during or after a meal. Limes are rich in vitamin C and contain antioxidants, which help to boost the body's natural defence mechanisms.

The juice of 2 limes
1 teaspoon salt or to taste
2 tablespoons caster sugar
700ml / 1¼ pints / 2¾ cups soda water
Thinly sliced lemons, to serve
Crushed ice, to serve

1   Blend the lime juice, salt and sugar in a jug and gradually pour in the soda water.
2   Stir until well blended and serve in tall glasses with crushed ice and sliced lemons.

Spiced Pineapple Punch

Preparation time: A few minutes
Cooking time: 20 minutes

Serves 6–8

Even though this drink contains warming spices such as cinnamon and cloves, it has a cooling effect when served chilled with lemons, oranges and mint, and is ideal during the summer months. It will keep in the fridge for several days.

450ml/16fl oz/2 cups water

4 × 5cm/2-inch pieces cinnamon
   stick

8 whole cloves

8 green cardamom pods, bruised

170ml/6fl oz/⅔ cup brandy

1 litre/1¾ pints/4 cups sweetened
   pineapple juice

2 tablespoons fresh mint leaves,
   chopped

Sliced oranges and lemons, to serve

1   Put the water and the spices into a saucepan and bring to the boil. Reduce the heat to low and cover the pan. Simmer for 20 minutes then remove from the heat and allow to cool, keeping the pan covered to preserve flavours.

2   When cooled, strain into a punch bowl and pour in the brandy and pineapple juice. Stir in the mint and chill for several hours.

3   Place the orange and lemon slices at the bottom of punch cups or glasses and top with the chilled punch.

Pomegranate Crush

Preparation time: 30 minutes   **Serves 4**

This is a pure and simple delight, both visually and to the palate. It is sweet with a slight sour under-tone and has a delicate bouquet. Pomegranate has become a regular feature on supermarket shelves. The skin should be a rich red because only these will contain the beautiful, burgundy, juicy seeds inside. Pale-skinned ones usually have pale seeds, which are not all that exciting.

For an exotic look, use pomegranate seeds to garnish pilaus, biryanis and fresh fruit salads. Simply sprinkle the seeds on top. Pomegranate seeds are delicious eaten on their own and contain plenty of fibre and vitamin C. The juice is known to be a great beauty aid, and Indian women use it to cleanse and purify the skin.

6 ripe pomegranates
Sprigs of fresh mint, to garnish

1   Halve each pomegranate and peel off the skin like an orange. If it is difficult to peel, hold a pomegranate half with one hand, cut-side down, and tap the skin gently all around with the handle of a large knife. Peel the fruit over a bowl so that you can collect every bit of the richly-coloured, delicious juice.

2   Once you have removed the outer skin, you will also need to peel off the white pith and membrane that hold the seeds together. They do come off quite easily.

3   Put all the seeds in a blender for about a minute, then strain the juice. Push the pulp through a sieve with a spoon to extract as much juice as possible. Serve chilled garnished with the mint sprigs.

Star Fruit, Orange and Pineapple Drink

Preparation time: 10 minutes   **Serves 4**

Star fruit, or carambola, from the tropics is available in our supermarkets from late summer to mid-winter. If you have ever wondered what to do with it other than just eating it as a fruit, try this exotic and delicious drink. Choose the fruits carefully as their sweetness varies a great deal. The ones with a rich, golden colour and broader gaps between the ribs tend to be sweeter.

3 ripe star fruits

1 small orange

125g/4oz/⅔ cup fresh pineapple,
    cubed

450ml/16fl oz/2 cups water

1 tablespoon caster (confectioner's)
    sugar, or to taste

1 teaspoon salt

¼ teaspoon freshly milled black
    pepper

½ teaspoon cumin seeds, dry-
    roasted and finely crushed

1 tablespoon lime juice

Crushed ice, to serve

1   Cut the star fruits into slices and remove the pips. Peel the orange and remove the pips and pith. Put them in a blender and add the pineapple. Purée and strain through a fine sieve.

2   Add the water and the remaining ingredients. Stir until well blended and the sugar has dissolved. Taste and add more sugar if necessary. Serve in tall glasses lined with crushed ice.

Tamarind Drink with Cumin and Mint

Preparation time: 10 minutes   **Serves 6**

In India, this is drunk for the digestive properties of cumin and mint. It can be served hot or cold.

1 tablespoon cumin seeds
1 teaspoon black peppercorns
1½ teaspoons tamarind concentrate
About 20 fresh mint leaves
1 teaspoon salt or to taste

1   Preheat a small cast-iron or other heavy pan over a medium heat and dry-roast the cumin seeds until they release their aroma and are just a shade darker (about a minute). Remove from the heat to stop them over-roasting. Cool and crush them lightly.

2   Put the peppercorns in a plastic food bag and crush them coarsely.

3   Put the cumin and peppercorns into a saucepan and add 1 litre / 1¾ pints / 4 cups water. Bring to the boil and add the tamarind, mint and salt. Reduce the heat to low, simmer for 5 minutes and strain through muslin or a fine sieve.

Bibliography

Achaya, K.T. *Indian Food – A Historical Companion* (Oxford University Press, 1988)

Reader's Digest. *Foods That Harm Foods That Heal* (Reader's Digest, 1987)

Reader's Digest. *Library of Modern Knowledge* (Reader's Digest, 1981)

Suppliers of Indian Ingredients

Avon

Bart Spices Ltd
York Road
Bedminster
Bristol BS3 4AD
Tel: 0117 977 3474
Fax: 0117 972 0216
(mail order available)

Berkshire

Medina Stores
27 Debeauvoir Road
Reading
Berkshire RG1 5NR
Tel: 0118 987 1171

Glasgow

Oriental Food Stores
303–5 Great Western Road
Glasgow G4 9HS
Tel: 0141 334 8133

Humberside

Indian and Continental Food
   Stores
69 Princess Avenue
Hull HU5 3QN
Tel: 01482 346 915

London

Patel Brothers
187–9 Upper Tooting Road
London SW17 7EW
Tel: 020 8672 2792

Dadu's Ltd
190–198 Upper Tooting Road
London SW17 7EW
Tel: 020 8672 4984

Asian Food Centre
544 Harrow Road
Maida Vale
London W9 3GG
Tel: 020 8960 3751

Middlesex

Asian Food Centre
175–77 Staines Road
Hounslow
Middlesex TW3 3JB
Tel: 020 8570 7346

Surrey

Atif's Superstore
103 Walton Road
Woking
Surrey GU21 5DW
Tel: 01483 762 774

Mail Order

Curry Club Direct Supplies
Tel/Fax 01746 761 211

Virani Mail Order
Tel: 01933 276 313
Fax: 01933 441 863

Fox's Spices
Mason's Road Industrial Estate
Stratford-upon-Avon
Warwickshire CV37 9NF
Tel: 01789 266 420
Fax: 01789 267 737

Natco Spices
T. Choithram and Sons Ltd
Choithram House
Wembley
Middlesex HAO 2BG
Tel: 020 8903 8311
Fax: 020 8900 1426

On-Line

Paul Campbell, exoticspice.co.uk

Index

About Cobra Beer

Cobra is a truly exceptional beer, brewed to an authentic Indian recipe, using only the finest natural ingredients (a unique blend of barley, malt, maize and rice) whilst retaining a premium strength of 5%.

Cobra is specially brewed to be extra smooth; it is double filtered and less gassy than other bottled beers making it the perfect accompaniment to Indian cuisine.

As well as being stocked in most major stores, Cobra is the first Indian beer to be sold in Harrods and is now established as the benchmark for quality beer in its own right. An award-winning beer, Cobra won Gold at the 2001 Monde Selection at the World Selection of Quality in Brussels, and received the Gold award for the second year running in 2002.

Throughout its history Cobra has remained true to its heritage. Cobra was first brewed in Bangalore, India and imported to the UK. In 1997 Cobra began brewing in Britain at Charles Wells, a 125-year-old family-run brewery and the largest independent brewery in Britain. With state-of-the-art brewing facilities, Cobra is brewed today by Charles Wells to the same authentic, Indian recipe.

Cobra Beer Ltd
Telephone: +44 (0) 20 7731 6200
Fax: +44 (0) 20 7731 6201
Email: cobrabeer@cobrabeer.com